Barbara Nyland

The Power & The Tories

The Power & The Tories

ONTARIO POLITICS — 1943 TO THE PRESENT

JONATHAN MANTHORPE

Macmillan of Canada
Toronto

ISBN 0-7705-1218-6

The Macmillan Company of Canada
70 Bond Street
Toronto M5B 1X3

Printed in Canada

Contents

ACKNOWLEDGMENTS

No book is entirely the work of one person. I should like to thank my wife, Dan, who discovered the worst sides of my nature while the book was being written; the patrons of the Southam Fellowship, who gave me the time to write the book; Ross H. Munro and John Zaritsky, with whom I worked in *The Globe and Mail* bureau at Queen's Park, and on whose articles I have drawn in some areas; Marilyn Grad and Kathy Williams in *The Globe and Mail* library, who helped scour the files for information; Doug Gibson, who did a splendid job of editing the manuscript; and finally the many people who provided information in confidence and who would have to leave town if their names were mentioned.

The Power & The Tories

1. Building the Big Blue Machine

Just below the surface, beneath the pleasant banter and the open smiles, there was tension as the ten men gathered in the private dining room in the lush surroundings of the National Club. It was, after all, a crucial meeting. On its results could rest the future of the Ontario Conservative party, the party which had ruled the province for the past 28 years. The ten men recognized that at all costs they must avoid the bitter rivalry and the suspicious, partisan hatred that had marked their conflict a few days before. They all wanted an alliance, but they were all proud men, the wounds of their recent contest were still painful, and none of them was about to be short-changed in any deals.

It was the end of February, 1971. As they had climbed the red-carpeted steps to the gleaming wood and brass front door of the club tucked discreetly among the banks and financial houses of Toronto's Bay Street, they had kicked from their shoes the remnants of the heavy snow that had fallen on the city on the night of February 12. That was the night when, after 13 hours of balloting, William Grenville Davis, Ontario's Minister of Education, had won the leadership of the province's Conservative party by 44 votes from Mines and Northern Affairs Minister Allan Lawrence.

Only 44 votes—that was the reason for the dinner meeting. The 41-year-old Education Minister had been heir-apparent to the throne of Premier John Robarts and should have won the leadership easily; but, hampered by a bad organization, labelled with a sneer as the establishment candidate, and forced by his opponents into a defensive campaign, he had just managed to scrape home. His near defeat had been a shocking experience both for Davis and for the people around him. He was going to have to fight an election within the next few months and it was obvious that if his own organization could only just garner him a majority of support from among Conservatives, it was unlikely to do any better among the voters. The thought of being the Conservative leader who led the party to defeat horrified Davis, a man who had almost been weaned and raised by the Conservative government.

Davis needed a new organization, and the best around seemed to be the one that had worked for Lawrence. Would it work for him? He was gently sipping a pre-dinner drink in the warm room waiting to find out. With him he had brought four men from his organization whose talents and advice he still trusted. They were Hugh Macaulay, the son of a wealthy family who turned a car dealership into another fortune and then turned to backroom politics; William Kelly, a vice-president of the Consumers' Gas Company whose ability to gather political contributions was to gain him notoriety at a later date; Clare Westcott, Davis's executive assistant and the supreme solver of political problems; and John Latimer, the owner of a commercial boys' camp in the Haliburton area and manager of Davis's leadership campaign.

It was not entirely for his political acumen that Mr. Latimer was there. He had the added qualification of being one of the few people in Davis's cadre who knew the four men on whom the new leader's attention was centred that night. All Davis knew of the men he had gone there to impress was their reputation as leaders of the new generation of Canadian political organizers. They were the men who had ousted John Diefenbaker and had made Robert Stanfield leader of the federal Conservative party in 1967. The key man was

Norman Atkins, advertising executive and political organizer without peer. "Advertising is my job, organization is my hobby," Atkins said once. Strange that a man should seek relaxation from the lively and colourful world of advertising among the dry charts and diagrams of organizational systems. But Norman Atkins pursues the dream of better organizational methods the way other hobbyists bound over summer fields in the hope of netting rare butterflies. If Atkins could be won over to Davis's side then no doubt the rest of the Lawrence people would follow. It all really hung on whether Atkins and his men took to Davis, could believe that the party under his leadership would move in the directions they wanted–and were offered roles in the new hierarchy.

In retrospect, the men who attended that dinner like to downplay its importance in the process of change-over from Robarts to Davis. But the alliance was vital to Davis and it established the political character of the Davis administration. The main impediment to the alliance was the incredible bitterness that had developed between the two groups in the course of the leadership campaign. Shortly before Robarts announced his decision to resign the leadership and the Premiership, the Atkins group had offered their services to Davis's men–and had been sloughed off without an explanation. They felt slighted, and went to Lawrence. The rivalry that grew in the campaign was so strong that when the voting machines broke down on balloting day, both groups seriously considered that the other side might have fixed the machines for their own advantage. So it was with some skepticism that Atkins and his team–Ross DeGeer, the young stockbroker who managed Lawrence's campaign; Paul Weed, who managed the campaign tour; and Eric Ford, Lawrence's fund raiser–waited for the dinner to begin.

Overlooking it all was the tall shambling form of their host, Roy McMurtry. The boyish-faced Toronto lawyer had his feet planted heavily in both camps. He had been Davis's friend ever since the two men had played football for the University of Toronto, and he had worked with Atkins, and Atkins' brother-in-law, Dalton Camp, in the campaign to topple John Diefenbaker from the leadership of the federal party. A back injury had kept McMurtry in hospital for much of the provincial leadership campaign; his physical discomfort was partly relieved by the thought that it excused him from the necessity of choosing sides in the battle between his friends. He had now cast himself in the role of honest broker and arranged the meeting. He thought it essential that once the steak had been eaten, and washed down with a few after-dinner drinks, it should be a united party organization that stepped out into the winter night.

McMurtry had put some time and care into arranging the meeting. The echoes of the last convention cheers had hardly stopped ringing around the rafters at the Maple Leaf Gardens before he and Hugh Macaulay were discussing the possibility of an alliance with the Lawrence organization. Macaulay was doubtful at first, largely because he was still bristling with suspicion and found the thought of an alliance unpalatable. But he could see the necessity for a meeting, and when the idea was put to him, so could Davis.

McMurtry did some telephoning. "Would you like to meet the man?" he asked Atkins. Atkins said he and his people would. What, after all, is the point of being a political organizer with nothing to organize? The obvious venue for the meeting was the Albany Club, social home of the Ontario Conservative party, but McMurtry rejected this. If the meeting were held there and failed, every Tory in the province would know about it within hours. It had to be somewhere neutral and private. He picked the National Club, watering hole for the most exalted Bay Street barons, and so jealous of its privacy that thousands of people walk past its red brick and stone Georgian façade every day totally unaware of what goes on behind those gleaming sash windows, the intricate wrought iron fencing, and the brass-fitted door of glass and dark oiled wood.

Unknown to McMurtry, Davis was approaching the dinner as far more than a pleasant social occasion to be played by ear. The evening before, Hugh Macaulay, William Kelly and he had a dinner of their own at the Albany Club and discussed how best to effect the conciliation. The soft approach was what was wanted, they decided. Keep the conversation light, show them they are wanted, stay away from confrontations and hard bargaining.

So at the National Club dinner Davis talked lightly about his view of politics and of the Ontario Tory party's situation, displaying the easy charm that comes naturally to him in small groups, but which somehow disappears when he faces a large audience or a television camera. The party must be opened up so that the grass-roots membership has some say in its affairs, he told them, echoing the demand of Allan Lawrence. The government must be overhauled, and a new era of responsive rule created. "The convention is over; I wanted to meet you and find out what you are thinking," he said at the end.

Atkins liked the man, his intellect, and his approach. As the party broke up he cornered the new leader. Atkins and his friends were going on for a final drink or two to a Toronto nightspot, Stop 33 at the top of the Sutton Place Hotel. Would Davis like to come?

"I would. I don't suppose I'll have the chance to do that sort of thing again," Davis replied.

With Toronto spread out below them and Davis opposite sipping a rum and orange, Atkins' favourable impression was reinforced. He had only met Davis once before, a brief encounter at the shoe-shine stall at the Park Plaza Hotel in 1963. He now found they had much in common, boating, football, and, of course, politics. They also discovered that they were both among the 15 per cent of the population who didn't believe that the introduction of the War Measures Act had been necessary to deal with the FLQ crisis in Quebec the previous October.

As the evening ended, Davis asked Atkins if he would work for him and Atkins replied that he would. That was all; but with that, the Big Blue Machine was created. Within weeks Atkins was the campaign manager for the forthcoming election, DeGeer was planning Davis's tour of the province during the campaign, and Weed was doing grass-roots organization. Meanwhile Macaulay was the new Premier's liaison man with the party, and Kelly was in charge of raising the $5 million Atkins estimated he needed to win the election.

Allan Lawrence, the man who had been the vehicle for the ambitions of the Atkins group, suddenly found himself out in the cold. He put on a brave face, but it was quickly apparent that it was just a matter of time before he tired of provincial politics, and the fine-sounding but fluffy jobs Davis gave him. In the fall of 1972 Lawrence quit the Legislature to run in the federal election and subsequently take his place among all the other hopefuls on the Opposition benches in the House of Commons in Ottawa.

In the spring of 1971 few people believed what many were to accept a few months later when the election returns were in, that the Conservatives had once again worked that unique Ontario miracle of regeneration. They had done it twice before. Power had been handed from George Drew to Leslie Frost to John Robarts—and now to the chubby small-town lawyer whose trousers tended to go baggy at the knees and whose shoes were invariably scuffed. On each occasion in the past the new man had re-established the party in the Legislature. In the fall of 1971 Davis did the same thing. He increased the Tories' number of seats in the 117-seat Legislature from 68 to 78, routing the best-organized campaign ever mounted by the New Democratic Party and driving the Liberals back into their traditional power base in the rural ridings of southwestern Ontario. It seemed that there might be some truth to the arrogant remark once made by John Robarts that the Tory party in Ontario could carry on governing forever.

"Regeneration" is the word the Conservatives use for their once-a-decade public extravaganzas to choose a new leader. It is as though the whole party attends a revival meeting at the fountain of youth, and after the total immersion is over they all arise with their once grey and flabby flesh now vibrant and muscular, their souls purged, and their minds razor-sharp. It is a marvellous spectacle which doubtless appeals to our half-erased pagan memories of old bulls and young bulls, the death of kings, springtime and harvest.

But although the regular changing of leaders is one reason why the Conservatives have maintained power in Ontario, it is not the most important; and to a large extent the whole operation is something of a sham. Behind the mask of change there are few real changes. The government still listens most attentively and sympathetically when special interest groups (particularly wealthy ones) speak, while it is more often than not arbitrary when dealing with the general public.

Premier Davis's first term was pock-marked with scandals which spoke not of a renewed, rejuvenated party, but of a party rotten with elitism, crumbling from within beneath the sheer weight of its preoccupation with maintaining power. The scandals (which we shall examine later) came close to Davis himself; while his personal honesty was never in question, his judgment in the choice of friends and advisers certainly was, even by the most loyal of his backbenchers. Conservatives publicly dismissed the scandals as being unimportant. The party, they argued, had been through such things before (as indeed it had), shaken off the dust and ashes of at least nominal repentance, and received yet another accolade from the voters.

The scandals were certainly not the whole story of the first years of Davis's rule, probably not even the most important part; but the speed with which they seem to have passed from the public's mind indicates how firm a grip the Conservatives have on Ontario. The electorate's liking for the Tories is so great that it is willing to forgive much. Because the Conservatives have been able to keep in reasonable step with the desires of the people, because the Conservatives are seen to be "safe" (Ontarians aren't risk-takers), and because the Conservatives have reflected Ontario's view of itself and its role in Canadian confederation, they have been able to maintain a successful electoral record. Being successful, they have attracted people interested in a provincial political career. Power attracts talent, and generally the Tories have attracted better candidates and better party organizers than either the Liberals or the NDP.

The case can be made that Ontario has been operating under a one-party system for the bulk of this century. As of the summer of 1974, the Conservatives had been in power for 56 of the years of this century. In 1905 the province saw the tail end of 33 years of Liberal rule. After that there have been only two interludes from Tory governments. From November, 1919, until the summer of 1923 the province briefly dallied with the United Farmers of Ontario led by Ernest Drury; and from July, 1934, to August, 1943, the Liberals, led by Mitch Hepburn (and the two men delegated to go down with the political ship he scuppered) were in power. It can be argued that those interludes represented no real diversion from the norm. The UFO was made up of small-"c" conservative farmers whose only claims to being radical reformers were beliefs in a few fiscal sleight-of-hand tricks, and in agricultural cooperatives. Mitch Hepburn, a former UFO member, was no reformer; he was a conservative who talked a good radical line.

The Ontario Conservatives differ from most dynasties in one rather significant way. They do suffer from elitism, they do suffer from a lack of imagination and sensitivity, but they have somehow avoided the most deadening fault of dynasties: the arrogant assumption of the right to rule. As each election comes round, the Tories whip themselves into a kind of Dervish dance of despair; the aim of the mad whirling is to convince themselves that they are going to be beaten. The result is the salutary one that they seldom take an election result for granted until the votes are counted. In the fall of 1973, about 18 months before an election could be expected, senior party organizers were already putting the fear of the NDP into party workers and whipping them on to greater efforts. This gift for self-hypnosis may well be the single most important reason for the Tories' success.

As a government, they have survived since 1943 not by a superior philosophy, but by superbly executed pragmatism. To a large extent the Conservatives have not led the province; rather, they have been dragged along by the needs and demands of its people. Changes in policy directions have generally been taken, not to anticipate a need, but when the need has become a problem, and the clamour for change has become so great that the political penalty for inactivity has outweighed the penalty for acting. "Do nothing until you have to, and then only as little as you can get away with," might well have been the catch phrase of the government.

Ontario has changed rapidly and radically since 1943. The economic picture has changed from that of an agrarian society centred on the family farm to a heavily industrialized society with large urban centres. In addition, the massive immigrations of people from all over the world, particularly since the Second World War, has completely altered the cultural and social make-up of the province. So far, the Conservatives have coped with the changes. But can they continue to do so? Their power base is still southern rural Ontario. Their greatest bulwark against defeat at the polls is the great belt of 34 seats from the Ottawa Valley to Lake St. Clair, in which adherence to the Tory party is part of the way of life. That allegiance has been stretched, perhaps to its limit, by such measures as the centralization of school and social services, and the introduction of regional governments. Increasingly—as in these examples—the Conservatives have been imposing the values learned in the cities on their rural power base. Much of what they are trying to do is necessary and logical—regional government is a prime example—but the introduction of the programs has been handled in a hamfisted and dictatorial fashion.

Rural discontent over regional government in particular showed itself in the Tory belt riding of Huron in a by-election in 1973 when the Conservative candidate was roundly defeated by the Liberal. This was a warning Davis could not ignore; if the Conservatives start losing seats like Huron to the Liberals, the only other party who can really compete with them in the rural south, then the end is nigh. So the government swiftly changed its whole method of introducing regional governments to give the areas affected much more say in the final scheme and much more opportunity to express their views. This appears to have headed off a confrontation at the polls on this issue.

By the summer of 1974 Premier Davis had certainly grown with the job. He handled his responsibilities with confidence where a few months before he was unsure and apparently indecisive. He still delivered prepared speeches to large audiences in a monotone, but he didn't display the anguish at having to speak that he used to. He had completed the round of hirings and firings that made it *his* Conservative party and *his* government rather than John Robarts'. He had introduced a mass of legislation, some of it important, much of it housekeeping. Despite his pronouncements to the contrary, he still didn't like the Legislature all that much, and spent little time there. But, then, he has always been an administration man, a child of the Conservative government who has come into his inheritance, not a hustings politician who has had to persuade people that he is the best man for the job. Yet, surprisingly perhaps, he is an excellent politician. His handling of the National Club dinner is but one example of his ability to deal with critical situations.

There may be many reasons for saying that the Conservatives no longer deserve the confidence of the Ontario voters, but as the Tories look over to the Opposition benches in the Legislature chamber they can justifiably allow themselves a little inward chuckle of confidence. Time and again over the past 30 years the Conservatives have been, to use Dalton Camp's phrase, rescued by "the gift of their opponents' folly". Since 1943 there has not been a credible alternative to the Conservatives. Part of the political history of the 1950s and 1960s is the rise of the NDP, child of the Co-operative Commonwealth Federation, and its failure in an age of quasi-socialism in North America and western Europe to do more than produce a vocal–though often talented–small third-party group in the Legislature.

In 1971 the NDP, under its newly elected leader, Stephen Lewis, was all set to take away from the Liberals the mantle of the official Opposition party, and perhaps even to force the Conservatives into a minority position in the House. Instead they were sharply slapped down by the Tories, and failed to get more seats than the Liberals. Ontario was not then, and shows no signs now, of being ready to accept an avowedly socialist party of any strength. Ontarians want social reform and more government services, but they appear to want these things from a left wing Conservative government. So the NDP has lowered its sights. It is no longer aiming to replace the Conservatives in the immediate future. Instead it is looking hopefully at the Liberal benches and planning in the next election to win the slightly more prestigious position of being the official Opposition party, a title of somewhat illusory significance.

In recent years the story of the NDP has been one of constant internal bickering between its two main groups, the trade unionists and the intellectual socialists. There have even been tribal wars, the most glaring example of which was the battle with the ultra-socialist and strongly nationalistic Waffle group.

The only strongholds the NDP now have are in the strongly union cities of Hamilton and Sudbury, but even here the NDP cannot be sure of its future, since in 1971 they lost the automobile manufacturing town of Oshawa, where the United Auto Workers union is politically dominant. Elsewhere, the NDP's association with the unions has not helped the party. The Conservatives have been quick to counter NDP criticism of United States' investment and control in Ontario by pointing out the power of the American unions in the NDP and suggesting that the union bosses in Washington are not without authority within the party.

Stephen Lewis took the party's lack of success in the 1971 election hard and he nearly quit the leadership. He is an astoundingly fine speaker and even the most anti-socialist, hoary, old Conservative backbenchers flock to the Legislative Chamber whenever he is scheduled to speak, simply for the pleasure of listening to him. But, as we shall see, Ontario has come to distrust fine orators, particularly clever ones. The results of the last election have made him painfully aware that he came over, especially on television, as strident and uncompromising. Lewis has now gone into political hiding; he occasionally rises to the surface to deliver a mild rebuke, but he has suppressed his instinct to make constant lunges for the Conservatives' political jugular. Instead he exhibits a world-weary, plodding determination to cultivate a respectable image for himself and his party, as though the only way to be accepted as an alternative to the Tories is to act and talk like a Tory, and to put forward a policy platform as close as possible to that of the Conservatives. The NDP could not be called socialist by any stringent definition of the term, anyway. They have retreated a long way from many of the traditional socialist policies—nationalization for example—and seem to be saying only that when the Tories have committed suicide the NDP will be there to do the things they did, but in a better way.

But the NDP, never having achieved power, can at least enjoy dreaming about the sweetness of that unknown pleasure. The Liberals are a sadder case. They have been in power.

They remember the taste of power, they see their brothers in Ottawa savouring it, but are completely incapable of attaining it themselves. Tantalus would have sympathy for them. They have tried every trick in the book to get their feet under the table. They have shuffled leaders like tarot cards. They have picked leaders no fewer than 10 times since the party fell into disarray in 1942. They have fought elections on issues of policy enshrined in laboriously produced manifestoes. They have damned the Tories for corruption. They have told the voters that it is simply time for a change. And all of it has been to no avail.

Over the years they have been pushed further and further back into the rural ridings of southwestern Ontario from where they came. On matters of policy they are squeezed between a left wing Tory party and a right wing NDP, so that the Liberals' alternatives become niceties of definition completely meaningless to anyone other than a constant observer of Ontario politics. Their organization is weak and lacking in talent, because any Liberal with ability and ambition naturally gravitates towards federal politics, where the Liberal party has the corner on power.

Leadership of the Ontario Liberals has been wishy-washy, and morale in the caucus low. In 1972 the leader, Robert Nixon, decided to quit, but reversed his decision when the Conservatives became embroiled in scandal after scandal. Late in 1973 he became a candidate for his own succession and won, though the strength of opposition to him indicated strong dissatisfaction within the party. He promised to change both himself and the party organization, and almost immediately made changes in personnel which at first glance would appear to be improvements. But the Liberals have much to overcome before they get within striking distance of the Tories. Still haunting them is the memory of Mitch Hepburn, the last Liberal elected to govern Ontario, who destroyed the Liberal party in the province and whose personal and political excesses opened the door in 1943 to three decades of Conservative rule.

2. "*Mitch*"

The second floor of Ontario's legislative building at Queen's Park is where the province's politics is most visibly expressed. Here is the Legislative Chamber flanked by the Government and Opposition lobbies, here is the Conservative caucus office, and such holy places as the Cabinet room, the office of the Premier, and the Lieutenant-Governor's suite. In these dim red-carpeted corridors the political mementoes of Ontario hang. Flags, photographs of members of the Legislature past and present—but mostly past—line the walls. Aging pictures of aging military governors of Upper Canada stare sternly down on the gaggles of school children and tourists who are led briskly along by the trim young tour guides equipped with megaphones and an alarmingly pat version of parliamentary history since Magna Carta. Lord Durham, the rosy-cheeked young gentleman whose ideas had a lot to do with it all, looks passively out into space as though he never had an idea in his head.

Just outside the Premier's office is a short stretch of corridor where hang the portraits of the recent Premiers of Ontario. Fine men all, they stand and sit in poses uniformly expressing their courage, principles, honour, dedication. The artists who painted these portraits idealized all these very different men into roughly the same picture of the civic virtues. All except one. At the far end, on the north side, is a picture unlike the others. It is of Mitch Hepburn, and the style is not that of the commissioned portrait painter who presents a cleaned-up, acceptable version of the man before him. It represents Hepburn as he undoubtedly looked in his last years.

The upright, challenging pose, so obvious in early photographs, is still there. There is the fierce dimpled chin, and the hands are thrust deep into the pockets of his grey double-breasted suit. But the suit hangs baggily round a corpulent figure, the face is rubicund with excessive good living, and, most striking of all, the light has gone from the eyes. The eyes are flecked yellow, troubled, and tired.

There has perhaps never been such a colourful period in Ontario politics as when this man Hepburn, the boy from Yarmouth in Elgin County, occupied the Premier's office from July, 1934, to October, 1942. And perhaps never has an Ontario politician been so completely seduced by power. He entered politics as a reformer pledged to end the authority of the financial and industrial magnates who represented to him and his fellow Liberals the heirs of the Family Compact. But he left politics the bosom companion–the pawn, even–of these men. His era began with an extravagant gesture to the crowd; he auctioned off all the limousines inherited from his Tory predecessor, "Honest" George Henry. It ended with his mind numbed by booze and his ears assailed by the chatter of the female camp followers who were part of the decor in his King Edward Hotel suite. It was all over for Hepburn by the time he was 45 years old. His health was broken, his friends believed him crazy, and his enemies earnestly wished that he would quickly succumb to his illnesses.

Hepburn was a man capable of the most intense and irrational hatred, but he was also capable of great charm and generosity towards his political opponents. Standing at his graveside, one of those opponents, Leslie Frost, said it was impossible to dislike Hepburn if you knew him. Nevertheless, he was devastating in his personal attacks on his adversaries, and ruthless in his attacks on his opponents' motives. His mastery of words was the base of his political power. Those who heard him speak recall that he could sway a crowd like no one before or since on the Ontario political scene. He was a spellbinder who could work his magic even when he was so drunk that he could hardly climb to the speaker's platform. There are still a few politicians around who follow the Canadian tradition of loosening up before a speech with the best part of a bottle, but, sadly, none of them are orators like Hepburn or Sir John A. Macdonald.

Hepburn's bequests to Ontario were mostly negative. He completely destroyed the provincial wing of the Liberal party; it has not yet recovered from his ministrations, and shows few signs of doing so. He rocked Confederation, and it took the provincial Conservatives some years of work to repair Ontario's tattered relationship with Ottawa. But Hepburn's most lasting endowment was that for three decades he continued to represent to Ontarians all that was unacceptable in a political man. His outrageous and crisis-ridden period in power is still remembered; the people of the province seem to believe that any repeat of that period should be avoided at all costs.

The Conservatives have been helped a great deal by Hepburn. As long as they have avoided excessive conflict, as long as their leadership has been quiet and measured, as long as they have moved with steady and predictable gait, as long as their sins have been within the bounds of what is forgivable on the scale of human frailties, they have been forgiven much. Ontarians will still toy with firebrands now and then, and will tolerate them in subsidiary roles; but should they seek leadership, the verdict of the people will be abrupt and final.

There is no doubt about when Hepburn made the move that finally destroyed him. It was January 18, 1940, and the setting was the Legislative Chamber at Queen's Park, a room whose massive gothic architectural impulses were, thankfully, restrained before they reached the outlandish reaches of the Victoriana of the House of Commons in Ottawa. A spectator in the public gallery at Queen's Park that day would have looked down, much as he would now, on tiers of leather-topped desks, mostly unattended, facing each other across a wide expanse of lush carpeting. Standing, speaking from one of the front row desks was a tall, handsome, austere man, impeccably dressed and groomed and with a hint of military arrogance in his bearing. Colonel George Drew, leader of the Ontario Conservative party, His Majesty's Loyal Opposition, was delivering yet another in his series of attacks on Canada's Liberal Prime Minister, Mackenzie King, for failing to push the nation into an all-out war effort in support of Britain.

Drew's enthusiasm for this subject didn't find much encouragement from the federal Conservative leader, Robert Manion. Manion felt, with justification, that Ottawa was the forum where such attacks should be made, and that if they were to be made it was he, Manion, who should do it. It was for Manion a delicate issue; he wanted to use it against King without losing support for the Conservatives from French Canadians, who had certain historical reasons for restraint in rushing the flower of their youth to the defence of Britain.

But Drew, sitting in Toronto rather than Ottawa, and as usual utterly convinced that he was in the right, felt no such constraints. He knew that if he didn't keep hammering away at the subject, other provincial Tories would. He also knew that Hepburn was not above taking a few off-the-cuff digs at King on the matter either. If the Liberal Premier of Ontario was not going to restrain his criticism of a Liberal Prime Minister, why should Drew? Even so, he was quite unprepared for what was about to happen.

When Drew eventually sat down, a Liberal backbencher rose to defend his party's national leader. He had loyally begun to quote from one of King's speeches when he was interrupted by his leader.

"Why should we be subject to that twaddle?" Hepburn interjected. "I ask to be associated with Colonel Drew in that attack on the King Government to which you refer."

The hatred that had simmered between King and Hepburn since the days when Hepburn served his political apprenticeship on the backbenches in Ottawa was about to boil over in public. But not before other Liberals jumped to defend King, as if by their numbers and verbiage they could expunge from the record the dreadful words their leader had spoken. But Hepburn was not to be deflected from the course he had chosen. He got up again holding a slip of paper with which he had been toying ever since Drew had begun to speak. His usual agitated state had become noticeably acute.

Hepburn had decided not only to confront King, whose motives on the war effort issue he mistrusted, but also his own provincial Liberal caucus. For Hepburn had decided on a confrontation with King, despite the fact that a short while before he had told his caucus that he would call off his running battle with Ottawa. So Hepburn bluntly told the Legislature that King had not done his duty to the country, and proceeded to introduce a motion "regretting that the federal Government at Ottawa has made so little effort to prosecute Canada's duty in the war in the vigorous manner the people of Canada desire to see."

The offhand remarks that Hepburn had been passing for some time about King were one thing—they could be discounted as part of the eccentric charm of the boy from Yarmouth—but this was quite another matter, a full-fledged motion of censure. So as the Speaker put the motion to the House, Liberal members scurried for the doors of the Chamber so as to avoid having to vote. Normally the Speaker would have only asked for a voice vote, with those in favour or opposed shouting aye or nay and the Speaker deciding by the volume of the responses which side had won. But Hepburn wasn't going to let it go at that. He called for a recorded vote, which required the division bells to be rung, the party whips to herd their members into the House, and each MPP to have his vote recorded in Hansard. Even so, a score or more of Liberal backbenchers didn't answer the call of the bells or the whip. Of the 36 hapless Liberals who did vote, 10 abandoned Hepburn and voted against the motion. The remainder joined the 18 Conservatives present to pass the motion 44 to 10.

In Ottawa, Mackenzie King received the news of the Ontario War Resolution with the closest thing to joy he ever exhibited. Drew and Hepburn had played into his hands. They had given him the very things he wanted—an excuse to fight an election, and a chance to clobber both of them and the federal Conservatives into the bargain. King was convinced that his restrained war policies were more in tune with the desires of the Canadian people than the strident demands of Drew and Hepburn were. He called the House of Commons into session on January 25 and promptly dissolved it to hold an election. King was right in his analysis; when the results came in he had won 178 seats to Manion's 39.

That election result was the beginning of Hepburn's long slide to rejection, defeat, and death. After years of sparring with King, the major confrontation had come and Hepburn had lost—and that losing confrontation proved to be a turning point in the politics of Ontario and the fortunes of the two main parties there. In politics the most important events often have their roots in the most inconsequential tiffs or slights. This was the case here. Hepburn's hatred of King stemmed from the time when as a young radical politician he was elected by the people of Elgin County (the area immortalized by John Kenneth Galbraith in *The Scotch*) to the House of Commons in Ottawa. Hepburn felt that his talents demanded that he be given a front row seat in the House. King, suspicious of this brash young man, refused and thus gained his undying enmity. As the years passed, Hepburn's hatred of King grew; but he chose to clothe it in a weave of dogma so that it appeared that it was the Prime Minister's *policies* and not simply the Prime Minister that Hepburn disliked.

In particular Hepburn felt that the only way to successfully push the war effort was to have a coalition government, as there was in Britain. King thought that behind Hepburn's war resolution was a plan to join up with Drew and fight a provincial election on the issue of a union government. If Hepburn and Drew could form a coalition in Ontario, there would be great moral pressure on King to do the same in Ottawa. But the plan failed and in the following months provincial Liberals began to voice their discontent with Hepburn more and more loudly.

Hepburn's government had been a one-man band from the start, and in the months between the war resolution scene in the Chamber and his resignation he consulted his caucus and Cabinet even less than before. His bouts of drunkenness became more frequent, and the already rudderless Liberal party began to break up. But he fought off calls for his resignation for nearly two years until quite suddenly, on a damp and drizzly afternoon in the fall of 1942, he drove to see the Lieutenant-Governor and quit. It was an uncharacteristic thing for Hepburn to do. *The Globe and Mail,* whose publisher George McCullagh was close to Hepburn, later suggested: "In our opinion what broke his heart and caused him to leave politics was the stinging blow he received after he had announced his intention to vacate the Premiership. He had expected the province to rise in protest."

The province did not rise. Hepburn was no longer the young firebrand from Elgin, but a prematurely aged dissipated wreck of a man; there were murmurs about his sanity, even among his friends.

Even in his leaving the Premiership Hepburn delivered yet another blow to the Liberal party. He appointed another anti-King Liberal to succeed him. The Attorney-General, Gordon Conant, from Oshawa, was sworn in as Premier the day Hepburn resigned. Not only was the Liberal caucus devoid of policy and imagination, it was now to be led by a dull pedantic soul who could call on no area of support from within the fragmented party. If *The Globe and Mail* was right in its opinion of Hepburn's motive for resigning, then the Premier might have been displaying a certain perverted logic in appointing Conant to succeed him. Perhaps he felt that he would benefit from being compared with Conant, and the expected cry from the countryside for his reinstatement would come that much more quickly.

As soon as Conant was appointed, events began to move swiftly. Two ministers resigned from the Cabinet in protest against the way the succession had been handled. The Provincial Secretary Harry Nixon (a King Liberal who had stood by Hepburn) made it plain as he quit the Cabinet that he would like to run for the leadership. The other man to leave was Farquhar Oliver, who was eventually to become a leader of the party. In the next few weeks pressure for a leadership convention—there hadn't been one since 1932—began to mount both in reaction to Conant, who pleased no one, and because of the way Hepburn had passed on the leadership without consulting the party. Late in the fall the Liberal caucus voted to hold a leadership convention after the spring session of the Legislature was over.

But Hepburn wasn't finished with them yet. Although he had resigned as Premier, he had retained the post of Treasurer, a portfolio he had kept, as was customary among Premiers, during his whole tenure. Hepburn offered to resign that post too, but Conant refused to accept it. So when Harry Nixon moved out of his Ministerial office in protest, Hepburn moved in. From this comfortable base Hepburn continued his attacks on King in the spring session of 1943. As his wording became more and more extreme and his logic more and more twisted it became apparent that if Hepburn was not prepared to leave what was left of the Liberal party, it was now prepared to leave him. In March of 1943 Conant decided to accept the resignation he had refused to consider five months before. Conant intended to run for the leadership at the convention, and he was conscious that there would also have to be a general election in the province within the next few months. Hepburn could be tolerated as an embarrassment to the party, but he had become a liability at the polls, and that could not be suffered.

The convention was held in April and Harry Corwin Nixon, father of the present Liberal leader, won it easily from Conant.

Grey is the adjective usually used to describe Harry Nixon, and grey perhaps he was. His politics were certainly grey, grey rural conservatism with a small "c". But after the extravagance of Hepburn he was predictable and safe, and he had more to him than Conant. There was, however, little that the cattle farmer from St. George near Brantford could do to save the Liberal party; his role was to go down with the ship.

Nixon called the election for August, 1943, and then, incredibly, campaigned on the record of the Hepburn government. The Liberals were defeated. Mackenzie King, noting the deficiencies of the campaign at the time, said the "greatest weakness of all was running on the record of the Liberals, which is really a thoroughly bad record."

Thoroughly bad? No doubt it was. Hepburn himself said his greatest contribution was legislation requiring the pasteurization of milk. No doubt it was an important piece of legislation, at a time when tuberculosis was rife, but hardly a substantial monument to nine years in office. But his term was also marked by some of the foremost labour legislation of the time, which was surprising considering Hepburn's virulently anti-union feelings (at the time of the Oshawa Strike he had raised what amounted to a private army of special constables to deal with apprehended, supposedly communist-inspired, violence on the picket lines). In reality Hepburn's Labour Minister David Croll was the author of that legislation.

In partial defence of Hepburn's lack of attainment, it can be claimed that he ruled through the depression and the war years when great legislative programs were not being enacted anywhere. Even so, he would probably not have done much better under other circumstances. So great was his lack of foresight that when he left office he believed that the province with its budget of $100 million a year and a population of 3.7 million people had reached a plateau in its development which would probably remain constant forever.

The editorial writers of *The Globe and Mail*, commenting shortly after Hepburn's death on January 5, 1953, said that they liked Hepburn personally. "As to his political principles, we express no opinion, for we are not aware that he had any. He was as much mountebank as politician."

In terms of his record as a legislator, Hepburn's bequests to the 1970s are small. But as a politician, his shadow has hung over provincial affairs for more than a generation and continues to do so. The Ontario Liberal party has not recovered from the debilitating effects of his leadership, and thus the quality of opposition to the Conservative government, and of the critical appraisal it has faced, has been lessened.

In the 1950s and 1960s the Liberals were obsessed with Hepburn. He was at once, to mix a metaphor, their Holy Grail of hopes of power and the albatross that caused them to while away the years in penitence for their failures. Hepburn was the only Liberal this century who had a formula to defeat the Conservatives, and at every leadership convention there is some group within the party that wants to return to it, while another group is just as determined to keep clear of such dangers. Such pro- and anti-Hepburnesque conflicts have been the mark of the multitude of leadership conventions the Liberals have held since 1943. Even at the convention in the fall of 1973, when Robert Nixon sought to retain the leadership, his main opponent, smooth-talking federal MP Norman Cafik, could be seen as the Hepburnesque contender, and the comparison was indeed made among delegates on the convention floor. The revelation that Cafik's debts had been paid off by a number of wealthy and influential people in his riding, and the fact that his candidacy was opportunistic in the extreme, did not prevent him from coming amazingly close to defeating Bob Nixon. His sweet-talking gravelly voice and his rugged ugliness wowed nearly half the delegates, and Nixon's victory was so slim that it was embarrassing.

Partly because of Hepburn, and partly for other reasons which will be discussed later, the relationship between the federal and provincial wings of the Liberal party in Ontario has always been bad. The federal wing has seldom been serious in its support of the provincial party. There have been occasional federal forays on behalf of the Ontario party, but the work done has lacked any real substance, enthusiasm, or meaningful result.

The Ontario Liberals were driven to again make Hepburn their leader in the mid 1940s and he schemed and plotted to regain power in a sadly frantic fashion. In the election of 1945 his rejection was complete. The people of Elgin County, who had stood by him through everything, at last left him too, and elected a Conservative. Hepburn, as he stumbled away from the election night gathering in St. Thomas, didn't really understand what had happened. He went back to his twelve-hundred-acre farm, Bannockburn, to a lonely existence. Few of his friends from the good old days came to visit him, but now and again people from Yarmouth would ask for his help and he would do his best. He even made a speech or two at political rallies and had them cheering, laughing, and clapping as he had in the old days. That pleased him. Then shortly before dawn on January 5, 1953, he died in his sleep in the room where he had been born. He was nearly fifty-seven years old.

3. *Colonel Drew*

While Hepburn was in his last paroxysms–equating King with Hitler and calling his policies Nazi–George Drew had had a vision, and he talked about it for some time before the 1943 election. It was a vision of a period of massive reconstruction after the war was over. Even in the darkest period of the war Drew talked confidently of the day when it would all be over and the people of Ontario could get down to the business of building the province to the economic and social level that was its destiny. And Drew was an unlikely messiah of the great social and economic revolution that was to begin in 1943.

Colonel Drew

Drew (who died in January, 1973) looked every bit the imperialist soldier, which in part he was. He was tall, and seemed arrogant and forbidding, although for all his bitingly partisan speeches, he was hesitant and unsure in his personal relationships. He was the ultimate Wasp in many ways, and some of his thinking was undoubtedly intolerant and reactionary. Some called him a stuffed shirt, others caught a glimpse of what was behind the stiff white shirt and lawyer's pinstripe and said he was just very shy. Possibly both analyses were true; certainly he was a very complex man full of contradictions whose contribution to Ontario and Canada has never been fully appreciated.

Drew's gifts to the Conservative party and government were threefold. He prepared them mentally and physically for the tremendous period of growth in the 1950s and 1960s; he recognized the desire in the population for social change, and geared the government to respond; and he set the style of the Conservative government—a style which has found acceptance among the voters in election after election. The style was once defined by a veteran Queen's Park correspondent as "untouchability". It's a clumsy word, but an apt one. George Drew was a controversial figure all his political life, which encompassed 42 years. This mysterious "untouchability" allowed him to sweep through a number of situations which would have left other men discredited. He always emerged utterly confident that he was in the right. The public did not always share his confidence, but he buried their nagging doubts with his energy. He advanced regardless, regrouping his support as he went.

It is hard to avoid military metaphors when talking about Drew, because he tackled politics in a very military way. His self-confidence was that of a man born and trained to command, and his election campaigns were fought with all the planning and foresight that goes into a military campaign; new political techniques, such as the use of radio and television, were avidly grasped as a general might grab the new weapon that will give him the tactical edge. He regarded politics as a constant battle with no final conclusion. And it is this sense of immediacy, the feeling that all the important battles are in the future, that has as much as anything kept the Conservatives in power.

George Alexander Drew was born on May 7, 1894, in Guelph, Ontario, the son of a lawyer and the grandson of another George Drew who sat as a Conservative in the first parliament after Confederation. It was a United Empire Loyalist family, and George Drew's devotion to the Imperial and Commonwealth ties remained strong throughout his life. His early schooling was at Guelph, but he later attended Upper Canada College and the University of Toronto. Besides the political tradition in his family there was also one of military service, and he joined the reserve force as a youth. In 1914 he left university to enlist in the Canadian Army, and was sent to Europe the following year. He was severely wounded in the left arm in 1916 and returned to Canada in 1917. He spent two years recovering after being invalided home.

With typical energy he then set out on numerous careers at once. In 1920 he became a lawyer and set up a practice in his home town. In 1921 he was elected an alderman on Guelph council and four years later he became mayor. He was appointed peacetime commander, with the rank of Lieutenant-Colonel, of the 64th Battery, Canadian Field Artillery, and he also started writing books about Canadian military history. For years he was pleased to be known as Colonel Drew, although later in his political career, when times had changed, the title was used pejoratively. But his favourite article of clothing remained the red and blue artillery tie.

His books, and particularly a magazine article called "The Salesmen of Death" (which was about private munitions manufacturers who had a vested interest in war, and which was translated into 30 languages), brought Drew to public attention in the later twenties and early thirties.

His growing reputation was enhanced in 1929 when he was appointed the province's first Securities Commissioner. In his five years in this job he succeeded in cleaning out many of the shysters, phony promoters, and swindle sheet publishers who then infested Bay Street, and he did so with a vigour that aroused astonishment among the public and alarm in some financial circles.

Ironically, it was Mitch Hepburn who propelled Drew into provincial politics. Hepburn had promised to clean out Queen's Park bag and baggage when he defeated George Henry, and in 1934 he did just that. It wasn't only the Conservative government's limousines that were thrown out in the course of Hepburn's housecleaning, he made a point of getting rid of senior civil servants as well, claiming that they were patronage appointees. Drew was one of those who got the chop. When Hepburn came into power Henry stayed on for a while as Conservative leader, but in 1936 a leadership convention was called, and Drew, with his background in municipal politics, his name, and his grudge against Hepburn, was a prominent contender. But he lost to Earl Rowe, who some twenty years later was to be Drew's deputy in the House of Commons in Ottawa and finally a Lieutenant-Governor of Ontario.

Despite his defeat in the leadership Drew was committed to Ontario politics, and he took the job of organizer of the provincial Conservative party. One of Drew's first tasks as organizer was to oversee the by-election campaign for the Tories in East Hastings in December, 1936. There was only one issue, the legislation Hepburn had recently passed to give Catholic schools a larger share of the educational tax dollar. The whole Conservative campaign was fought on viciously anti-Catholic lines. Hastings was and is a staunch Orange county, and all Hepburn's arguments about equality and fairness to Catholics fell on historically deaf ears. Rumours—unauthorized, of course, by the Tories—flew among the doughty farmers of Hastings, claiming that Casa Loma in Toronto was being prepared as a Papal residence and that the crowns on highway signs would be replaced by romanish crosses.

Hastings was not then (and, as we shall see later, is not now) very subtle in its politics, and Drew did nothing to raise the level of debate. In fact he was said to be responsible for one of the strongest electoral appeals to racial prejudice in modern Canadian history.

He told a reporter that he intended to state in a speech in

the riding that the French were a defeated race and that any rights they had were only theirs because of the tolerance and generosity of English Canadians. This was printed as a report of the speech, because the reporters couldn't go to the meeting, and Drew vehemently and repeatedly denied having used it in his address. He may not have done, but he certainly said it to the reporter.

When the votes were counted in Hastings on December 9, 1936, the traditional Tory riding had asserted itself more strongly than ever and trebled the Conservative's majority over the Liberal candidate. The following year Hepburn repealed the School Assessment Act.

Despite all the bitterness of the East Hastings election, within five months Drew and Hepburn were active allies in one of the strangest chapters in the province's political history. In the United States the growth of the Committee for Industrial Organization had been accompanied by violence and sit-down strikes. Early in 1937 the CIO spilled over into Ontario from Michigan. Hepburn was horrified, and when the CIO was involved in organizing a strike at the Oshawa Plant of General Motors he became frantic. He sent word to Ottawa that he wanted a detachment of the RCMP to deal with anticipated violence on the picket lines. When Ottawa took a less serious view of the situation than Hepburn did, and offered to mediate the strike, he flew into a rage and ordered the Mounties withdrawn. He then raised a private army of 400 special constables instead. Most of them were university students, who lounged around Toronto playing cards and exercising with dumbbells.

Hepburn's fear was Communist infiltration of Canada through the unions and it was a fear played on—and perhaps sown in the first place—by his friend George McCullagh, publisher of *The Globe and Mail.* McCullagh was something of a young financial wizard and a heavy investor in Ontario industry, particularly mining, and thus had a fairly practical motive for not wishing to see an active union movement in the province. So all-possessing was Hepburn's fear of subversion by the CIO that when the strike ended, in the last days of April, 1937, he took steps to see if a government made up of a union between the Liberals and the Conservatives could be formed.

Colonel Drew

Hepburn met alone with the Opposition leader Earl Rowe in a downtown hotel. At that meeting it became clear that not only the influence of McCullagh's views on trade unions was driving Hepburn towards a Liberal-Conservative union; he was also propelled by a desire to get at Mackenzie King. Drew's view was that if there were Liberal-Conservative government in Ontario and Quebec, Canada would be well controlled, and what King did in Ottawa would not matter much. Hepburn apparently shared this feeling, but Rowe didn't. He was utterly astonished by the proposal, and delayed giving an answer to it. But before he could decide how to deal with the situation, the story of the impending coalition came out in *The Toronto Star*. There was some furious back-pedalling. Both Hepburn and Rowe denied that the suggestion of a union had been made. On May 6, the day after Rowe's denial, Drew's resignation as party organizer was announced. Drew said he was resigning because he was in complete agreement with Hepburn that the CIO should be prevented from exploiting Canadian labour and he therefore disagreed with Rowe's policy that labour should have freedom to organize however it wished.

But Drew's real reason for resigning was because Rowe would not accept the Liberal-Conservative union government idea. Drew had in fact implored Rowe on several occasions at the end of April, 1937, to agree to a union government, and had made it known that he would join up with Hepburn if his party leader would not. He had been offered the post of Attorney-General in the coalition government by Hepburn.

Hepburn's Liberal party organizers told him that his hard line against the CIO was popular in the province while Rowe's stance was not. Hepburn called an election. Drew ran as an independent Conservative in Wellington South riding and battered away at Rowe from one side while Hepburn thumped at the other. The former Tory organizer used the Communist threat to Canada in the shape of the CIO and the merits of union government as his main issues. The party system was too confining in provincial politics, he told one audience, and there was no good reason for maintaining it. If that was not trouble enough for Rowe–at one point he was forced to disavow Drew entirely–McCullagh also stumped the hustings physically and editorially in favour of Hepburn and Drew. The publisher of *The Globe* knew nothing about politics and had very little sense of the democratic process. But as a businessman he believed in efficiency, and he thought a union government would be efficient.

The 1937 election, Hepburn's last, was a fine victory for the Liberals. They dropped only 4 seats to 66, the Tories gained 6 for a total of 23 seats. Drew, however, was defeated.

But not for long. A year later, at the end of 1938, Rowe resigned the Conservative leadership. At the convention in the Royal York Hotel in December that year he revealed to the delegates that Drew had quit as party organizer over the union government issue and not because of the party's labour policy. He felt that Drew had betrayed him in the 1937 election and he said so. He may have felt like Caesar stabbed by his lieutenant, but he spoke like Brutus. "Who is here among you so doubtful a Conservative that he would form a coalition with our common enemy? Him only have I offended. I lost an election, but I saved you a party."

Drew already had the convention sewn up, and his response to Rowe's impassioned speech was terse. He had believed in coalition at the time, he said. "I may have been mistaken, but I was honest. Personally I shall do everything I can to unite the party for the purpose of defeating Mr. Hepburn." With the help of a party organizer named A. D. McKenzie from his home town of Guelph, Drew won the leadership on the first ballot, and in the new year he entered the Legislature after winning a by-election in Simcoe East. When the House opened on March 8, 1939, for the spring session, Drew faced Hepburn across the red-carpeted floor of the Legislature.

Looking back, Drew's actions throughout this period are somewhat perplexing. To some degree, however, they are in character. He certainly maintained an uncompromising hatred of Communism throughout his life. Indeed, in his latter years as a member of the Board of Governors of the University of Toronto, it was unkindly, untruthfully, but rather widely whispered that his main contribution to the work of the board was a long annual diatribe against the evils of Communism as it pertained to the increasingly vocal and active student movement.

But why did he go for the idea of a union government? He was, after all, "the most Tory of Tories", and having any truck with Grits was surely anathema to him. The influence of McCullagh may have had something to do with it. Certainly, the two men were very close; when McCullagh died, Drew married his widow. Or Drew may have felt that the times demanded such action. It was the Depression, unemployment rates were high, the bread lines long, social injustice horrific. Drew was a decisive man who needed action, and he may well have believed that the only way to deal with the situation was to treat it as a disaster, pool resources, and do away with party squabbling for the duration.

For Drew to take his belief in union government to the extent of actively campaigning in the 1937 election against his boss of a few months before may seem excessive. Whatever Rowe's failings as a party leader, he deserved better treatment than that. But the party Rowe led was fragmented and disorganized, and Drew was never a good team player in any other post than captain. He showed this clearly during his tenure as High Commissioner to Britain from 1957 to 1964. Far from accepting lightly the sinecure of this comfortable diplomatic post, he pursued what was in fact an independent foreign policy, and actively counselled Britain against joining the Common Market. It was an entirely improper thing for a servant of the Canadian government to do off his own bat, and was of considerable embarrassment to Ottawa. But it was typical of Drew to be outspoken on matters about which he felt strongly.

Drew had said on the night of the leadership convention that elected him that he would do everything he could to unite the party and to defeat Hepburn. Once he was in the Legislature he set about doing it. At first his speeches were somewhat pompous, and Hepburn had great fun twitting him, especially as Drew was easily riled by personal jibes. But his performance improved as Hepburn's decline became more and more apparent.

Around Drew at that time were the men who were to be, with him, the founding fathers of the current era of Conservative rule. They were mostly of United Empire Loyalist stock, Protestant, and they usually represented small-town Ontario. They had something else in common, too. Like

Drew, the war that was then beginning in Europe had special meaning for them. Leslie Frost, the man who was to become Drew's Treasurer and successor, was wounded near Arras in World War I and invalided home. Leslie Blackwell, later one of Ontario's outstanding Attorneys-General, lost a leg at Passchendaele. Thomas Kennedy, who was briefly Premier and who was the political patron of a young lawyer named William G. Davis, was wounded in the arm and face by shrapnel at Loos.

To all these men Drew's message of preparation for a period of massive reconstruction and expansion after the Second World War was over had a special poignance. They had had similar hopes in 1918, and had seen them come to little or nothing in the ten lost years of the Depression.

Drew worked hard at getting his message over and at building up the riding organizations of the Conservative party, but he could not be separated from controversy for long. On January 12, 1942, he charged that large numbers of untrained men were included in the Canadian Expeditionary Force sent to Hong Kong, which was almost immediately captured by the Japanese when the colony fell on Christmas Day, 1941. Fearing the effect this statement could have on recruiting, Mackenzie King set up a Royal Commission under Sir Lyman Duff to investigate. The hearings were held in secret and the Commission's report discredited Drew's charges. But he was not to be deflected and he repeated his allegations. King wouldn't tolerate this, and Drew was charged under the Defence of Canada regulations. There was an immediate public outcry in Drew's favour and three weeks later Ottawa was forced to drop the charges.

The Canadian government had always maintained that it anticipated that the troops would complete their training in Hong Kong and that the swift Japanese assault was unexpected. Drew said this was rubbish; the government knew when the ships were despatched that the colony was likely to fall any day. When the evidence heard by the Royal Commission was finally made public, it showed Drew to be right; but many questions about the expedition remain unresolved.

Drew, therefore, was much in the public eye at a critical

time. Generally, things were moving well for him. He gave a picture of vigorous leadership of a united party at a time when Hepburn was dropping towards the nadir of his life and the Liberals were in complete disarray. Drew spoke of a bright future when the Liberals had nothing to say, no ideas, no policy. He also knew that the people of Ontario, like people elsewhere, wanted more and more social services from their government and would vote strongly for the CCF if given no other choice.

On July 9, 1943, a few days after Harry Nixon called the election, Drew set out his election platform, the 22-point program for the social and economic development of the province. The main point was a promise of sweeping municipal tax reform, including payment by the province of 50 per cent of the cost of education, money which had previously been raised by property taxation. Other plans included the provision of universal medical, dental, and other health protection (dental care has not yet been introduced); an immediate increase in the mothers' allowance; complete revision of the educational system to equalize educational opportunity; increases in the old age pensions; the establishment of an Ontario Housing Corporation–something that was not to happen for nearly 20 years; and the removal of Ontario Hydro from the political arena, where it had caused some fine scandals. Even as a semi-autonomous satellite commission, Ontario Hydro continued to cause problems; and in the 1970s Premier Davis considered putting it back in full public view as a Crown corporation.

Much of Drew's document was aimed at the development of Ontario's agricultural and resources industries. He foresaw the establishment of produce marketing boards for farmers, and the nationalization of stockyards by the province to eliminate speculation and manipulation and to guarantee farmers fair prices. Mining was to be encouraged by the easing of the tax burden on that industry, and all measures that discouraged prospectors from finding and developing new mining properties were to be removed. The forest industry could employ hundreds of thousands more people than it did, Drew asserted, and he promised a massive program of timber management and reforestation. Amazingly, the man who had reacted so strongly to the Oshawa Strike also assured Ontarians that his government would introduce legislation granting the province's workers "the fairest and most advanced" laws governing labour relations in the country. For the times his labour policies *were* reasonably progressive.

Newspapers at the time commented that the 22-point program was a document unparalleled for a generation both in its content and in the very fact that it existed as a testimony of a party's well-rounded policy program. The 22 points were certainly an important factor in the Tories' victory when the votes were counted on August 4, 1943. They had won 38 seats, the Liberals were cut to 16 seats from the 66 they had held, the CCF were close behind the Conservatives with 34 seats, and two Communists were elected.

It was a halting start to the most successful era for the Conservatives in the history of Ontario. Drew's Tories formed a minority government; they were outnumbered by 52 seats to 38 and maintained in power by the Opposition parties. But the Liberals and the CCF had agreed in fact not to overthrow the Tories for the time being. The Liberals were completely demoralized after the strain of purging themselves of Hepburn and their election defeat. The CCF, under Ted Jolliffe, felt that they had to go along with many of Drew's proposals, and were watching and waiting for the right issue on which to bring Drew down.

Drew, meanwhile, carried on as though he had a majority. He set about implementing his 22-point program and his chief political aide, A. D. McKenzie, got busy establishing a network of helpers out in the ridings who could keep him informed of problems and the mood of the electorate.

In the fall of 1944 Drew provoked the Opposition to actions which were to lead to the next election. He hit out at the federal government's proposed family allowance legislation, which he called "iniquitous". This roused Hepburn from the torpor that had afflicted him since he was evicted from the Cabinet two years before, and he began rattling away at the Tories with, apparently, all the force and ability of his performances in the 1930s. But Drew now had the measure of Hepburn and was not as affected by his jibes as he had been. Harry Nixon, however, unable to find any weapon with which he himself could attack the Conservatives, began to believe that the old Hepburn had returned to succour the Liberals; in December, 1944, he asked his caucus to elect Hepburn party leader again. It did.

Back in the saddle, Hepburn in his first major speech early in 1945 vowed to bring down fire and brimstone on the heads of the Tories. He was dedicating himself to the destruction of Toryism root and branch, he said. To begin the crusade, Hepburn and Nixon visited Jolliffe's office. There Hepburn announced his belief that Drew had become so unpopular that an effort should be made to persuade the Lieutenant-Governor, Albert Matthews, to call on Jolliffe's CCF party to form the government. Jolliffe replied that he didn't think the time was ripe for Drew's overthrow, since the people would prefer to wait until the war was over before going to the polls again.

A few weeks later Hepburn had another crack. He invited Jolliffe to his new hotel suite at the Park Plaza, and over a bottle of whisky the two men discussed the idea again.

As a means of persuading the Lieutenant-Governor to call on Jolliffe to form the government without the necessity of an election, Hepburn suggested he and the CCF leader put out a press release to the effect that Drew had lost control of the Legislature. They would allow the idea to ferment, and then would visit Matthews with the request of a change of Premiers. Hepburn was sure this would force Matthews to call on Jolliffe without an election having to be called. Jolliffe, however, was not convinced that Matthews would be duped by a trumped-up campaign of this type, and refused to go along with the plan.

While Hepburn was plotting the downfall of the Tories, Drew himself was fervently hoping that his party would be defeated in the House so that he could go to the people; he was confident that he could win a majority of the seats and the full authority to implement his twenty-two points. His wish was answered on March 22, 1945, at the end of the Throne Speech debate.

Before the House was a CCF motion mildly criticizing the government for its legislative plans. Hepburn, however, had decided that the time had come to dump the Tories and he introduced a strongly worded amendment blasting Drew for plans to require a religious education in public schools. Seeing what was happening, Jolliffe decided to deny Hepburn the pleasure of bringing down the Conservatives. The CCF leader allowed his followers to vote as they wished on the Liberal amendment and, as he expected, it was defeated. One of the two Communists in the House attempted to remove all ambiguity from the original CCF motion, but Drew waved him down and said his government would stand or fall on the result of the vote on that motion.

First the Speaker turned to the CCF and they all rose to vote in favour of their motion of censure. The Speaker then turned to the Liberals. Hepburn rose, followed by the other Liberals, and the packed public galleries were treated to the strange spectacle of the Conservatives joyfully throwing papers into the air to celebrate their own defeat. It was the first and only time that an Ontario government has been defeated on the floor of the House.

The election campaign began quietly enough and continued that way until the night of May 24–11 days before the June 4 polling day. On that night Jolliffe, without consulting his party, told Ontario over the radio that Drew was maintaining in the province a paid government spy organization–"a Gestapo", Jolliffe called it–to try and keep himself in power. There was instant uproar throughout the province. Drew and his Attorney-General, Leslie Blackwell, angrily denied the allegation, but the story gathered momentum and two days later Drew ordered a Royal Commission inquiry under Mr. Justice A. M. LeBel.

It was the first of many scandals for the Conservatives, and it seemed that it could not have come at a worse time, just days before the election. But it was Jolliffe, who opened the door to the closet where the Tory bones rattled, who was punished. From being the official Opposition with 34 seats his party was cut right back to 8 seats, and Jolliffe himself was defeated. The Liberals changed little, keeping 14 seats, but Drew was given the mandate he wanted, 66 seats out of the 90-seat House.

Even before the election Jolliffe had produced telling evidence of his charges–names, dates, affidavits–and at the

Royal Commission inquiry he told a colourful story. He said that a provincial police captain named William J. Osborne-Dempster operated the spy group out of a secret headquarters above an abandoned garage in Surrey Place near Queen's Park. The purpose of this group, Jolliffe said, was to spy on CCF members in the hope of linking as many of them as possible to the Communist party. He said Osborne-Dempster's identity was kept secret, his name did not appear on government payrolls and his reports to Drew and Blackwell were signed only with the code D-208. The group, according to Jolliffe, attended union meetings and drew up lists of suspected Communists. It then made these lists available to selected industrialists.

Other evidence indicated that Osborne-Dempster had indeed prepared at least 41 reports which included information on thousands of Ontarians with leftist leanings, among them Jolliffe, Hepburn and former Liberal Labour Minister David Croll. With Drew sitting on a comfortable majority when the hearings were going on, the findings of the inquiry were of only academic interest.

Mr. Justice LeBel, in his report, said there was no evidence that Drew was operating a secret police force in the terms that Jolliffe had implied. The report stated that Osborne-Dempster was officially engaged in anti-sabotage work for the Ontario Provincial Police and Blackwell should have stopped Osborne-Dempster when the reports of the political activities of CCF members started arriving on his desk. That was the only major criticism of the government that was felt necessary.

Another strange situation went unremarked. It was shown during the inquiry that besides being paid by the OPP, Osborne-Dempster was being financed by a violently anti-socialist pest exterminator by the name of A. M. Saunderson who was famous at the time for a series of advertisements he purchased in Toronto newspapers to put forward his strong political views.

Looking for a scapegoat to blame for their poor showing in the 1945 election, the CCF laid it all at the door of Jolliffe, saying that he had mis-timed his "Gestapo" statement and aroused a sympathy vote for Drew. There may have been an element of this in the election result, but it was not the whole story by any means. The question really was not why had the CCF done so badly in 1945, but why had they done so well in 1943. The CCF share of the popular vote in the 1937 election was 5 per cent, but in 1943 it rocketed to 32 per cent. In 1945 it dropped back down to 22 per cent, where, roughly, it has stayed since. In 1943, also, only about 58 per cent of registered voters turned out to vote. This was undoubtedly partly because of the war, but probably also because it was an August election. The Conservatives and Liberals have traditionally had trouble getting their supporters to the polls in mid-summer elections, while the CCF and NDP have not had as much trouble.

Another factor in the CCF's 1943 showing was undoubtedly the wave of sympathy for socialist philosophies and the hope of a better, fairer world which swept the western democracies in reaction to the war. Winston Churchill was defeated by these sentiments in Britain immediately after the war.

The main reason for the CCF's poor showing in 1945 was not Jolliffe, but Drew. In his two years as Premier, Drew had established a vigorous government and had moved with reasonable despatch to implement many of the famous 22 points that he, Lincoln-like, had pencilled on the back of an envelope before the 1943 election. People still didn't love him, but he had imparted his vision of a prosperous, thriving Ontario, and had caught the province up in his own enthusiasm. He had also appointed A. D. McKenzie as party organizer.

McKenzie was a brilliant man and a brilliant organizer who established an amazing network of contacts throughout the province. This network allowed him to see that problems arising in the ridings were dealt with promptly, and that the Conservatives got the credit. He had a Conservative ward heeler not merely in every riding, but in every poll in the province. It made the Tories part of daily life in Ontario, or, to use an appealing Maoist image, the party moved in the community as do fish in water. Even today, Mr. Davis and his organization are living off the strength of that creation.

Now, with a secure majority, Drew set about laying the

groundwork for the economic expansion of the 1950s and 60s. As is often the case in politics, one of the most important moves was one that seemed comparatively uninteresting. There had been debate for some thirty years about changing Ontario's electrical system from 25 cycles to 60 cycles, the same as that in the United States. Government after government had put off making the change because of the cost, but Drew felt that the change was essential to the industrial development of the province, and in typical style bulldozed his way through the criticism for spending $400 million on the project. As well as being a tremendous boon to industry, the change-over also made household appliances cheaper, and thus available to a wider section of the community.

Drew also began modernizing Ontario's highway system, and started the Department of Planning and Development to oversee the social and industrial changes of the time. He introduced a new penal system with the emphasis on reforming criminals rather than merely punishing them. But Drew is probably best remembered for two actions in this period: the importation of 10,000 skilled British immigrants, and the reform of Ontario's liquor laws.

Early in 1947 Drew was on one of his frequent visits to Britain when he met a man at a party who operated a charter airline with landing rights in Canada. The Premier made a spur of the moment decision and arranged with the man to fly immigrants to Canada. As a result, a pool of highly skilled workers was airlifted to Ontario between the summer of 1947 and the fall of 1948. They filled the places created by Drew's work to expand the economy, and provided a basis for industrial development in the next two decades. It wasn't a terribly popular move at the time. There was a lot of feeling that the immigrants were taking jobs Ontarians should have had, but Drew maintained that without these imported skills the province's development would have been slow and tortuous.

Those staunch supporters of Drew who remember him with awe and affection lay great emphasis on his visionary qualities and the courage with which he pursued courses he believed right, even though they might be unpopular. The liquor question was such a course. Ontarians are at their most hypocritical and their Calvinist worst when discussing liquor, and even now the province's drinking laws are uncomfortable in the extreme. They are still aimed at making the drinker, whether he or she is merely an occasional social drinker or a hardened tippler, feel as uncomfortable as possible with their sin. No Ontario government has ever been concerned about voter reaction to the gouging prices it charges for wines and spirits, for who in Ontario will complain when the abject sinner has to expiate his depravity by parting with gold?

In 1934 Hepburn had, against considerable opposition, introduced beer parlours, but in 1947 the only place hard spirits could be bought legally was from a government liquor store. The result was that hotel rooms around the province were the setting for wild and wonderful scenes, because travellers who wanted a drink were forced to buy a bottle and take it to their rooms–and, as everyone knows, bottles have a habit of being drunk. Drew found the situation ridiculous, and tending to promote drunkenness rather than the reverse.

Not only were hotel rooms the bar rooms of the province, but bootlegging was rife. Taxi drivers did a thriving business running backwards and forwards to the moonshine depots, and cab drivers who remember those days recall that some policemen were not above keeping a watch on the routes to and from the bootleg outlets and levying a personal tax on the laden cabs.

Not long before the 1948 election was called, the Drew government passed an order-in-council permitting cocktail lounges in the province. Retaliation from the hard-line "drys" was quick and devastating. When the votes were counted on June 7 the Conservatives had lost 13 seats to the CCF. The result was 53 for the Tories–still a majority–and 21 for the CCF. The Liberals kept their 14 seats and the two Communist members also stayed.

Among the 13 Tory casualties to abstinence was Drew himself who was defeated in High Park riding by the teetotal CCFer William Temple. Drew said he wasn't concerned about his personal defeat. After all, he reasoned, there were other seats that could be made open to him. He had changed seats before, he could do it again. But he never did. Drew had become interested in federal politics and the post-war future of the whole country. Some said that he called the 1948 election two years before he needed, because he anticipated that the federal Tory leadership would become available, and that with the provincial election behind him he would be in the forefront of the candidates.

A month after the June provincial election, federal Conservative leader John Bracken announced his resignation. Drew entered the fall leadership convention and defeated Donald Fleming and John Diefenbaker.

But in his parting Drew left consternation at Queen's Park. He had given no hint of what he intended to do about the provincial succession, and one or two hopefuls, particularly Leslie Blackwell, were concerned that Drew intended to will the leadership to a favourite. Now it was as though Drew had packed his bag and disappeared up Highway 7 to Ottawa leaving only a cloud of dust behind him. The first authoritative statement the Ontario Cabinet Ministers received of their future was on the Monday morning after the federal leadership convention when they read their morning *Globe and Mail.* Because of the close relationship between McCullagh and Drew, *The Globe and Mail* was regarded as something of a mouthpiece of the administration; that day it proclaimed that 69-year-old Thomas Kennedy, the Agriculture Minister from Peel County, would be named Premier. The story went on to say that after two years Kennedy would step down in favour of Robert Saunders, a former mayor of Toronto who was then Hydro chairman. That might well have been in Drew's mind, or perhaps even McCullagh's. But Conservatives who were in positions to know at the time do not remember that as ever being a likely prospect.

Blackwell and others were furious at the story and at Drew. A Cabinet meeting was called; there it was decided to hold a party meeting to which four delegates from each riding would come to sort out the succession issue. Blackwell was well known, intelligent, and full of clever ideas; he wanted the leadership convention immediately that fall, confident that he could win.

But the delegates were not so sure they wanted to be rushed, and they put off the convention until April, 1949. The timing was crucial for a 54-year-old lawyer from Lindsay named Leslie Frost, who had been provincial Treasurer since 1943. Frost was virtually unknown, but he got the support of A. D. McKenzie, and the two used the winter well to gather grass-roots support. As the convention approached, another leading contender for the leadership, Highways Minister George Doucette, threw his support behind Frost, killing Blackwell's chances and ensuring Frost's victory. On May 4, 1949, Leslie Miscampbell Frost, the most successful politician in the province's history, was sworn in as Premier of Ontario.

And what of Drew? Old-time Tories still ponder what might have been. George Drew as leader of the Tory Opposition in Ottawa fought two elections against Louis St. Laurent, in 1949 and 1953, and was badly defeated on both occasions. But during that time Drew greatly increased the Conservatives' share of the popular vote, whittling away at the Liberals and setting the stage for Diefenbaker. Drew loyalists wonder what might have happened if their chief had stayed on one more time and become Prime Minister, and whether he would have introduced nationally the kind of program he nurtured in Ontario, and what state the country would be in today if he had. But even his most ardent fans say that Drew could not long have survived as leader either in Ontario or in Ottawa. "Drew never stopped to think what the public would think before he did something. It was whether it was the right thing to do that concerned him. This was one of his weaknesses," one Conservative said. "He was alienating his middle of the road support and it could only have gone on for so long."

4. *Old Man Ontario*

Meeting Leslie Frost was a physical experience that can be compared to receiving the ministrations of a chiropractor. In a conversation Frost never relied on the pull of his words to keep his audience with him, he preferred to trust the grip of his large bony hands, which maintained their grasp until everything to be said had been said. His cue was the simple introductory handshake, and while his right hand was vigorously squeezing and pumping away, his left hand had taken a firm hold on the upper arm or shoulder of the already slightly bemused person he had met. As the one-sided conversation progressed, Frost, still keeping a firm hold on the right hand, would drape his left arm around his companion's shoulders and start working away at the muscle with his strong blunt fingers. And all the while the kindly, confidential words would come tumbling smoothly out of this tall, silver-haired genial man. When it was over and Frost had moved on, you felt from your aching muscles that you had done a day's work, and that you had met someone rather extraordinary.

And indeed you had. Leslie Frost ruled—it's the only word for it—Ontario for 12 years, gave the Conservatives election victories which have not been matched before or since, and drew from the people of Ontario feelings of personal loyalty and friendship which have survived his leaving politics and his death. Frost liked to characterize himself as a small-town lawyer with his roots and understanding embedded deep in the province's rural and village communities. This was partly true, but it was also a part he liked to play. Once at the federal-provincial conference, surrounded by the country's top politicians and civil servants, Frost leaned back in his chair and said: "Well now, sir, I look at this from the barber chair at Lindsay."

It was an attention-grabbing line, as he undoubtedly intended it to be, but it was also true. He did look at things from the perspective of Lindsay (population 12,000) where he and his brother practised law, and which was an archetype of southern Ontario towns of the 50s. Through all his years in government he never lost touch with the nature of his constituency, rural and small-town Ontario. That was the basis of his political strength. But he was certainly no rustic innocent elevated by some quirk of fate to the halls of the mighty. Leslie Frost wielded political power and played the political game with peerless ease and devastating effectiveness. The opponents whom he shattered time after time came to call him "The Silver Fox".

Frost was born into a political family in Orillia on September 20, 1895. His father, William, had been mayor of the town and had gained the name "Daylight Bill" for his efforts to have daylight-saving time introduced. Leslie Frost got his unusual middle name from his godfather Andrew Miscampbell, a Conservative member of the Legislature. Orillia in the early 1900s was of consuming amusement to Stephen Leacock, who immortalized a slightly exaggerated version of it as "Mariposa". Young Les Frost took it much more seriously. Here were the primary values of sobriety, charity, and loyalty with which he characterized small-town Ontario throughout his life. He and his younger brother, Cecil, went through high school together in Orillia and together broke off further studies to join the Simcoe Regiment and go to France to fight in the Great War. Leslie was wounded in the hip at Neuville Vitasse in the spring offensive of 1918. He spent some seventeen months in hospital, but never fully recovered from the wound, which gave him considerable pain in later life.

After the war the two Frost brothers completed their studies at Osgoode Hall Law School and set up practice in Lindsay in 1921. They also both married the daughters of John Carew, MPP for Victoria riding. Leslie married Gertrude Carew in 1926. She was a strong-willed woman who didn't always see eye to eye with her husband on political matters. "For instance, when he voted for cocktail bars, I stuck with the drys. I never take anything stronger than a cup of tea."

Initially, Cecil was the politically active wing of the family. While Leslie tried unsuccessfully to win Victoria for the Conservatives in the face of the Hepburn sweep of 1934, Cecil was working away in the party. He served as president of the Ontario Conservatives from 1938 to 1943, when he was succeeded by, of course, A. D. McKenzie. He died in 1947. Leslie tried again to win Victoria riding in 1937, and this time succeeded. Gertrude was not all that happy about her husband's voyage into public life and he promised to give it up soon–it was twenty-six years before he was to fulfil that promise.

In 1943 Drew appointed him Minister of Mines, and Treasurer. Even after he became Premier, Frost hung on to the Treasury until 1955. In the Frost budgets the old Orillia virtues shone through, virtues of thrift and money in the bank. It was not until his last budget, in 1961, that the prolonged tax-sharing battle with Ottawa prompted Frost to introduce a 3 per cent sales tax.

The Conservatives have been lucky–even they would not claim it was all foresight–in getting the right leaders at the right time. Frost was certainly the right man to implement Drew's 22-point program for the development of the province. He could explain in his easy drawling way all those great changes to the farmers on the back concessions and get their support as Drew could never have done. Frost's philosophy of government was a very simple one. "There is no magic in government," he once said. "After all, government is business, the people's business. Good government is therefore a matter of common sense. Our creed is that more people lead to more industry, more jobs, more wages and more opportunity, and from these come more productivity and more revenue."

It was a simple creed, and also simplistic. Frost recognized that as well as people, development needs capital investment. He looked to the United States for dollars, and made Ontario a safe haven for American investment. Indeed, U.S. investors were so coddled that in 1953 the president of the New York Stock Exchange was moved to comment, "We envy the environment in which capital is encouraged to work in Canada and the respect accorded the risk-taker." In the 1970s Frost's successors were to wish that slightly less "respect" had been accorded the "risk-takers" and that there had been somewhat more insistence that Ontario should not be tied to the whims and fluctuations of the U.S. economy.

Frost maintained in later years that he was not all for

selling out Canada's resources in the drive for quick money. "Just because the United States has gutted their resources they shouldn't be allowed to gut ours," he commented once. But this was an afterthought of his later years.

It was on a sea of billions of dollars of U.S. investment that Frost floated the post-war boom in Ontario. The problems of the prosperity that this boom brought were the ones that Frost faced—the kind of problems every political leader would *like* to be faced with, perhaps, but problems none the less. "If you look at it from the standpoint of simply developing a great country, from a materialistic standpoint, not having regard to the betterment of the people, then, of course, in the end it will crush you," he said once. "It has to be a partnership between the two philosophies of economic advance and human betterment."

With the revenue that came pouring into the Treasury, Frost set out to deal with the staples of human betterment. Everywhere there was building; building roads, building hospitals, building schools, building hydro-electric projects, and building the St. Lawrence Seaway. And as Frost built, he changed the face of Ontario so that he knew it less and less. Political power may have remained within view of the barber chair at Lindsay, but increasingly the driving force of the province was the cities, which were growing in size and muscle. With urbanization came problems that Frost and his followers from the small towns could only react to, not predict. But Frost did respond, and responded successfully, with pragmatism.

The art of governing pragmatically was one of Frost's main lessons for his successors. He also showed them the value of changing party leaders before they become stale, and particularly before they find themselves out of office. Frost was Premier for 12 years, John Robarts for 10. Changing leaders about every 10 years has become the first canon of the Conservative party liturgy.

The Conservatives have, perhaps, put excessive faith in the principle of regeneration, of changing leaders. In 1971, the key phrase of the leadership convention to replace John Robarts was the "new wave", and tremendous trouble was taken to ensure that the convention would be a good show.

It was of supreme importance to the organizers that the party must be seen by the public to be vibrant and on the threshold of change. In fact, the stage management was more effective than the reality of what was happening in the party.

In latching on to the idea of regular changes in leadership the Tories have played down the importance of Frost as the man who made the Conservatives part of the way of life across southern rural Ontario. But Frost didn't do it by himself, as is sometimes suggested. Behind Frost was a figure largely unknown outside political circles. This was George Drew's old lieutenant, a Toronto lawyer by the name of Alexander McKenzie, usually known (in a political world already supplied with Alexander McKenzies) as A. D. McKenzie. McKenzie was the supreme political organizer and adviser. From the time Drew made him provincial organizer in 1942 until his death in 1960 McKenzie kept a tight grip on the Conservative party, arranging nominations for candidates, running elections, establishing and maintaining a network of local Conservative organizers and agents who acted as the channel to Queen's Park for people with problems. Frost relied heavily on McKenzie. The two men had breakfast together almost every day and often met in the evenings as well at the Royal York Hotel, where A. D. could be found in the Black Knight Room by Tories who had "problems" to be solved. McKenzie's death had a great deal to do with Frost's decision to resign the party leadership in 1961. Altogether McKenzie engineered 6 provincial elections and 20 by-elections, and won the lot.

McKenzie had already organized three provincial victories when Frost moved into the Premier's office in May, 1949. It was a comfortable office to be in. The government had a clear majority, it had a program and it wasn't short of funds. But one of Frost's first tasks was not entirely pleasant. Drew, preparing for a federal election campaign, wanted the support of the strong Ontario organization which he had helped create. But his overtures to Frost got him nothing but a flat refusal.

There was no love lost between the two men; in fact they disliked each other rather strongly. But sheer malice was probably not the only reason for Frost's reluctance to get involved in federal politics. Even while he was Treasurer in Drew's government, Frost had been trying in vain to recreate the Ontario-Ottawa relationship that Hepburn had so effectively destroyed. Coming out strongly for Drew against the federal Liberals at a time when the Liberals were unlikely to be beaten would not help his hopes for a reconciliation.

Frost had a lot of time and effort invested in his drive for a truce with Prime Minister Mackenzie King. As Treasurer he had even frequented Ottawa cocktail parties in the hope that he would be allowed a brief encounter with the Prime Minister. But Mackenzie King was not to be mollified. All Frost won was repeated polite brush-offs.

In 1950 Frost finally soothed King into a show of friendship, but it was too late, since King had retired two years before. Frost was asked to officially open the home of William Lyon Mackenzie, the Prime Minister's grandfather, which had been restored by the City of Toronto. Frost was dubious. William Lyon Mackenzie had been, after all, one of the most virulent opponents the Tory party had ever known. But the Premier's advisers persuaded him to accept the invitation from the City fathers. After it was over Frost received a letter of thanks from King and an invitation to come to Ottawa for a talk. But the meeting never took place; King died a week later.

(According to legend, King's reverence for his grandfather's old house on Bond Street once put him in an embarrassing situation. The house had come down in the world since the great rebel lived there and at one point was a brothel. Mackenzie King was once in the area and, despite the efforts of his more knowledgeable companions to dissuade him, insisted on strolling by the house. He knew nothing of the activities then going on behind that honoured façade and was gazing reverently, hat in hand, up at the building when a lady threw open one of the upstairs windows and began to coax this shy potential customer inside. King was at first unaware of the import of the advances being made to him, but when the truth dawned on him, he fled.)

So King died unreconciled with Ontario, but Frost had

already been busying himself with King's successor, Louis St. Laurent. The new Premier and the new Prime Minister met at the burial of *The Ottawa Journal* publisher P. D. Ross in Ottawa in June 1949. Frost recalled St. Laurent putting him arm around his shoulder and suggesting they have a talk. It was a long talk, first at the Prime Minister's office and later at his residence on Sussex Drive; at the end of it mutual friendship and respect had developed. It was a relationship that was essential to the building of the St. Lawrence Seaway, but it didn't hinder Frost from publicly and loudly pushing Ottawa for more grants and for the right to raise more taxes.

So Drew went into the 1949 federal election campaign without Frost's provincial support, and got beaten. But in 1949 Frost had an election of his own to worry about. It was an October by-election in Leeds riding in south central Ontario, good rural Tory country. On this occasion, however, the Conservative candidate was facing not only the Opposition candidates, but also the concentrated wrath of *The Toronto Daily Star.*

The Star was traditionally a Liberal newspaper. But Frost had aroused it to a peak of anti-Tory rage that summer when the Charitable Gifts Act was passed by the Legislature. The Act prevented any non-religious charitable trust or foundation from owning more than 10 per cent of the capital stock in any company. *The Star* believed, with justification, that the Act was aimed at the foundation set up by *The Star*'s former owner, Joseph E. Atkinson, to run the paper after his death in 1948. Hell had no fury like it. *The Star* berated Frost and the Act with every pejorative adjective acceptable in a family newspaper, and it used them in every square inch of space it could find between the masthead and the comics.

When the by-election was called, *The Star* set up a special newsroom in Leeds riding. Every day the paper devoted a considerable amount of space to the campaign, often three pages, and it gave out free copies of the newspaper to everyone in the riding every day. A familiar sight in that fall of 1949 was *The Daily Star* truck trundling down to Leeds with its cargo of free papers.

One of the Conservatives involved in that campaign recalls that some of *The Star*'s news stories at that time were none too subtle and were, as it turned out, destructive of *The Star*'s case. The Conservatives won the by-election without difficulty. But Frost allowed the Atkinson foundation a two-year extension on its seven-year deadline within which it had to get rid of at least 90 per cent of its *Star* interests. In the end, in 1958, five directors of *The Star*, who were also trustees of the Atkinson estate, were allowed to buy the newspaper. Considering that it was one of the largest selling newspapers on the continent, that *The Star Weekly* magazine was included as were all the printing equipment and the paper's offices, the rumoured buying price of around $25 million was something of a bargain.

After the sale, *The Star*'s criticism of the Frost government seemed to die down to a mere shadow of its former flaming splendour.

From the beginning of his tenure as Premier, Frost travelled the province, cutting ribbons, opening schools, hospitals, roads, and touring factories, meeting thousands of non-political people. He went to political meetings as well, of course, but at those he was mostly facing the converted, and what was the point in that, other than to keep the fences mended? He hardly ever made political speeches lambasting the Opposition. He preferred to just chat about the good things the government was doing, gently weaving the audience into the web of his charm.

It was all easily and deftly done. "Hello, my name's Frost. I work for the Government," he would say as he toured factories. There was no great heralding of the coming, no hushed anticipation of the presence, no sprawling entourage that would make a Medici jealous. And if he spotted a Liberal in his audience he would spare a few pleasant words for him. "How unlike Mr. Drew," everyone thought. Drew never used the word "Liberal", only the word "Grit", which was spat out with distaste. "What a gentleman this Mr. Frost is, and one of us, too. Not all puffed up like Mr. Drew." Frost made it easy for the middle-of-the-roaders to follow him.

Opposition members were certain that the genial Frost was not the real one. The real Frost, they contended, was a reactionary who ruled Ontario as a fiefdom from behind closed doors, and only turned on his calming charm in public. Frost certainly had a fearful temper and he chewed out his ministers unmercifully on occasion; but he had no difficulty going straight from a harsh dressing-down session to a meeting with a delegation in his outer office where he would appear full of smiles and avuncular joviality. The Liberal leader at the time, Farquhar Oliver, called him "the closest I know to Dr. Jekyll and Mr. Hyde. No one can do it just like him."

The Premier kept his Ministers on a very tight rein, allowing them little independence. It was common in the House to see Frost wave down a Minister who had been quizzed during Question Period and answer the question himself. The annual presentation of estimates of expenditure is the time when Ministers usually get the chance to show their knowledge and understanding of their portfolios. On one occasion Frost interrupted a Minister 17 times while the Minister was presenting his estimates to the Legislature.

It was a moderate series of governments that Frost led, and it was an inward-looking Ontario that he managed. He got on well with Quebec Premier Maurice Duplessis, but there was no strong call for Frost or Ontario to show much understanding of Quebec. Ontario didn't really care about anything that was going on outside its borders. The big issues were things such as highway construction. Over the period of his Premiership hundreds of millions of dollars were poured into road building. The Macdonald-Cartier Freeway alone cost $400 million, and $220 million was spent on the Ontario section of the Trans-Canada Highway. Frost called it a frontal attack on the province's transportation problems and said that no small-scale nibbling would do. Considering that his first budget in 1949 was only for $300 million *in all*, it's an astounding record.

The decades-old dispute between the United States and Canada over construction of the St. Lawrence Seaway was brought to a head by Frost, with the support of his new friend Prime Minister St. Laurent. Ontario told Washington that if they didn't want to contribute any money to the multi-million-dollar project, then the province would go it alone with New York State. In later years Frost maintained that his statement was no bluff and that he would actually have preferred the project to be a joint venture between Ontario and the State. But, bluff or not, his threat caused the U.S. government to make a final decision, and the Seaway construction began.

One of the benefits of the seaway development was more hydro-electric facilities. There had been severe power shortages after the war and, in response, major plants were developed on the Ottawa River and at Niagara Falls as well as on the St. Lawrence. In his search for power for the new industries in the province, Frost also encouraged construction of the natural gas pipeline from western Canada to northern Ontario.

In social, as opposed to physical, development, Frost's government moved at a cautious pace. Provincial hospital insurance was finally introduced after years of public demands, and discrimination in employment and housing was outlawed. But it was generally at the final hour, when the political penalty for inactivity outweighed the penalty for doing nothing, that such measures were taken.

There were exceptions. In 1954 the Frost government attempted to deal with the problems of growth in the Toronto area by establishing a metropolitan system for the City and the surrounding 12 municipalities. It was the first of its kind in North America, and it worked largely because of the great personal friendship between Frost and the first Metro Toronto chairman, Frederick Gardiner. It continued to work because successive chairmen and premiers got on reasonably well. The system was stretched badly in 1971 when the halting of the Spadina Expressway rocked the relationship between chairman Ab Campbell and Premier Davis. But harmony was again achieved with the appointment of Paul Godfrey as chairman, and the granting of more powers to Metro.

In 1953 Frost was invited by Governor-General Vincent Massey to an informal dinner in the vice-regal splendour of Rideau Hall for U.S. President Dwight Eisenhower. It happened to be on the day of Mrs. Eisenhower's birthday and it was a merry little private get-together. At one point during the evening the President took Frost by the shoulder (a case of the biter bitten) and said: "You people here have a great country with great possibilities, so don't let them ruin your water. We have ruined ours in the States with our growth of population so that the great beautiful rivers that flow into the Atlantic and down through the Mississippi Valley and so on are contaminated.

"You should remember this," Eisenhower emphasized, "that really pure water is one of your greatest assets. But when you've got a lot of it, you don't think about it." Frost chewed over in his mind what Eisenhower had said, and on the way home that night came up with the idea of establishing an Ontario Water Resources Commission. The first chairman of the commission was a young, newly-elected MPP from London, named John Robarts. Frost gave him the chairmanship because he wanted to see how Robarts would manage responsibility and (the deft political hand at work again) because London was suffering a water shortage.

Donald MacDonald, leader of the CCF and later the NDP, once called Frost "the great tranquillizer" for his ability to smooth over potentially troublesome issues. It was an ability that was tested to the full, for the Frost era was one of great scandals as well as of great development. But when Frost fought his first campaign in November, 1951, he and his party were untroubled by charges of government misconduct and he won the greatest victory in the province's history, taking 79 seats in the 90-seat House.

Frost's personal integrity was never seriously challenged throughout his entire career. But when he went to the people again in June 1955, the Liberal leader, Farquhar Oliver, was able to charge that the government appeared with its hands "dripping with guilt" as a result of recent scandals over highways contracts. In January, 1955, Highways Minister George Doucette, the man whose support had assured Frost of the Premiership, resigned after three construction companies were fined a total of $215,000 and six employees of the Ministry were jailed or fined for conspiracy to defraud the government.

The story goes that before Doucette had his interview with Frost in January, 1955, he jauntily assured reporters that he was not going to resign. A changed man emerged from the corner office a little while later and announced in a low voice that he had decided to quit the Cabinet.

Frost's technique for dealing with the scandals was swift and decisive. He fired the miscreants and then called an election. After the elections, he considered all former wrongs erased from the record. It was a method that worked; in 1955 the Conservatives were returned with another massive majority. They won 83 seats in the expanded 98-seat House. Among the winners was Doucette. "The people with their unerring judgment by the ballots confirmed that there was nothing to this, and endorsed the Government," Frost said after the election.

But in 1958 Frost had to deal with another scandal. This one involved the buying by Cabinet Ministers of stock in the Northern Ontario Natural Gas Co. Ltd. (NONG) before general sales to the public began. Three Ministers resigned after an inquiry into the affair. They were Mines Minister Philip Kelly, Municipal Affairs Minister William Griesenger, and Lands and Forests Minister Clare Mapledoram, who ignored a directive from Frost to sell his stock.

The following year after the whole affair was apparently over, CCF leader MacDonald charged in the Legislature that the affair included Frost himself and the highest echelons in the Tory party. According to MacDonald, the Tory *éminence grise* A. D. McKenzie had drawn an annual retainer of $6,000 as legal adviser to the gas company, had owned NONG shares and had actively peddled the company's stock among MPPS. The CCF leader found it difficult to believe that McKenzie had not told Frost of the NONG stock dealings by Cabinet Ministers, particularly those of Mines Minister Kelly, before the inquiry began. Kelly had resigned early in 1958, ostensibly to seek a federal seat. MacDonald contended that Frost had misled the Legislature—the most serious offence that can be laid at the door of a member of that gentlemanly association—when he repeatedly asserted that he knew nothing of Kelly's stock dealings and that they had nothing to do with the Minister's resignation.

"I have never suggested the Premier was personally involved in these pipeline deals," MacDonald said. "Like Sir John A. Macdonald and William Lyon Mackenzie King, the Premier is personally incorruptible. But like Macdonald and King what he is willing to do to protect his party is another story, and represents a completely different moral code."

Frost replied with a spirited defence of his old friend A. D. McKenzie. Hitting out at MacDonald, he lost his temper for the first and last time in the Legislature. "You're chittering like a pig in trough," he shouted, red-faced, at MacDonald. "Get down in the sewer and get yourself covered in it. You're a character assassin." It was an outburst Frost regretted, particularly when he got home to Lindsay. His wife, Gertrude, angrily ordered him to apologize. He did.

In 1959 the province was due for another election and Frost again sought the "unerring judgment" of the people in June. Even though the Conservatives lost some seats, they maintained a clear majority. The Tories won 71 seats, the Liberals 22, and the CCF 5.

In May of 1960, less than a year after organizing his last successful election campaign, A. D. McKenzie died. He had been ill with heart trouble for some time and in the last years his meetings with Frost, which had often been twice daily, grew less frequent. The Premier trotted out the usual bland words of condolence and sorrow for the obituary writers: "I have known him intimately for twenty years or more. He was a very quiet person, shy and very self-effacing," Frost said. Observers at the time had another perception of McKenzie; they believed him to be the power behind Frost and the true architect of Tory election victories since 1943. That view probably belittles Frost and glorifies McKenzie more than either deserves.

There is no doubt that McKenzie's tremendous knowledge of Ontario's political scene was—and to some extent still is—an essential factor in the Conservatives' success; but he could not have succeeded without Frost or Drew, and neither of them would have been so strong without him. In his nearly twenty years at the senior levels of the Tory party, he kept well out of the limelight. The records show less than a handful of assessments of him by contemporary reporters, a few stories on his involvement in the NONG scandal, and the reports of his funeral. For the rest, the record simply shows, each year from 1943 to 1960, his re-election to the presidency of the party.

Newspapermen, always suckers for the elusive, may have inflated his importance slightly because they could never get to McKenzie for a true assessment of his role. He avoided them and shunned publicity. Publicity, McKenzie stated, was meant for candidates and political parties, not for organizers. Veteran Queen's Park reporters therefore remember him as being aloof and difficult to deal with. Sensing that there are no cloaks without daggers, the reporters deduced that at the breakfast meetings each morning, McKenzie primed Frost for the day. "Leslie wouldn't even go to the john without McKenzie's say-so," was one newsman's belief. It is difficult to believe that a man like Leslie Frost, a cool organizer if ever there was one, would allow himself to be organized. There is no doubt that Frost leaned heavily on McKenzie for advice, but he was not the man's puppet.

Conservatives who remember McKenzie have a very different picture in their minds from that of the newsmen of the time. They remember a man of brilliant intellect and imagination, who made himself available to the MPPS each evening at the Royal York Hotel to listen to and deal with the problems that had arisen in the ridings during the day. These day-to-day problems in the constituencies were precisely what McKenzie had organized himself and the party to handle. For the ordinary MPP, getting his constituents' mundane problems solved is what getting re-elected is all about. Getting MPPS elected, and then re-elected, is the essence of getting the party elected again and again. So McKenzie kept a very close eye on what was happening across the province. He is said to have known more people personally than anyone else in Ontario. He naturally took a very deep interest in the selection of candidates for elections. So deep was his interest in this matter that he often found it necessary to take this delicate question out of the hands of the riding associations, which, encumbered by rules aimed at ensuring fairness in contests for candidacies, could make mistakes. A.D. preferred to choose the candidates himself.

One thing about McKenzie that sticks in the mind of everyone who knew him was his phenomenal knowledge of the works of Shakespeare. Apparently he could recite Shakespeare's plays, line by line, for hours on end. No doubt a close study of Shakespeare gives as good a political education as any, and no doubt the recital of the same at length can, on occasion, head off a distasteful interview or befuddle the inopportune importuner. A useful skill, without doubt.

McKenzie was one of the more shadowy important figures that Ontario has produced. But there have been others who have marched purposefully through the background of events as though they knew what the whole business was really about, and that it didn't have much to do with what was happening on centre stage. One such was Alex MacLeod, Labour-Progressive member for Bellwoods riding in Toronto from 1943 until 1951. Labour-Progressive may have been the label, but MacLeod and his fellow MPP from the neighbouring riding of St. Andrew-St. Patrick, Joe Salsberg, were Communists, albeit moderate, socially-acceptable Communists. Both men were consummate orators and in the darkest days of the Liberal party's depression after the 1943 election, these two provided the main day-to-day opposition to Drew in the Legislature. Later, when the Russians marched into Hungary in 1956 they both quit the Communist party.

Both MacLeod and Salsberg were befriended by Frost, and he often sought their advice and counsel. Even after MacLeod was defeated, he remained a potent force whose thinking was elicited on major topics. Early in the 1960s he returned to Queen's Park, this time on the staff of the new young Minister of Education, William Davis. Serving as a mixture of adviser and speech writer, MacLeod exerted influence until his death in 1969. But his son David is following in his footsteps. David MacLeod also worked in the Ministry of Education and moved to the Premier's Office with Davis in 1971. Most recently, David MacLeod was working with the Minister Responsible for Youth, Margaret Birch.

Clearly the friendships that grow in the community of the Legislature have little to do with the daily pantomime of adversity acted out between political parties and political men on the floor of the House.

Frost could probably have become Prime Minister of Canada had he wished. He was offered a chance at the federal

Tory leadership in 1956, when he was the most prestigious Conservative in the country, but he turned the offer down. Gertrude wouldn't have stood for it.

The Ontario Conservatives have never shown much inclination to assist their federal counterparts at election times (the federal Liberals have the same attitude towards their provincial brethren), but in 1957 Frost threw the full weight of his political organization behind the new federal leader, John Diefenbaker, and helped to make him Prime Minister. Frost lent his aid again in 1958 and got considerable credit for the Diefenbaker sweep in that year, as the federal Conservatives won 67 seats in Ontario.

After Alex McKenzie's death in 1960, rumours began to circulate that Frost would retire from the Premiership and leadership of the Conservatives. The stories gained momentum in the spring of 1961, and in the summer Frost said they were true. A leadership convention was planned for the fall. Though there was no pressure on him from the party to quit, and although his powers were undiminished, Frost had recognized that for him to stay on would be to court disaster for the party. His contemporaries were answering the call of the Reaper or the more welcome one of comfortable retirements. "This is a young person's world. Young people should run it," Frost said a few years later, when he began shedding the company dictatorships he gathered after quitting politics. He felt the same way in 1961. He had changed his world and made himself an anachronism in the process.

So Frost stepped down from the Premiership to allow a younger man to take over. This, people said at the time, was just another example of his sense of timing. He knew that the time had come for the Conservatives to perform their trick of regeneration. Others wondered about that sense of timing, and on reflection came to the conclusion that Frost was not as sensitive to the desires and needs of the public as was commonly believed. Hospital insurance, for example, was introduced in two other provinces 10 years before Frost introduced it in Ontario, the country's richest province; and even then Ontario introduced it when federal aid for the program was forthcoming.

Ron Haggart, a columnist for *The Toronto Star* at the time, wrote that "George Drew believed in ideas. Leslie

Frost believed in things. Nothing symbolized the administration of Leslie Frost more than the fact that the disgraceful, crowded and smelly hospital for retarded children at Orillia, subject to pleas for help for years, could be reached by the most modern and expensive, four-lane, boulevarded expressway." Such harsh judgments were being mouthed in the wings, but at centre stage there was nothing but laurels for Frost on his retirement.

Even his bitter enemy of 12 years, *The Toronto Star* itself, greeted the news of his retirement with an editorial entitled "Mr. Frost's fine service". The editorial noted that when Frost came to power in 1949 the population of the province was 4 million, and that in 1961 it was 6 million. The 1949 Ontario budget was $300 million, and the 1961 budget was over $1 billion. In a rather obvious reversal of its previous editorial stance, *The Star* said that Frost's personal integrity had never been questioned, magnanimously choosing to forget its own queries of a couple of years before at the time of the NONG scandal. Frost's crime, *The Star* said, was that he was too trustful and too loyal.

Loyalty to one's associates and trust in their honesty and competence is a natural sentiment and a very useful defence for any special interest group. The professions of law and medicine have survived unmolested for years by maintaining that to question the inner workings of their societies is to question their collective honour. Frost felt somewhat the same way about the Conservative party. He considered that his win in the 1955 election had wiped the crimes involved in the highways scandal from the sheet of political debits.

Obviously, this is an astounding position to take, since it means that so long as a man or party can get elected, their competence or their honesty means nothing. It is a precedent that has now become part of Ontario's political heritage, and that has been invoked again and again to smother criticism. It is one of the more unfortunate aspects of Frost's legacy to the province, because it puts power and loyalty to the dynasty above justice and intelligence. It breeds an arrogance that has prompted countless Conservative Ministers over the years to respond to Opposition party attacks by asking, "How many seats have we got and how many seats have you got?" It is the ultimate exhibition of power that the

Conservative government uses when it feels unsteady on its feet or just plain unsure of itself. Premier Davis, in his early halting days as leader, used the trick often to cover his uncertainty and taunt his adversaries.

But the picture that remains of Frost should not be of a glad-handing charlatan of a country lawyer who managed, by political craft and smooth talking, to ride the boom years and dismount before being thrown. If hindsight over the gulf of a decade shows in sharp relief some inadequacies in his tenure, then it is also true that he in part was responsible for the changes in Ontario society and thinking that have drawn his own deficiencies into focus. Ontario's problems are still largely the problems of over-abundance and how to manage it. They are the best problems to have.

Frost was the beneficiary of nicknames like no other Premier—the Laird of Lindsay, the Silver Fox, the Great Tranquillizer—and in his last years he was called Old Man Ontario. That was a name he liked, a name invoking timelessness, wisdom, and respect. Yet in the end even Lindsay appeared to Old Man Ontario to have changed. As he walked down the streets of the town he found everything changed. "It's got so I don't know the people any more. And most of them don't know me."

5. *John Robarts, Management Man*

"I'm a management man myself. This is the era of the management man . . . I'm a complete product of the times." Enter John Parmenter Robarts, management man. It is one of the paradoxes of Ontario politics and politicians that Leslie Frost, the great hustings politician, dealt with things, and Robarts, the non-political bureaucrats' dream, dealt with ideas.

When Robarts' childhood is considered, it is not difficult

to see how the metallic blend of management man with steel nerves and an iron constitution developed. Robarts was born in Banff, Alberta, in 1917 and his early years were unsettled. His mother died when he was three years old and his father, Herbert Robarts, remarried seven years later. Robarts senior was a bank manager, and the family moved around the country from bank to bank in those early years before they finally put down roots in London in 1930. Robarts finished his schooling in that city and went on to its university, the University of Western Ontario, from which, in 1939, he graduated with an honours degree in business administration.

John Robarts

In the summers Robarts operated a newsstand on the old excursion boat, the *Chippewa* (a floating hotbed of romance for young Torontonians in those days), which plied between Toronto and Niagara. Even this limited form of ships and seamanship enthralled the university student and in 1940, at the age of 23, he enlisted in the Royal Canadian Navy as an ordinary seaman. But talent will out, especially in wartime, and a year later he was commissioned a sub-lieutenant. Over the next four years he served in all the major theatres of the war at sea—the Mediterranean, the Atlantic, the Pacific, and was mentioned in dispatches for bravery during the Battle of Salerno.

He got home leave in 1944 after his ship was blown up. While he was home he married Nora McCormick, who had been his girlfriend since his college days; it was to her that he had confessed ten years earlier that one day he wanted to be the Prime Minister of Canada.

But in fact his drive to fame had a slow beginning. When the war was over he went to Osgoode Hall Law School and graduated in 1947. He practised law in Hamilton for a year, turned down an offer to join a Toronto law firm, and moved back to London. The first plunge into politics came two years later; in 1950 he was elected alderman for the city. The political game proved to be to his liking, and in the provincial election the following year he ran as the Conservative candidate in London North and was elected.

The records show little happening in the life of John Robarts for eight years after that, but it was a busy time for him. As well as fulfilling his duties as a backbencher in Toronto he was nipping back to London as often as possible, to keep his law practice going and to see his family. He did, however, make one substantial mark on the records during that period. In 1955 he was appointed chairman of the Select Committee on Toll Roads and Highways Finances, which was set up to help Frost decide how best to pay for the miles of asphalt he was bequeathing Ontario. Robarts was credited with influencing the government's decision not to establish toll roads, but to pay for the construction out of revenue. In that, Robarts relieved the people of Ontario of one of the most aggravating burdens for the traveller: the toll gate.

There were some good times for Robarts in Toronto. He shared an apartment with his running mate from London South, Ernie Jackson, and another new boy to the Legislature, James Auld, from Leeds. The three of them worked hard, but they played hard as well. There were sports cars, good food, and drink, and rollicking evenings listening to Dixie and jazz on the Yonge Street strip. Robarts, looking and living rather like an untormented political version of Ernest Hemingway, enjoyed it all.

But after seven years his political career hadn't progressed much and he seriously wondered whether or not he should contest the 1959 election. His buddy, Jackson, had already decided to return to London and his flourishing insurance business. But Frost, who had appointed Robarts chairman of the Ontario Water Resources Commission a few years before to further test the backbencher's mettle, stepped in. He made Robarts a Minister without Portfolio, and the decision to stay at Queen's Park was made. In 1959, after the election, Robarts was given the Education Ministry, an important post in Frost's last years.

But it was now the summer of 1961 and Frost had announced that he was going to step down from the leadership. The August sun shone brightly as Robarts walked along the trail towards his lakeside cottage at Grand Bend. He had been considering his future for some weeks; now on the trail beside Lake Huron he decided that he would become a candidate to succeed Frost. Before he left the Legislature, Jackson had said jokingly that when Robarts was ready to go for the leadership, he would be there to run his campaign. So once his decision was made, the next step was to contact Jackson. Fortunately, all of London's aristocracy moves to

Grand Bend for the summer (just as the Regency court in Britain moved to the resort of Brighton) and a few minutes later Robarts was sitting on Jackson's cottage lawn.

Jackson's recollection of what happened next is rather folksy. They were going for the leadership. But they had no idea of how to go about it, and no lists of candidates. All they had was a road map of Ontario. So they decided to start campaigning in the east, and work west towards home. The next day they bundled themselves into Jackson's car and drove across southern Ontario to Ottawa. They booked in at the Château Laurier Hotel late in the day and telephoned the riding presidents in the Ottawa area, asking to meet the local delegates to the leadership convention.

The delegates trooped in to meet them, riding by riding. At these meetings Robarts displayed the charm that was so conspicuously absent from his public oratory, a man was delegated to push Robarts' cause locally, and then the two London boys drove off west. This was the pattern of their campaign. As it progressed, Jackson's organizational talents developed so that as the convention approached he stayed in Toronto, organizing, while Robarts roamed the province.

Toronto was going through a late fall warm spell when the leadership convention opened on Monday morning, October 23, 1961. The scene of the final act was to be the Varsity Arena two days later, but the build-up was conducted in bars and hospitality suites in hotels around the city as the various candidates' followers cajoled, sweet-talked and bullied support out of the delegates.

Jackson had built up an organization of some 400 workers, among them a number of MPPS such as Charles MacNaughton and William Stewart from Robarts' home area. These two operated as a team to bring in the vote for their man and were called (not altogether kindly) "the Bobbsey Twins" by the supporters of opposing candidates.

The delegates were faced with a problem as they filed into the arena on the warm wet afternoon of October 25. The main problem was the long shadow of Leslie Frost, whom many delegates thought irreplaceable. Some thought that the best bet was to elect one of Frost's protégés, James Allan, the provincial Treasurer and an old-man-Ontario type, for a few years until a new man could be groomed. Others turned towards the Attorney-General, Kelso Roberts, a Toronto lawyer who was considered by everyone to be a gentleman with an appealing touch of eccentricity. Indeed, he was unconventional enough to ride a bicycle to work at Queen's Park every day from his home near St. Clair and Avenue Road. In the 1950s and 1960s that was a sure mark of non-conformity, since at that time one could travel the length and breadth of Toronto without seeing a bicycle. For the delegates who cared to take a chance that Wednesday there was the magical, mercurial Robert Macaulay, a man whose aura was clearly visible even to those without the slightest psychic tendencies. Against this varied and colourful field John Robarts did not stand out. He was everyone's second choice.

But being everyone's second choice in a race with no clear favourite was perhaps the best spot to be in. Just so long as you had a solid basic pool of support that would stick with you while some of the other candidates dropped out, you were all right. So Jackson organized his workers into a corps that would enable him to keep tabs on the convention. He drilled them in the tactic of grabbing the supporters of defeated candidates as soon as possible and getting their support. And to be sure that he could keep an eye on his team and find them at a moment's notice from his command post in a trailer, he dressed them all in bright yellow blazers.

After the first ballot was counted in mid-afternoon, Kelso Roberts was in the lead, with Robarts second and Macaulay third. Robarts was doing better than anyone had imagined he would. The gap between first and second spot was not wide enough for Kelso Roberts to get a bandwagon rolling and increase his lead, and on the second ballot he slipped into second place behind Robarts. As the voting went on through the afternoon Robarts maintained the lead, but not by much. The break came at the end of the fifth ballot when, as low man on the totem pole, it was Macaulay's turn to be dropped before the next vote. His supporters were numerous enough to give the victory to whichever of the two remaining contenders he guided them towards. The crucial decision was his.

Macaulay was perplexed and upset at his own defeat and

he stood silent for a few moments, his forehead creased. As he stood there a young lawyer named Allan Lawrence came over. Although he was a member of Macaulay's law firm, Lawrence was working for Kelso Roberts. Now he asked which way Macaulay was going to go, but Macaulay didn't appear to hear him. Macaulay's campaign manager, another young unknown in the party, William Davis, said to Lawrence, "I'm sorry, Al."

Macaulay turned to those around him and said: "Go tell our people to vote for Robarts. We don't want Roberts." With that he left his seat, and strode smilingly over to Robarts. He greeted Robarts warmly, pointed to the campaign button that Robarts was wearing, and said, "Hang it on me, John." Robarts was only too happy to oblige.

That clinched it for Robarts and he won the leadership on the sixth ballot by 976 votes to Kelso Roberts' 633.

"I would rather govern than be governed," Robarts once told a reporter who asked why he had gone for the leadership. But governing was not so simple at the beginning. Robarts was not well known—nobody had stature in Frost's Cabinet, apart from Frost—he didn't appear to be particularly clever, and he had the stamp of the dull Ontario establishment all over him. Physically, he had a chunky, formal handsomeness which was almost too symmetrical to be appealing. What was worse, the province was suffering from a recession and unemployment was high. And within his first weeks as Premier he was faced with a scandal of far-reaching effects over gambling and organized crime.

Robarts wasn't all that worried about his poor image—quick loves soon burn out. He was content to quietly work into the job. But the unemployment situation could not be ignored, and dramatic public steps were required. He turned to Robert Macaulay, already the Minister of Energy, and appointed him Minister of Economics, Trade and Development as well. Macaulay quickly became known as "the Minister of Everything" as he whizzed around the province and the world organizing "the trade crusade" which was his answer to the employment problem. The trade crusade, which urged the people of the province to buy Ontario-made products, and provided financial incentives for industry to come to the province, worked well and improved both the balance of trade and the employment picture. For some time Macaulay's power seemed to rival Robarts' own; but perhaps it only seemed so because Macaulay was so visible while Robarts preferred to stay hidden.

Macaulay's frenzied expenditure of energy appeared to tell on his health. In 1963 he collapsed on his way into the Legislature, victim of what seemed to be a heart attack. As Macaulay was carried out, his executive assistant, Clare Westcott—faithful to the end to the trade crusade's ideals—attempted to cover the Minister's shoes, which clearly proclaimed "Made in Italy". After a period in hospital, Macaulay announced that ill health dictated that he must leave the Legislature, which he did a few months later. But far from leading the quiet life of the invalid, Macaulay joined one of the largest law practices in Toronto and set busily about making money and a reputation as one of the most successful and well-connected planning and real estate lawyers in the business.

Macaulay, of course, had not had a heart attack. What had happened to him was what often happens to defeated candidates in Tory leadership conventions—they suddenly realize that their political future is pretty bleak. Macaulay had been thinking about leaving for some time and had even talked jokingly with his staff about staging some kind of dramatic scene at which to announce it. So when he did collapse, at least one of his people thought that the whole thing was a fraud. It wasn't. The faint was genuine, but it was a faint brought about by a mixture of influenza and a touch of angina. And it allowed Robert Macaulay to retire from politics and leave centre stage to his boss, John Robarts.

Problems with organized crime were to dog Robarts for half of his years in office. They began shortly before Robarts became leader when a woman court reporter for *The Globe and Mail* told her editors that organized crime existed in the province and should be investigated. Two other reporters, one of them named Harold Greer, were put on the assignment with her, and the trio spent three months tracking the story down. At the end of their investigation they wrote a report showing that social clubs used for syndicated gambling were being issued charters by the Provincial Secretary's Department, and that the proceeds of illegal gambling were being used to finance legitimate business enterprises in the province.

Heeding the advice of its lawyers, *The Globe* refused to publish the story, on the grounds that more proof was needed; Greer speculated that senior editors of the newspaper were aware of Frost's then unannounced intention to step down, and they didn't wish to embarrass the Premier in his last days in office. But the failure to publish so enraged Greer that he took himself and his story off to the Liberal party leader, John Wintermeyer. Wintermeyer, with Greer as his speech writer, loosed *The Globe* story in the Legislature in a two-and-one-half-hour speech in November, 1961. Robarts appeared shaken and, over the objections of his Attorney-General, Kelso Roberts, set up a Royal Commission inquiry under Mr. Justice Wilfred Roach, who spent 66 days investigating the charges.

Mr. Justice Roach found an alarming increase in gambling in Ontario, but he did not conclude that it was ruled by a syndicate of criminals, nor did he believe that police action against the gamblers had been suppressed by the Attorney-General's department. He did say, however, that there had been an unfortunate association between a late member of the Frost Cabinet and two gamblers he called "public menaces". He also recommended that the deputy commissioner of the Ontario Provincial Police and a district inspector be fired for turning blind eyes; both officers resigned.

The Royal Commission didn't expose the government rot that Wintermeyer felt sure was there, and in the lead-up to the 1963 election, he attempted to hammer home his claim that the government was corrupt by waging a campaign on the theme "a scandal a day". But Robarts had been working hard in the two years following his appointment to the Premiership. He had made a lot of changes in the Cabinet so that many of the time-serving Ministers inherited from Frost disappeared. The bright new Ministers had jockeyed an abundance of legislation through the House by the time the 1963 election was called. The abundance included more money for Separate Schools—that perennial sticky subject in

Ontario—portable pensions, a legal minimum wage, grants for the construction of Toronto's subway (a genuinely radical move), redistribution of the electoral boundaries to give the urban areas better representation, and more relaxed liquor laws.

The electorate decided that they liked dour Robarts better than fervent Wintermeyer and returned the Tories in the election with 77 seats, 6 more than they had had. The Liberals gained 2 from 22 to 24, as did the NDP (successor of the CCF) who went from 5 to 7. The attentive reader will no doubt consider it a somewhat unusual election when all the parties gain seats and nobody loses. The answer is simple. The size of the House had been enlarged from 98 to 108 seats. The real story is in the popular vote, where the Conservatives increased their percentage by 2 to 48 per cent. The Liberals dropped 2 per cent to 35 and the NDP stayed about the same with 16 per cent. Wintermeyer resigned shortly afterwards and Farquhar Oliver was called back until a leadership convention could be arranged.

The year after the election came phase two of Robarts' problems with the question of organized crime. A piece of legislation was drafted which was known technically as Bill 99, but became known colloquially as "the police state bill". Its aim was to give the police powers to deal with organized crime, a praiseworthy aim. It would, however, have allowed people to be held for questioning indefinitely without being allowed to see a lawyer, and without charges being laid.

The magnitude of the powers became apparent at a press conference given by Attorney-General Frederick Cass after he introduced the legislation. Cass defended the Bill, agreed that the powers it gave were "dangerous" and "drastic", but said these powers were necessary to deal with organized crime. Robarts was not aware of the reaction to the Bill until that night when he attended the legislative Press Gallery's dinner and dance in the Royal York Hotel. He was chatting by the bar with a group of reporters when another came charging across the ballroom waving a copy of *The Globe and Mail*'s first edition. The paper had blazed a damning editorial over the front page, which gave the story a status among reporters it had not had earlier in the afternoon.

When the Bill came up in the Legislature in March of 1964 the Opposition parties were itching to go. Andrew Thompson led off for the Liberals and in his flowing Irish accent presented a detailed indictment of what he saw as the government's authoritarian tendencies. His oratory was so fine that on the basis of that one speech he became the darling of the Press Gallery, and over the next few days there appeared a multitude of stories on the general theme: "Have the Liberals found their new leader?" The question may have been rhetorical, but the Liberals, still dreaming that the ability to spin a web of words the way Mitch used to do was the road to power, answered "Yes", and made Thompson their leader a couple of months later.

The clamour against Bill 99 grew as the debate continued, but Robarts allowed the days to slip by without taking decisive action. It was only when he realized that opposition to the Bill was just as strong on the Conservative benches as it was across the floor and that he would not be able to carry his own people with him when the Bill came up for the approving vote, that he decided to drop the Bill. But he defended the legislation even as he discarded it.

Cass resigned and spent a few years languishing on the backbenches before being appointed Speaker of the House. Robarts maintained afterwards that the Bill only brought together police powers which already existed in other legislation, and that it was Cass's mishandling of the affair which created the crisis. That was true. But the crisis had also been caused by Robarts' failure to withdraw it once the strength of the reaction to the Bill became apparent.

Robarts' response to the police Bill crisis was to set up the Commission on Civil Rights headed by the former Chief Justice of the Ontario Supreme Court, J. C. McRuer. The Commission worked away diligently for four years and produced a mass of reports aimed at remodelling much of the province's legal system. In general the Commission redefined the rights of anyone who came before a court, tribunal, commission, or who was up against bureaucracy in general. The safeguards proposed by McRuer became the standards to be followed in the activities not only of existing judicial and quasi-judicial bodies, but also of any new bodies created in the future. The Commission also produced an improvement in the professionalism of the judicial system; this was most noticeable at the level of magistrates, who were re-named provincial judges and from whom much higher standards of behaviour and judgment were demanded than previously.

Civil rights was a popular area of reform, and Robarts put much emphasis on it. There was the added advantage that it was not an expensive area in which to develop initiatives.

Robarts was not a good politician. Yet, particularly in his latter years as Premier, he exerted tremendous authority in the Legislature, partly because of the stature he had achieved in the country at large. There was always a marked difference in the atmosphere when Robarts was sitting in his seat in the Legislature. He was in absolute control and everyone, Opposition included, took their lead from him. Occasionally his deep gravelly voice would boom out, calmly deflecting a question or rambling on in a monotone about the splendours of Conservative rule; but he didn't have to speak to make his presence felt.

He didn't have to speak to make his presence felt in the halls of the Conservative party, either. When he became leader, Robarts had made Ernie Jackson his liaison man with the party. What happened was that Jackson, who knew Robarts' political thoughts without having to ask, ran the party.

Jackson suffered in comparison with A. D. McKenzie, who had worked long, hard, and successfully at keeping the party unified and happy, by means of liberal doses of patronage. But Jackson felt that the electorate had changed and become far more sophisticated. There were not as many dyed-in-the-wool Grits and Tories around, he felt. Instead there was now a much larger body of independent voters who were looking for action and efficiency from their politicians. In this he was right, but his method of attracting this vote was to present Robarts, and to a lesser degree the government, as the epitome of those characteristics, action and efficiency—and the party went by the board.

"Ernie was the most powerful man in the party," said a former Conservative official in 1971. "At first we used to see him down at headquarters, but after the '63 election, he, like Robarts, started to get fat, and he had neither the time nor the inclination to keep the machine well-oiled. It got so we would have to go down to London once a month to see if there was anything on Ernie's mind and to fill him in on what was happening."

Eventually, one Robarts aide recalled, Jackson's only concern was that there should be enough money in the party coffers to fight an election. "The way Robarts neglected the party was bad for the morale of the troops," the aide said. "They stopped caring, too, and by the time he left, it was pretty rusty and creaky."

This was reflected in the polls at the 1967 election, when Robarts lost seats, even though his own reputation was at its peak. But even his colossal neglect of the party apparatus was not able to destroy the grass-roots allegiance to the Tories that Drew, Frost, and McKenzie had built.

Instead of McKenzie's well-oiled machine, the Conservative party became a small group of people around Robarts whose power derived from their closeness to the Premier's ear. Many, though not all, of them came from London, where they were the leading figures in the community. Some of them represented old money, others had grown wealthy in the boom of the fifties. Their common marks were a cool disdain for those outside the circle, and a horror of publicity. They were also very genial and engaging people to those accepted within the fold.

The extent and complexity of the London power structure was not to be exposed to public view until 1973 when John Robarts was long gone as Premier. During the Legislative Committee's inquiry into the awarding of a contract for the construction of a new head office for Ontario Hydro, one of the unsuccessful bidders, a contractor from London, told how he had tried to get fair consideration of his proposal. His story of those whose aid he tried to enlist reads like a "Who's Who of the 1960s Conservative Party". So intertwined were their relationships, and so abrupt the end of their power when William Davis became Premier, that the story deserves a close look, and will be dealt with in a later chapter.

It is not remarkable that Robarts, the Management Man,

should feel more comfortable dealing with fellow managers than with the shareholders, which helps explain why he was seen to be remote by the electors. To people outside management circles, managers are a little-understood phenomenon.

Even in his dealings with the media, Robarts preferred to communicate direct with the brass quietly and privately. Frost had an open-door policy with reporters, who would saunter into his office and sit down with their feet up while the Premier let flow what he assured them was the inside dope. And it *sounded* like the inside story, until they had time to quietly reflect on their notes and discover there was no meat there. Robarts never bothered with such exercises. Over whisky and steak he would be charming and helpful to an editor or publisher; but to the front-line reporter, who accosted him for some comment or other, there would only be a belligerent "Waddayerwant?", and a terse dismissal.

It was not a government that accepted public scrutiny with pleasure, and the Press Gallery at Queen's Park was a grudgingly tolerated nuisance.

The management syndrome was of considerable political importance because its central element was planning. Both Frost and Drew had recognized the need for managers and planning. Frost had hired some of the first "experts" brought into the civil service. But Robarts set business philosophy at the very heart of government. It was Robarts, for example, who set up the Committee on Government Productivity, a group charged with suggesting ways of reorganizing the Ministries and the decision-making processes in government. Significantly, the group was made up of senior civil servants, and very senior figures from the world of business and industry.

The result of this commitment to planning was that the government moved the focus of its attention several years into the future. Naturally, this had a disruptive effect on the civil service for a few years. But the effect on the Opposition was devastating. They too had to try and push forward their horizons without the resources in expert staff to be able to do it. They have never closed the gap.

The Opposition parties may not have been able to keep

up with what was happening, but, unfortunately for the Tories, neither could the voters. In the 1967 election, with a Legislature expanded to 117 seats, the Tories won 69 seats and slipped 6 points to 42 per cent of the popular vote. The Liberals also dropped from 35 to 32 per cent of the share of votes cast, but this worked out to be 4 more seats, a total of 28, than they had had before. The big winners were the NDP. Their share of the popular vote went up 10 per cent to 26 per cent and the number of seats they held climbed from 7 to 20.

But then, it was something of a non-campaign that the Conservatives ran in 1967; the catch phrase could well have been "The Province Is Strong". Robarts and the record were the themes, and the record was impressive. It included major social reforms such as the introduction of a partial medical insurance plan, a free legal aid system, the Go Transit system for commuters, increased prosperity, expenditures of over a third of the budget on education, and vastly improved relations with the federal government.

Even though he had allowed the party structure to crumble, Robarts' record and his stature as a national figure were enough to win him elections—with help from Frost's political ghost. As early as June 1963 the country had seen that it wasn't dealing with just another inward-looking Ontario Tory. In that month Robarts went to Quebec City and showed a state dinner audience his passionate feelings about Canada. Canada must be a partnership in fact, in spirit and in purpose, he said. "I am certain that the two great peoples who first established our Confederation are ready to make a greater effort to make it work and succeed. Let us do everything to unite and nothing to divide," he said. It was a theme to which Robarts was to return again and again, and as he reiterated it he became more and more a national figure. His sympathy for Quebec in its fiscal arguments with Ottawa, his friendship with Quebec Premier Daniel Johnson, and his introduction of French-language education to Ontario all did much to maintain national unity during the Quiet Revolution of the 1960s in Quebec.

The peak of his reputation as a national statesman was in 1967 when he, John Robarts, Premier of Ontario and not

Prime Minister of Canada, called the Confederation of Tomorrow Conference. It was a measure of his power and influence that the other nine Premiers happily left the convening of this meeting, with its wide-ranging debate on the future of the country, to Robarts when he first suggested it to them the year before.

Robarts was at his most non-political when talking about national unity, and indeed he got very angry at people who attempted to draw politics into the debate. But many observers—there is never a shortage of cynics among politician watchers—hunted around for political motives for his actions. The natural conclusion to reach was that Robarts intended to seek the leadership of the federal Conservative party when Diefenbaker was persuaded or forced to go. Robarts, however, never showed any serious signs of being interested in moving to Ottawa, apparently having forgotten his teenage confession to his wife-to-be. Much to the displeasure of the federal wing, Robarts and the Ontario Tories never gave much visible help in national elections. On at least one occasion, Jackson, who doubled as the party bagman, steadfastly refused to give federal fund raisers his lists of sources of provincial contributions; not surprisingly, this struck the federal boys—great team players all—as being remarkably uncivil. Robarts did make a few appearances on behalf of Robert Stanfield in the 1968 federal election, but took care not to get in so deep that his relationship with Pierre Trudeau would be difficult if the new Liberal leader won.

Robarts, the non-politician, never had any qualms about pinching good ideas from wherever he could find them, and he found a number in the speeches of the NDP members. Both Frost and Drew had recognized that the times required that the Conservatives sacrifice traditional Tory principles in order to maintain support and to provide needed programs; but Robarts took this idea well beyond the bounds of his predecessors' thinking. Frost had come to rely, by necessity, on pragmatism. For Robarts pragmatism was the only way to operate, and he did it extremely skilfully. On occasion he tried too hard to find consensus, and every change in law seemed to wait on the findings of plodding commissions and committees which investigated the situation to the point of screaming boredom. It could certainly be said, however, that when the legal changes were eventually introduced, everyone had had their say.

The province never knew Robarts very well; managers are remote people. It had some idea of his toughness, which was on display in his battles with Ottawa over tax sharing. Robarts maintained that Ontario must have a greater share of income tax or face "fiscal nightmare" and deficit budgets. He hired economists equal, if not superior, in quality to Ottawa's to help make his point: but he was constantly rebuffed. He was to pass on the nightmare and the battle with the federal government to William Davis. But Robarts did manage to balance the books without a tax increase until 1970.

That battle demonstrated one kind of toughness. What was seldom heard of was Robarts' incredible physical toughness, for he kept his private life very much out of the public eye. The public didn't see him talking the night away with copious amounts of whisky—and then striding off to the office none the worse for wear. They didn't see him scouring the north woods' lakes and streams for trout, when he would delightedly abandon the luxuries of Toronto for the rigours of the trail and the fishing camp.

Few even of his close associates saw the full glory of his rage. Cabinet Ministers who had been foolish found it a good idea to keep out of Robarts' way for a while. One who didn't get far enough away to avoid the full force of Robarts' temper commented: "I have never been chewed out by anyone the way John Robarts has chewed me out." This Minister had also served under Frost, who had no small reputation himself in the dressing-down department; but the shaken Cabinet member made it clear where his terrified vote would go in any formal comparison between the two: "When John gets mad he makes Les Frost sound like a Sunday School teacher."

An offshoot of the centenary celebrations of 1967 was a rise in Canadian nationalism. This should have pleased Robarts, the statesman who was always calling for national unity. But, paradoxically, Robarts had little time for the nationalists' demands for policies which would give Ontario a greater degree of economic and cultural independence. He and his Trade and Development Minister Stanley Randall held that the province needed every United States investment dollar it could get, and further maintained that this in no way undermined Ontario's political independence. The glib-tongued Randall (he once told a meeting of perfume manufacturers that he saw in his audience "the sweet success of smell") loudly and laughingly taunted the Opposition parties for bringing up what he called "a phony issue" whenever the question of economic dependence on the U.S. was raised in the Legislature. Robarts made some concessions to the Opposition by putting restrictions on the export of raw materials in an effort to create more processing plants in Ontario, but his general response was to warn that restrictions on American investment meant unemployment for Ontarians.

In his last few months in office he bowed to those who saw Ontario's cultural integrity threatened by the number of media being taken over by U.S.-based interests. In response, Robarts set up the Ontario Royal Commission on Book Publishing. The establishment of the Commission was one of Robarts' last major acts as Premier. While it was undoubtedly an important recognition of Ontarians' growing awareness of the need to protect and nurture their own culture, the commission is writ larger on the calendar of those last few months than perhaps it deserves, probably because there was nothing much else happening.

It was typical of Robarts to avoid any great final demonstration demanding popular acclaim before he left. If he cared much for what people thought about him, he never showed it. He was his own critic and his own judge. Perhaps the Ojibway summed up Robarts best when they named him Pau Bai Mirin Way Moouch–The chief who brings glad tidings.

6. *Waiting for Robarts*

On a high summer afternoon in 1970 Robarts and Ernie Jackson were again sitting on the lawn of Jackson's cottage at Grand Bend. It was a day very much like the day nine years before when the two men had unfolded a road map of Ontario and decided to drive to Ottawa in the morning. A lot had happened in those nine years; Robarts' hair, once brown, was now steel grey, and the short-back-and-sides of 1961 had become a modish mane curling over his collar. Always chunky, he was now bordering on the pudgy. The strong jaw line was still there, but now it sagged slightly at the edges. The years were showing on Jackson, too. The work and the play had not etched their way into the features of Robarts the way they had with Jackson. He looked by far the more grizzled and worn of the two friends.

Robarts had been thinking for about nine months about stepping down, relinquishing the Premiership and the leadership of the Conservative party. Now with this last great career decision in the balance, he went to chat it over with Jackson before coming to a conclusion. The Premiership had been hard on his family life, he had been a member of the Legislature for nearly 20 years and he felt he had given enough of his life to the public service. He was 53 years old and wanted to get out, do some fishing and sailing, and get into the business world to make some money before he retired. Both Frost and Drew before him had found powerful and wealthy men eager to welcome them to the most distinguished board rooms in the country.

The names of former Premiers of Ontario looked good on any company's letterhead and certainly did not harm the company's chances of a respectful hearing whenever it was necessary to talk to governments. Robarts hoped for the same corporate welcome.

So, for all these reasons, Robarts decided to go. The next question was how best to do it, and, more important, *when* to do it. There had been some speculation a few weeks before that Robarts would call a snap election in the summer of 1970 on the issue of the federal government's proposals to change the Canadian tax system. Finance Minister Edgar Benson's White Paper on Taxation had angered large sections of the community, and a federal Conservative party poll at the time, which included some provincial questions, indicated that the Ontario Tories could pick up 8 to 12 seats in an election fought on the tax issue. But Robarts, apparently with thoughts of resignation in his mind, hadn't acted.

There were still two years to run before there had to be an election in Ontario, but it had become customary for Premiers to call an election every four years instead of waiting out the whole five-year term, for fear of being charged with clinging to power. So Robarts was looking at the spring or fall of 1971 as possible election times. He wanted to give his successor sufficient lead time into an election, just as he had had, so that meant having the leadership convention either in the fall of 1970, or early in 1971. This would give the new man the chance to present a Speech from the Throne outlining a legislative program, and a Budget spreading the goodies around, before going to the polls.

A large federal Conservative convention was planned for the fall, so Robarts, to avoid confusion, picked the first few weeks of 1971 as the best time for the convention. He told Jackson to organize the preliminary work of choosing a Toronto location, deciding which party committees should be formed to oversee the event, and renting every available hotel room around the convention hall.

Jackson got together three of Robarts' closest and most trusted associates to help him with this work. They were (Fast) Eddie Goodman, a bright rubber ball of a man, who was a federal Tory bagman and had organized the national party's leadership convention in 1967; Joe Barnicke, a morosely charming Toronto real estate broker who had tremendous authority in the property business because of his political connections, and who was therefore charged with finding the convention space and the hotel rooms; and Toronto advertising executive Peter Hunter, the president of McConnell Advertising.

News of Robarts' decision was restricted to a few close

friends, but by the middle of September suspicions and rumours were beginning to circulate. However, September and October, 1970, brought other events to occupy Conservative minds and bring joy to their hearts.

Through all his seventeen years as the leader of the handful of men who represented the NDP in the Legislature, Donald MacDonald had never been seriously challenged. It was not until the party amounted to something that aspirants began to appear. The first try was made in 1968; in that year Jim Renwick, MPP for Riverdale and federal president of the party, ran against MacDonald. But Renwick lost, largely because he didn't have any great support from the NDP caucus, which then numbered 20.

In the following year, 1969, a by-election was called in Middlesex South and the NDP campaign was organized by a 31-year-old firebrand named Stephen Lewis. Middlesex South was in John Robarts' backyard, the countryside around London, and hardly, observers thought at the time, fertile ground for socialist doctrine. But the NDP candidate won, and Lewis got a lot of the credit. His stock in the party rose and his position was further strengthened a few months later in January, 1970, when he was appointed the NDP caucus spokesman on labour matters. This was crucial to him because it put him in daily contact with the leaders of the trade unions affiliated to the NDP whose disciplined vote could make or break would-be party leaders.

In the middle of June, 1970, Lewis announced that he would be a candidate for the leadership at the fall convention. On June 25 MacDonald said he would not run for re-election. Although MacDonald did not say so, it had become apparent to him that he would be unlikely to win if he did run, and even if he did maintain his position it would look very much like the Old Guard clinging to power. MacDonald had lost that necessary base of support, his own caucus, 14 of whom were committed to Lewis. They were mostly younger men who felt more in tune with Lewis than with MacDonald.

There was also a touch of discontent with MacDonald, particularly among the northern members, over the question of money. At that time the total pay for an MPP was around $10,000, which NDP members from the north, with their heavy travel costs, found it impossible to live on. Their incomes were not bolstered by lucrative appointments to government boards and commissions as were the Tories, and they had asked MacDonald to press Robarts for more money. Their leader certainly approached the Premier, but his approach had been without immediate results. Some of them felt that he had not pushed the request hard enough.

Despite Lewis's popularity, there was a forceful element in the party that didn't want him as leader, and certainly didn't want him to win unchallenged. The role of a sacrificial lamb fell to Walter Pitman, MacDonald's deputy. Pitman was the NDP critic of the government's Department of Education, then the top-spending Ministry, under William Davis, and the quality and moderate delivery of his arguments in the House had won him respect on all sides. But he could not match Lewis's speed of thought in debate, or Lewis's devastating oratory, either. Pitman knew from the outset that he had no chance of winning, but he was determined that the delegates should have an alternative candidate to vote for if they wished.

During September and October, 1970, the two candidates diligently toured the province discussing policy issues and generating a considerable amount of publicity for the party. But by voting day it was obvious to everyone that the outcome was not in doubt. The union vote, which made up nearly half the delegates, went strongly for Lewis. The powerful United Auto Workers was delivered to him almost as a block. Lewis won by 1,188 votes to 642 for Pitman.

The Conservatives received the news of Lewis's victory with glee. His strident tones, hawkish appearance, and apparently uncompromising socialist philosophy would allow them to fight the next election on their favourite theme: the real threat of a socialist government in Ontario. Before the NDP convention the Robarts Cabinet had conducted a little poll of itself, and the results were quietly leaked afterwards. The Ministers, it was reported, regarded Pitman as the greatest menace to the Tories, because his "moderate" style could win seats from them in their rural power base. Any gains that Lewis made would be at the expense of the Liberals in the urban areas.

After Lewis's victory, this piece of bravado was leaked in order to convey to the public that the Tories were not rattled. To the business community their message was different and simple: "It's either us or them. Which would you rather have?" The industrialists and businessmen didn't have to ponder long over that one, and dollars started pouring into the Conservatives' war chest.

During October, more and more Conservatives came to believe that Robarts would resign. Around the middle of the month William Davis, the free-spending Education Minister who had been working towards the leadership for eight years and was considered the heir apparent, made the decision to become a candidate. Shortly afterwards, before that decision had been made known, he received the telephone call which was to establish his course in the campaign.

Davis was in his sessional office in the legislative building when the call came through from Charles MacNaughton, the Treasurer, and Robarts' right-hand man in the Cabinet. MacNaughton, who was known as "hard nosed Charlie", said he wanted to come over straight away and talk. A few minutes later MacNaughton was sitting in Davis's sessional office on the third floor at Queen's Park. Davis was never a man to express his personality in his choice of decor, and the room had all the character of a Holiday Inn lobby. The furniture was Public Works number one issue, Ministers, for the use of, and that was it. The surroundings did nothing to detract from what MacNaughton, the stalwart but sometimes blinkered party workhorse, had to say. He told Davis that he wanted to support him for the leadership. "I know the natural thing for me to do is to support Darcy McKeough, but I want to support you, and I want to be your campaign manager," MacNaughton said. Certainly it would have been natural for MacNaughton to support McKeough, for the young Municipal Affairs Minister was, like him, from southwestern Ontario and was his political protégé. But now MacNaughton was offering his prestige and abilities to Davis.

This was an offer the Education Minister could not refuse, and he was deeply moved by it. Davis had worked hard to develop a wide base of support out in the rural ridings, and having MacNaughton on his side would add enormously to the support he had gathered. Not only would the Treasurer bring a fair amount of southwestern Ontario with him, his influence would also ensure that Davis got the support of the bulk of the Conservative caucus, and this would have a ripple effect in the ridings.

But there were some negative sides to MacNaughton's offer as well. MacNaughton was part of the Old Guard Tory establishment and he was well known as Robarts' number two man in the Legislature. His support might well identify Davis as Robarts' candidate, and consequently as someone who was not going to deal with all the dissatisfactions that were welling up within the party as a result of Robarts' neglect. But, on balance, MacNaughton was such an important figure that his offer was a blessing.

At this time Davis was having preliminary discussions with some of his close political advisers. One was Clare Westcott, his executive assistant, who had been Robert Macaulay's executive assistant before the "Minister of Everything" resigned. Then there was Ron Webb, Davis's law partner in Brampton. Another was Hugh Macaulay, Robert's younger brother who was a director of the Ryerson Polytechnical Institute while Davis was Education Minister. Then there was another member of the Ryerson Board, William Kelly, a vice-president of Consumers' Gas. Ryerson and Robert Macaulay's 1961 leadership campaign were to be common bonds among most of the senior people on Davis's campaign organization.

At the beginning Davis's dilemma was one of timing. He was the heir apparent and thus was expected to set the pace; and yet Robarts had given no public indication that he would leave, and was still replying to questions about his rumoured retirement by saying, "These rumours are simply that." What was Davis to do when approached by the Press or by Conservatives outside his own circle? He didn't want to raise antagonism among Tories by appearing to jump the gun and have a campaign going before Robarts announced. Since it was important to avoid seeming disrespectfully eager, it was decided that all inquiries would be deflected by saying that there was no campaign organization being built and nothing would be happening unless and until Robarts made a statement. This decision was to rebound on Davis with great force.

Waiting for Robarts

While Davis and his men were lying low and waiting for Robarts to move, another group was becoming active. In the middle of October, 1970, a meeting was held at the North Toronto home of a lawyer named Donald Guthrie. Mr. Guthrie had been Robert Stanfield's personal representative in Ontario and the men who gathered at his house were the people who had gained their experience making Stanfield the federal Conservative leader in 1966 and 1967. They were the young Turks of the Conservative party, the aggressive young men with the new ideas. From the world of advertising there was Dalton Camp, former federal party president, the egg-head of the party, and his brother-in-law Norman Atkins, the organization wizard. There was stockbroker Ross DeGeer and Paul Weed. Weed ran a collection agency and had been Guthrie's assistant on the Stanfield campaign. There was lawyer Roy McMurtry; an insurance broker named Chad Bark; an investment counsellor named William Saunderson; a federal Tory fund raiser named Patrick Vernon; and financial consultant Eric Ford, Stanfield's tax policy adviser.

These men knew that collectively they were the most sophisticated political organization in the country, and they wanted to be in on the provincial leadership race. To an outsider it would have been a strange scene to watch. Here was a group of the fastest political gunslingers in the country calmly sitting around deciding that they wanted to be in the up-coming range war, but not yet certain whose side they wanted to be on. They talked for some time back and forth about whom they should support. Guthrie and Bark were for supporting Allan Lawrence, the Minister of Mines and Northern Affairs, partly for the excellent reason that they were close friends of his. Others were for offering their services to Bill Davis. In their politics these men were federally oriented, and Davis had shown more interest in helping federal Tories than the other possible candidates for the provincial leadership. No one there, apart from McMurtry, knew Davis well, but everyone felt warmly towards him and his record. For example, in 1965 Davis had offered to help

Dalton Camp to get the Tory nomination for Peel. Camp declined the offer, ran in Eglinton and was defeated. When Camp ran in Don Valley in 1968, Davis campaigned for him in the riding. Thus in the end the consensus of the meeting was that they would approach the Davis people first, with Lawrence as a possible second choice, but no one really thought that they would have to bother with second choices.

Paul Weed was delegated to make the initial approach to Clare Westcott, whom he knew quite well from their work together on previous campaigns. But when Weed called Westcott and asked if any campaign organization was being put together and went on to offer the services of the Camp-Atkins group, all he got was the agreed-on stock answer—nothing is happening, Robarts hasn't resigned yet, we'll let you know when anything happens. Weed and his gang were furious. They knew for a fact that preliminary organization work *was* being done for Davis, and they considered the response to their approach a studied insult. Now thoroughly paranoid, they began to wonder aloud if it was the presence of Camp in their group that had caused the rebuff. At that time the intense feelings aroused by Camp in the federal leadership battle in 1966 and 1967 had not died down. The mere name of Camp was enough to raise the blood pressure of Diefenbaker loyalists. Perhaps, the Camp-Atkins group figured, Davis felt that being associated with them would lose him a lot of votes.

But the Camp group also had a pretty good opinion of their own value as a political machine and their collective pride was hurt by the brush-off. They liked to be in on things from the beginning and have a hand in the formation of the campaign from the ground up. Westcott's line about calling them when anything happened didn't go down well, because it implied that they would be coming into the organization in subsidiary roles. That was not an idea that appealed.

Westcott didn't find out till a few days later what the effect had been of his chanting the appointed response; when he did find out, he was shocked. When Weed called he had not been aware of the import of the inquiry. Westcott had taken it to be just a casual offer.

A little while later Davis visited McMurtry, who was in

hospital with a back injury. McMurtry asked him about the brush-off and Davis, who by this time knew what had happened, replied that it was done without his knowledge. McMurtry said that it was a pity and that Davis was in for a rough fight.

Davis was. Don Guthrie and Chad Bark went to work on their friend Allan Lawrence, and after much dithering persuaded him to run, and to ask Atkins to organize the campaign. (Camp decided to stay in the wings of the whole affair.) At first Atkins wasn't completely sure that he wanted to work for Lawrence, but in the end he agreed to do it. Part of the agreement was that he and his group would get paid for their work.

By the middle of November the rumours had so solidified that it had become a question of *when* Robarts would make his announcement, not *whether* he would.

And then, finally, on December 8, a brief notice went up on the board of the Press Gallery at Queen's Park: Premier Robarts would hold a press conference in the press conference studio that morning. As the time approached, hordes of photographers and reporters gathered outside the second-floor Premier's office, beneath the gilt-framed portraits of Drew, Frost, Hepburn, Nixon, Conant, and Kennedy. With a few minutes to go, Robarts strode briskly out of his office with his deputy and secretary to the Cabinet, Keith Reynolds, keeping step beside him. Photographers scuttled backwards down the corridor ahead of them, snapping away with their cameras. Robarts and Reynolds exchanged a few inaudible words, the words of men under close scrutiny who wished to appear calm, as they walked down the wide main staircase. And then Robarts was sitting behind the table in the packed studio with the television lights blazing.

He had enjoyed it all, he said. There had been some fine achievements, but it was time to go and hand over to a younger man. The convention would be on February 12 next year. He answered a few questions, indulged in a little philosophy, and that was that. Always the master of the anti-climax, Robarts even managed to make the announcement of his impending resignation into a workaday occurrence.

During the course of the morning the Press Gallery had

been informed that Allan Lawrence would be holding a press conference shortly after Robarts had finished. There was no doubt in any of the reporters' minds that Lawrence would announce his candidacy at that press conference, and Lawrence hung around outside the studio while Robarts was holding his press conference. But when the Premier left, one of Robarts' aides went up to Lawrence and told him it would be "injudicious" to announce his candidacy so soon after Robarts had made his statement. "This is John's day," Lawrence was told. The Lawrence press conference was hurriedly cancelled.

It had become clear by this time that even though no one had yet declared an interest in Robarts' job, five Cabinet Ministers were likely to go after it. Despite his eagerness on December 8, Lawrence was blowing hot and cold, but would undoubtedly declare in the end. Davis was a certainty. Robert Welch, the Provincial Secretary, was a likely starter, as was Bert Lawrence, the Financial and Commercial Affairs Minister. There was some doubt about Darcy McKeough, the Municipal Affairs Minister, following the loss of the support of his mentor, Charlie MacNaughton, but he was still a strong possibility.

There was a sixth possibility, Alan Eagleson, the party president. Eagleson was certainly playing his role as the impresario of the event for all it was worth, and with all the theatrical aplomb he usually reserved for hockey stars' salary negotiations. He held numerous press conferences to explain the organization of the convention and consistently refused to rule out his candidacy, though no one else seemed to be particularly interested in whether he ran or not. On December 15 it became known that Eagleson had been involved in a major behind-the-scenes battle over the committee, headed by Ernie Jackson, that Robarts had set up to do preliminary organization work for the convention.

Jackson's committee had appointed chairmen to ten organization sub-committees, but the fifty-four-member party executive, led by Eagleson, had refused to ratify the appointments. Their refusal was evidence of mounting concern among the party rank and file that "the Establishment" was attempting to steer the leadership in Davis's direction. Jackson was forced to expand his committee to include Eagleson as well as the executive director of the party Arthur Harnett, and Harnett's assistant Hugh Latimer.

Feelings in the party were now running so high that the following day, December 16, Robarts had to steel himself for the demeaning task of going to a meeting of representatives of the party executive to assure them that they were solely responsible for the running of the convention.

On December 20 Davis was in New York at the end of a three-day stay spent discussing the purchase of programs produced by Ontario's Educational Television Authority by the NBC network. That night, from his hotel room, Davis telephoned every Conservative member of the Legislature whom he had not already talked to. His message to each of them was the same. "This is Bill. I just thought I would let you know I am going to be back in Toronto tomorrow. I'm down here in New York on business and I am going to be announcing my candidacy within the next few days."

And he did, on December 21, the next day, after paying a very large phone bill when he checked out of his hotel.

7. The Heirs to the Throne

William Davis's drive towards the leadership had peaked, as the political analysts say, about three years before December 21, 1970. The day he announced his candidacy, his fortunes as the heir apparent to Robarts, as the man who revolutionized education in Ontario and as the whiz kid of the government were already in decline. Three years before, these accomplishments would have brought him almost unopposed into the corner office on the second floor at Queen's Park. But by the end of 1970 the great leap forward in school building, in equalizing educational opportunities, and in rationalizing the administration of education had become a liability.

In the mid-sixties the reformation in education had marked Davis as a young man going places, and he helped the image by streaking across the province at a rate of some 124,000 miles a year, to open new schools and chat about the great things that were happening in his department. Then, as they always do, the bills started coming in, and the province realized that almost half of the provincial budget was being spent on education. Parents began to look at the lush carpeting in the new schools and the cupboards full of equipment that didn't look as though it had ever been used—and then they looked at their tax bills, and wondered what kind of revolution this had been.

A couple of years before, when Robarts was at the height of his reputation, being heir apparent wouldn't have been a bad thing either. But Conservatives had begun to feel the impact of Robarts' neglect of the party. They had lost seats in the 1967 election and they had unexpectedly lost Middlesex South in the by-election of 1969. Robarts and his small cadre of confidants seemed unconcerned with the physical condition of the party and deaf to the voice of the grass-roots membership, particularly the young membership. To be a Robarts man at the end of 1970 was to be a fat-cat establishment figure, self-satisfied, manipulative, and scornful of the frustration in the party.

Whiz-kiddery also had lost its glamour. It had been rather marvellous to see all these great minds brought to bear on the problem of education, such as in the Ontario Institute for Studies in Education. But the public's intellect could not keep up with the seething minds fermenting ever more complicated and expensive educational systems. The public believed that it had a firmer grasp on reality than these thinkers in their towers, both of which were as costly as ivory. Davis was the deviser of this program of intellectual rocketry, and thus took the blame for it.

And so Davis entered the leadership race on the defensive. He was everyone's target, and his campaign was to justify what had been done. He had to win support, yes, but more important he had to keep the loyalty of the supporters he had gathered during the best of his eight years as Minister of Education.

Nevertheless, William Grenville Davis, 41 years old, was no political wreck that December. He was a product of the twenty-seven years that the Conservatives had been in power. The party had weaned him, reared him and shaped him in its own image, so that within his make-up as a politician and administrator could be found many of the salient elements that characterized the Tories at that time.

Davis had Drew's sense that in some areas traditional Tory principles must be sacrificed and ideas taken from the political left if the party was to retain power. Indeed, that concept had seeped into the Tory mentality so thoroughly that a conscious rejection of conservatism was no longer needed. The party had changed. Some of Frost's feeling for political fighting at the hand-to-hand level had been absorbed by Davis, but it was overlaid by an almost excessive gentility which, though socially admirable, was something of a handicap when parrying the jugular lunges of a leadership race. His greatest debt at that time appeared to be to Robarts. Though his opponents may have found much to criticize, Davis as Minister of Education had established himself as a fine administrator. He had complete control of his huge department and an encyclopedic knowledge of what was going on within its walls. He had an answer for every query and a retort for every criticism.

Physically Davis did not have what was considered a necessity for every successful politician at the time, charisma. He was a chubby 5 ft. 10 in. tall and wore his rather featureless face like a mask; only in trusted company was the mask allowed to slip into something more comfortable, an easy, Cheshire-cat grin. The Davis wardrobe ran to a few badly cut suits whose most lively colour was navy blue. The trousers were generally baggy at the knees and the shoes invariably scuffed like a small boy's. Davis was the last one to be concerned about his sartorial image, and the aides who eventually decided that it needed changing were to have one heck of a time getting him to a decent tailor.

The physical image was not improved when he began to speak. His monotonous delivery and convoluted grammar defied the attention span of even the most eager listener. At Queen's Park there is a legend that once, though no one can remember quite when, Davis spoke a sentence in the Legislature that took up half a page of *Hansard* (about 300 words). Even if that is not true, it does indicate that his manner of speech was so remarkable that it created a mythology. For some reason the ultimate torture for Davis was the use of the first person singular. He would go to any lengths to avoid the word "I". In the early stages of the leadership campaign he was asked at a delegates' meeting why he thought he would make a good party leader. "We are relatively young. We have had some political success, and I think we say things when we feel they have to be said though they may be unpopular," Davis spluttered and hurriedly scanned the room for another question.

It took Davis a lot of time and effort to overcome (even partly) this embarrassing sensitivity about himself and his ideas. It was also symptomatic of a trait which isolated him in his decision-making; for while he liked to have people around him who would tell him exactly what they thought, he seldom responded in kind.

Davis was born on July 30, 1929, the son of Albert and Vera Davis, in Brampton, then a small town about half an hour's drive from Toronto. Bill Davis's father was the Crown Attorney for the area and it was a pleasant middle-class childhood. The family was in the upper echelons of local society, with all the feelings of responsibility and duty that entailed. In the summer there were the holidays at the family cottage on Townsend Island, about fourteen miles from Honey Harbour on Georgian Bay. The island remained Davis's favourite summer retreat in later years, and a regular sight on Friday afternoons was a Department of Lands and Forests float plane leaving Toronto Harbour on its way to the island with the Davis family on board.

Though comfortable and well established, the Davis family didn't belong to the Ontario elite. Neither Ridley nor Upper Canada College moulded the young Davis boy. He went to public and high school in Brampton where his early academic career is remembered as being "average". After three tries he—surprisingly, perhaps—won a prize for public speaking. The suspicion lurked in his mind for many years, he once said, that the school eventually gave him the prize because his father supplied the money for the award each year, and they were concerned that the funds might be cut off if they didn't.

However undistinguished his academic achievements may have been thus far, they were enough to get him into the University of Toronto. He took most interest in political science, history and English, and got his degree with a B average. Davis also plunged into the joys of football, played for the intermediate intercollegiate team, and made a friend of one of the stars of the first team, Roy McMurtry. From the University of Toronto Davis went to Osgoode Hall law school for four years, where he again earned a B average. He was called to the bar in 1955, and set up in practice with his father in Brampton.

Before he was called to the bar, Davis married his girl friend from his U. of T. and Osgoode Hall days, Helen McPhee, who came from Windsor. They had four children, Neil, Nancy, Katherine, and Ian. In March, 1962, Helen Davis died after an operation for a colitis condition. Davis's second wife was Kathleen Mackay, from Chicago, whose parents had a cottage on an island in Georgian Bay not far from the Davis summer home. Kathleen had been a friend of Davis's sister, Molly, and in January, 1963, shortly after Robarts had given him the education portfolio, Davis and Kathleen were married in Chicago.

In small-town Ontario in the 1950s (and even now) business success and politics were intertwined. Albert Davis introduced his son to the Conservative party early in life. When he was in his early teens in the 1940s Davis worked on the campaigns of federal members for the area, Gordon Graydon and John Pallett, as well as for the provincial member Tom Kennedy.

Davis nearly went straight into federal politics. His most influential mentor in Peel was the federal member, Graydon. Davis got his basic political education from Graydon and developed an interest in federal political questions, particularly external affairs. If events had run their natural course Davis would have sought the Conservative federal candidacy after Graydon retired. But in 1953 Graydon died. Davis was still at law school, and not yet ready to jump into politics. John Pallett won the nomination and the riding.

Tom Kennedy had represented Peel riding in the Legislature since 1919. He lost only one election, in the Hepburn sweep of 1934, but got back again in 1937. Kennedy was Agriculture Minister for 14 years, and, very briefly, between Drew and Frost, he was Premier. He was a leading figure in both those regimes. Like Frost, Kennedy could wrap himself around an audience with home-spun sentimentality, and if all Kennedy's emotional stories weren't strictly factual, no one really minded.

Kennedy took a shine to the young Davis, and one day in 1958 he marched him along to Frost's office at Queen's Park. "I'd like you to meet the next member for Peel and a future Premier of Ontario," Kennedy said. What Frost replied and what Davis said is not recorded. Davis is the lone survivor of that meeting, and his recollection is only that Kennedy said some very complimentary things. At 28, Davis had all the qualities Kennedy was looking for in a successor. He had plenty of experience of campaigning, he looked solidly honest, came from good local stock, was a United Church member and a Sunday School teacher, and family man.

So, on December 7, 1958, with Kennedy nodding approvingly on the platform, Davis was nominated the candidate for Peel riding. Davis entered the Legislature after the general election of June the following year, but with difficulty. Prime Minister John Diefenbaker in Ottawa had just cancelled production of the Avro Arrow airplane. At the Malton plant in the riding, where much of the work was to have been done, there was consternation. While the technical experts assembled for the project hightailed it to the U.S. in search of jobs, the regular workmen had nothing to do but stay at home, collect unemployment cheques and complain. When young, fresh-faced Bill Davis came knocking on their doors he was reminded that he belonged to the same party as Mr. Diefenbaker and was sent none too politely on his way. Davis did, however, beat the Liberal candidate, architect and town planner Anthony Adamson–but only by 1,400 votes. Davis recovered handsomely in 1963 when he won by 14,000 votes.

William Davis, MPP, saw out the Frost years from about as far back on the backbenches as it was possible to go. But when Frost resigned the leadership in 1961 the time for action came. Davis had met Robert Macaulay about 10 years before when Macaulay became the member for Toronto Riverdale. Macaulay was always somewhat ambivalent in his friendships—he might bare his soul one day and stalk by without a word the next—but he liked and trusted the young MPP from Brampton. Davis was attracted by the intellect and imagination of the "Riverdale dynamo" and agreed to manage his leadership campaign when Macaulay asked him.

They lost to Robarts, but as kingmakers they had to be reckoned with. When Macaulay was given the empire of Energy, Economics, and Development, Davis was given Macaulay's former post as vice-chairman of Ontario Hydro, which upped his salary from $7,000 to $17,000 and convinced him to make politics a full-time profession. After he became Premier, Robarts held on to the Education portfolio for a year. But in a major pre-election shuffle in October 1962 he gave the job to Davis. As a Hydro commissioner and a caucus member Davis had shown himself to be clever, and he was well liked by most of the caucus members. And it didn't go unnoticed that Robarts was giving a top job to a young man who only a year before had organized an opposing leadership campaign. That couldn't hurt party unity.

Davis's experience of education administration amounted to a spell on the Brampton Public School Board. But he quickly came to know his Ministry, and realized that it needed a thorough shake-up. He shook it till its bones rattled. As one bystander put it: "He shunted aside, eased out or neutralized a large number of officials so set in their ways that more modern observers feigned surprise that they did not sign documents with quills." In his early days in the Ministry Davis backed the formation of the Ontario Curriculum Institute and later the Ontario Institute for Studies in Education, the School of Graduate Studies in Education and the Department of Educational Research. To staff his Ministry and these groups he enticed the best minds he could find to work for him.

The innovations came thick and fast. Most were pushed through simply because Davis knew more about them than anyone else and could argue opponents inside and outside Cabinet to a standstill. He argued his political enemies to a standstill when he decided to amalgamate rural school boards into regions so as to make the standard of educational facilities in rural areas equal to those in the cities. There were predictions that he had committed political suicide, but he appeared to win over most of the vocal opposition. However, during the 1971 leadership campaign it became obvious that many Tories on the concession roads were anxious about loss of contact with their local schools, the long bus rides their children had to take each day to the new centralized schools, and the large increases in their tax bills that had accompanied the move to county boards.

Possibly Davis's greatest failure as Education Minister was that he couldn't sell the academic advantages of amalgamation to the parents. His greatest success was probably the introduction of 20 colleges of Arts and Technology, known as community colleges, which offered skilled training to students who were either unable or unwilling to go to university. The community colleges were the concrete result of Drew's realization that the province must have technicians if the economy was to expand and diversify.

In the late '50s Davis had first come across a coiled spring of a young man named Clare Westcott. After a varied career which included spells as a Hydro lineman and a reporter for *The Toronto Telegram*, by reason of stalwart service to the Conservative party Westcott had become Macaulay's executive assistant in the Energy Ministry. As vice-chairman of Hydro Davis was in and out of the Energy Department, and when Macaulay bowed out in 1963, Davis took Westcott on as his executive assistant.

It was a happy association. Westcott was a compulsive worker, the supreme solver of political problems, and hander-out of favours. As Davis shuttled around the province for eight years opening schools, attending meetings, making friends, appointing people to committees, he may not have had his eye on the goal of leadership; but Westcott certainly did. "He's holding IOU's he doesn't even know about," Westcott commented smugly during the leadership campaign. No pleasant gesture was too small for Westcott, no policy question too large for him to have nothing to say about it. In addition Westcott developed an astonishing network of friends and informants, not only within the Ontario civil service, but also throughout the province, in all sectors of life. He operated a one-man intelligence service which was capable of getting as accurate a reading of the mood of Ontario as any.

There was a pyrotechnic quality to Westcott's energy which drew attention away from the coolness of his brain. It was not uncommon to see him carrying on conversations on two telephones at once and writing memos to his secretary at the same time. For anyone who telephoned Westcott and found himself in the middle of one of his three-part-harmony conversations it was a troubling experience. Westcott had almost an addiction for telephones, and without one close at hand he became fidgety and restless. Meal times, particularly in restaurants, were torture. After going through all the possible arrangements of the cutlery on the table he would make swift sorties from his table to chat with acquaintances he saw dining close by.

In 1967 Davis was at the crest of the first wave of his political popularity. Dalton Camp, then president of the National Conservative Association, had engineered the calling of a leadership convention in September that year, and, in the spring, it appeared almost certain that Davis would be among the candidates. By the middle of May Davis had almost decided to run, encouraged by a deluge of mail and phone calls from potential supporters.

He intended to run as the youth candidate, the bright young Tory, but two things made him change his mind. One was the entry of Nova Scotia Premier Robert Stanfield into the campaign. Davis respected Stanfield's abilities and knew his own campaign could only be a token effort in comparison. His second reason for not running was illness.

In July Davis was forced to spend eight days in hospital for tests after suffering from back pains, headaches, dizzy spells, and numbness in his legs, all resulting from a football injury in his youth. After leaving hospital he was required to cut his regular work pace drastically, and was certainly in no condition to wage a leadership campaign. He could not have beaten Robert Stanfield, but a good showing and a switch to federal politics would have made him an influential figure in line for a Cabinet post if the Tories won in Ottawa, and for another crack at the leadership after Stanfield left. At 38 years of age Davis had time on his side. But he didn't let the federal leadership convention go by without noticing him. He was chairman of the policy committee and thus played an important role in diverting the convention from a destructive showdown between the Diefenbaker and Camp factions.

The organization that gathered around Davis for the provincial leadership contest in 1971 was the remnants of Bob Macaulay's supporters in 1961–and they had not learned much in the interim. At the head of the organization was Charles MacNaughton with the post of campaign chairman. The campaign manager was John Latimer, the genial operator of a boys' camp who had worked on the Macaulay campaign and who was later to be important in the reconciliation with the Atkins group. Bob Macaulay's younger brother Hugh, already retired in his early forties after having made his nest-egg selling Pontiacs, had been with Davis from the first discussions on how to run the campaign. He was with MacNaughton on the campaign committee. William Kelly was vice-president and director of marketing of Consumers' Gas and did much of the fund raising for Davis's campaign. Jack Gorman, an unsuccessful Tory candidate in Nipissing riding a few years before, and thereafter found to be just the man to be executive assistant to the president of Ryerson, organized Davis's campaign tour of the province. The reader will recall that both Hugh Macaulay and Kelly also did duty as board members at Ryerson. Paul McNamara, owner of the Ports of Call restaurant in Toronto, a favourite Tory hangout at the time, was involved in forming policy statements for Davis. Robert Byran, of James Lovick Advertising, and president of the Conservative Riding Association in Ontario South, was chairman of the publicity committee. Another man from Lovick Advertising, Ab Mellor, a member of Davis's riding association in Peel North, looked after Press liaison.

As it turned out, this selfless work by two of its staff didn't do Lovick Advertising much good. It had had a pretty good share of the Ontario government's advertising contracts, but after the leadership changed an agency named Camp Associates–president, Norman Atkins–moved into government work in a big way, and Lovick Advertising and a few other Tory agencies found themselves getting smaller slices of the pie.

Ward Cornell, well known as a dull but cheerful commentator for "Hockey Night in Canada" on television, who had ties to the Robarts London establishment, worked part time with the Davis tour organization. Travelling with Davis as he criss-crossed the province was Ronald Webb, his law partner from Brampton, and John Gillies, a former *Globe and Mail* reporter who was on a leave of absence from his post as press officer for (wait for it) the Department of Education.

From the start Davis had the support of a third of the Conservative caucus of 68. This support was to grow as the campaign proceeded, and was the crucial factor in Davis's slim victory. That support saved him, but it also marked him as the establishment candidate and helped nurture the opposition to him.

Having announced his candidacy, Davis was left standing alone as the only candidate over Christmas and New Year. Robert Welch and Bert Lawrence were expected to announce early in the new year, but Allan Lawrence appeared to have lost his early enthusiasm, and Darcy McKeough seemed to have dropped out of the picture altogether, after having been touted as Davis's biggest challenger a few weeks before.

In fact McKeough's star had been rising steadily over the previous few years, as Davis's declined. He was the favourite son of the southwestern Ontario Tories. He counted not only MacNaughton among his patrons, but also such people as John White, who took over Ernie Jackson's riding of London South; Agriculture Minister William Stewart from Middlesex North; such party notables as Eddie Goodman; and many of those from the London establishment, including Jackson, with whom McKeough had class bonds.

McKeough, a large slab of a man with a voice like a blunderbuss loaded with tin-tacks, had aristocratic pretensions. He was known as "the Duke of Kent" in which county his home town of Chatham lay, and it was not a nickname that displeased him. But he saw the funny side of this pose, too, and enjoyed putting on a good performance as the red-baiting red-neck in the House, particularly since the New Democrats generally received his jibes with affronted seriousness.

For years the party power brokers had patted McKeough on the back when the subject of leadership came up and said, "Yes, Darcy, your time will come." It was implicit in this support and encouragement that behind it was the sanction of the man to whom all McKeough's patrons owed their allegiance—John Robarts. So in the summer of 1970 McKeough had been given equal odds with Davis to win the leadership. But in the first days of the new year he found himself alone; all his friends were in the Davis camp.

McKeough had all the right credentials. He was 37 years old, the youngest member of the Cabinet, came from a well established Chatham family and had followed the family tradition of involvement in municipal politics before being elected to Queen's Park. There was a thriving wholesale plumbing business back home and a spacious family compound south of the town near Lake Erie. He had been to school at Ridley College, an exclusive private school at St. Catharines, and had married Joyce, the daughter of Conservative Senator David Walker.

When MacNaughton came to him in summer and told him that Robarts was leaving and that he, MacNaughton, was going to work for Davis, McKeough's first feelings were of disbelief. The disbelief became shock as he saw all his other powerful supporters either overtly or covertly going to the Education Minister. Over the Christmas and New Year break McKeough turned over in his head the problem of whether or not to run. He could still muster a considerable amount of support from his home area, and could pick up some high-quality organizers and workers from other areas. They wouldn't be the big names, of course, but good enough to put on a decent showing. It was obvious that there was a lot of discontent in the party with the way the leadership was being set up for Davis, and this protest vote might well be mustered into a strong campaign. At 37 years of age he had nothing much to lose by running.

He called a press conference within hours of having made up his mind. Although it was a Sunday evening, on January 3rd, grumbling reporters were summoned to McKeough's Ministerial office at the corner of Bay and College streets and told the news. The group that McKeough had put together for the campaign included Joe Martin, who had been executive assistant to former Manitoba Premier Duff Roblin; McKeough had got to know Martin when they both worked for Roblin, as had other important London Tories, in the 1967 federal leadership contest. There was also Douglas Bassett, one of the sons of the Bassett communications empire, which included *The Toronto Telegram* and CFTO television. Then there was Ted Rogers, of Rogers Cable TV, and a couple of bagmen, W. H. Watson, a political ally from Chatham, and Murray Webber, a Toronto developer.

The next day, January 4, Bert Lawrence, the 47-year-old Minister of Financial and Commercial Affairs, announced that he too would be a candidate. Bert Lawrence had nothing much in the way of a campaign organization and his main strength was his likeable personality and his intelligence. He never exhibited any political muscle, but the delegates enjoyed sitting down with him for an hour or so and chewing over issues in a more forthright way than they could with the other candidates. The delegates emerged from these meetings inspired and impressed, but Lawrence was never able to translate these feelings into votes. The bulk of his support came from his home area around Ottawa.

Meanwhile, Allan Lawrence, 45, the Minister of Mines and Northern Affairs, had been vacillating. After the Atkins group's overtures to Davis were rebuffed, Lawrence's friends in the group, Don Guthrie and Chad Bark, encouraged Lawrence to run, and before he had finally decided, arranged a meeting with Atkins. At first Atkins wasn't sure that he could work for Lawrence, and there were several long discussions before Atkins agreed to run Lawrence's campaign.

There was obviously a protest vote to be gathered from people who believed that Robarts was trying to steer the leadership towards Davis; but was Allan Lawrence the right man to collect that support? Lawrence had the right kind of irreverent image to make him a natural anti-establishment candidate, but perhaps he was a bit too irreverent. He had become known as a maverick in the Legislature for his record of speaking and, on occasion, even voting against the government. Indeed, it was widely believed that Robarts took Lawrence into the Cabinet in 1968 to shut him up. He was given the junior post of Mines and Northern Affairs, and by hard work built an empire out of it.

Thus, at the leadership convention Lawrence could count on solid support from northern Ontario, and should have been able to weave his Bay Street-Rosedale lawyer background into a fair vote from Toronto. He was not terribly subtle in his thinking on policy, but had a clipped, uncompromising way of speaking that was quite powerful in its impact. His ingenuous, self-deprecating sense of humour was quite appealing, and even though he was balding, he had a boyish face and smile which made him look younger and less stodgy than Davis. Lawrence was also a natural for television. He was one of those people whose image leaps out of the screen at the audience, all his appealing qualities magnified. And if there was something the Atkins group knew about, it was the use of television.

But no sooner had they struck a bargain with Lawrence, than he began to have doubts about running. Earlier he had come close to showing a disreputable craving for power by planning to announce his candidacy moments after Robarts had made his retirement statement (Lawrence's people insisted their man had only wanted to deliver a personal tribute to Robarts); now Lawrence went off the idea of being Premier altogether. The date had been set for him to announce, but a few days before he told his team that he wasn't going to go through with it. Someone called Lawrence's wife Moira, who was staying for the weekend at the family cottage near Lindsay. Mrs. Lawrence, an impressive woman with at least as much political experience and acumen as her husband, called him at once and persuaded him to stick to the original plans.

On the morning of January 6 the Queen's Park press corps was treated to the most theatrical of all the candidates' announcements. They were invited to a large meeting room at the Westbury Hotel where about a hundred chairs had been set up facing a podium; the podium was adorned by a picture of the province's coat of arms pinned to the front, and it was flanked grandly by the Ontario flag. While hostesses poured coffee for the bemused reporters, more and more smartly-dressed young people trooped into the room. It slowly dawned on the reporters that they were heavily outnumbered by Lawrence's supporters and were about to be subjected to an "event". When Lawrence and his wife entered the room, this cheering section rose as a man from its seat, clapping and hollering; they also booed and hissed the reporters who, as is their custom, refused to be awed by the proximity of greatness and remained firmly and defiantly seated.

A lively speech had been prepared for Lawrence, which was to set the tone for the campaign. Abandoning the stance taken by the other candidates that this business of choosing a new leader was a gentlemanly affair which should be conducted without malicious attacks on one another, Lawrence hit out fiercely at Davis and the costs of education. To the noisy glee of the cheering section he announced that it was just ridiculous that education would take up $1.5 billion or 43 per cent of the Budget in 1971, and he pledged himself to cut it back to 33 per cent. Government spending and the rotten condition of the party became Lawrence's two battle cries, and they proved to be the right ones to draw the Tory dissidents to him.

Two days later, January 8, Robert Welch, 42, the Provincial Secretary, held a quiet press conference at Queen's Park and said that he too would be a candidate—and then immediately got into trouble. He was asked what policies he would be discussing and putting forward during his campaign. Welch replied that he wasn't going to discuss policy, because if he were elected leader on the basis of specific policy proposals this would break the decision-making authority of Cabinet. This was reasonable enough. The other candidates had all made some concessions to the feeling that the event should not appear to be purely a power contest by producing slight policy proposals to give a gloss of intellect to the proceedings. Welch stripped that away, and suddenly found himself facing a hostile press corps which grilled him for three-quarters of an hour on the general theme, "What kind of defunct campaign is this that has no policies?" When it ended Welch staggered from the room, obviously shaken and upset. He never lived down that beginning to his campaign, even though in the end he produced more policy papers than any other candidate. In politics, first impressions can last a lifetime.

Welch, the member for Lincoln riding, which surrounded St. Catharines in the Niagara peninsula, didn't have much of a campaign organization to begin with. It amounted to not much more than a few friends and supporters from his home area. But before the weakness of his organization became generally apparent, a strange thing happened; four people closely associated with Robarts joined Welch's campaign. They were Don Martyn, Robarts' executive assistant, who became campaign manager; Ab Campion, executive assistant to Robarts' old flat-mate, James Auld; the head of the Conservative caucus research department, Nes Lubinski; and Charles Greco, the owner of the La Scala restaurant—a favourite Tory eating place—who was the former president of the Metro Toronto Conservative Association, and Robarts' election organizer in Toronto.

To many people, the meaning of all this was clear. Robarts wanted the convention to give the appearance of being a good fight, so that the party would be revived in the eyes of the public. Welch's campaign seemed likely to be weak, and Robarts had stepped in to help it along so that the plum wouldn't fall too easily into Davis's lap.

This analysis was hotly denied by the Robarts people on Welch's campaign. They had all voluntarily chosen to work for the Provincial Secretary, they insisted; but the rumours that they had been assigned persisted.

Welch managed to gather a significant amount of support, much to the surprise and chagrin of Darcy McKeough who was most damaged by it. A puckish man with a loud laugh and a penchant for bizarre plaid jackets, Welch's pleasant manner and abilities as a speaker gathered him a good proportion of the uncommitted vote that didn't fancy either Davis or Allan Lawrence.

So with all the contestants signed in, the character of the game was already set. Davis had been marked as the heir, but was unsure that he could keep hold of the silver spoon. The Lawrence people were angry at the intended anointing and had coolly determined to stop it. McKeough and Welch hoped to be everyone's second choices and thus the compromise candidates who would streak through at the last moment. Bert Lawrence hoped the party would decide that what it really needed was quiet kindly intelligence rather than power.

If indeed the affair was being arranged so that the leadership would go to Davis—but only, like a professional wrestling bout, after the appearance of a good fight—the mastermind underestimated the abilities of Norman Atkins and his gang.

8. *The Candidates on the Stump*

The extravaganza began in earnest on January 14 when the candidates—minus Davis, who had already made campaign arrangements of his own for the day—flew up to Ottawa for the first of seven scheduled all-candidates' meetings. A hungry press corps followed, eager for their first glimpse of the four contenders matching wits before an audience of delegates from the Ottawa area. The results of the first round were inconclusive. Robert Welch made a good delivery of a rather woolly speech in which he promised that he would lead a "consultative government" that would ask people who received government services to help in the formulation of the policies affecting those programs. Still keeping away from setting out firm policies, Welch attempted to set out the roles of the party leader and Premier. Inevitably, the whole thing became rather abstract and incomprehensible.

Darcy McKeough looked the audience straight in its collective eye and willed them to believe that beneath that "young fogey" exterior there lurked the soul of a Walter Gordon economic nationalist who was also a good Tory. McKeough's speech was better prepared than Welch's, but his delivery was not as good. His saw-edged voice was pitched a little too high for comfort, but he made up for it by the firmness of his delivery, his size, which was something over six feet, and a face which was distinctive and was not too handsome to be a political liability. McKeough made a little dig at the federal government for not giving Ontario a better tax deal, and Allan Lawrence later did the same. No visit to Ottawa is considered complete by Ontario Conservatives unless such an attack is made.

Lawrence also attempted to get over to the delegates the feeling that on their votes depended the future direction of the Conservative party and its success in future elections. The delegates greatly enjoyed hearing this; it had been some time since the party sachems had thought that they had anything at all to offer. Bert Lawrence, on his home ground and with his friends and supporters about him, went out of his way to comment that neither he nor the other contenders there that night had entered the race simply to give the appearance of a contest for the leadership. His remark only served to add to the grumbling in the background, and gave the "conspiracy theory" the stamp of official recognition.

If anyone had forgotten that what was really happening was that the province had entered the first stage of the build-up to a general election, they were reminded of it the next day. The Liberals, envious of the amount of attention the Conservatives had already been able to generate, told newsmen that a recent poll showed that the Liberals were increasing their popularity at the expense of the NDP. The poll was of one thousand people and was taken the previous November and December. It showed the Liberals to be the most popular party in the province, with 27 per cent of the people behind them. The Conservatives were next with 25 per cent, while the NDP trailed with 18 per cent. About 30 per cent of the population was undecided. It turned out during the course of the day that the Tories also had a poll (all parties can produce comforting figures when necessary) which showed them to be holding on to 42 per cent of the popular vote, with the Liberals at 31 per cent and the NDP at 27. The polls gave the Liberals a little fillip, but Stephen Lewis showed no signs of alarm that his party was going down the drain.

In fact the Liberals' poll had only marginal application for Ontario. It was taken shortly after the federal Liberal government introduced the War Measures Act in response to the October kidnappings in Quebec, a move which was widely praised in Ontario so that the provincial wing of the party gained a momentary surge of popularity. Equally, the provincial NDP suffered because the party's federal wing had been publicly opposed to the Act. The Conservatives' poll was probably a more accurate reflection of the standings of the parties at the time.

Allan Lawrence's attack against education spending on the day he announced his candidacy had been the talking point of the campaign so far, generating wisdom in the heads of editorial writers and sending reporters scurrying after Davis for comment, comment which he refused to give. In the province and in the Tory party Lawrence's criticism was sweet music to many ears, and on February 15 Bert Lawrence, in London, joined his name-sake on the issue. He deplored the extraordinarily lavish spending on educational research, and promised to reorganize the system of allocating funds. He said friends had indicated to him that they were disturbed that elementary school children "were having a good time but not learning anything" and high school students were "plagued with regimentation". A couple of days later, in North Bay, Allan Lawrence reiterated his point, to keep the pot boiling. But still there was no reply from Davis.

It is almost an overstatement to say that Davis was campaigning. He was certainly travelling the province and meeting the delegates, but beyond that physical movement there was little of substance. By nature Davis does not like scraps and he was not prepared to dive into the leadership race feet first. What statements he made in the first few weeks were turgid and irrelevant. When he asked for questions from meetings of delegates his answers were masterpieces of circumlocution. He and his organization felt they could win with ease. They believed that all that was required was for people like MacNaughton to remind the delegates that, like the bulk of the caucus, he was supporting Davis, for Davis to be wheeled in to shake a few hands and exchange a few pleasantries, and the delegates would have no doubt about which way they should vote.

The constitution of the Ontario Progressive Conservative Association set out clearly how delegates to the leadership convention were to be chosen. But about this time alarming stories began to surface, stories that indicated that some people considered that the regular fairly open method of delegate selection left a bit too much to chance. The executive of the party began to get complaints about rigged delegate nomination meetings. The constitution said that each riding association must call an open meeting of its membership at which 10 delegates and 10 alternates were to be selected by ballot. In addition, the delegation should be made up of four men, four women, and two members of the Young Progressive Conservative Association, if there was one in the riding. If there was no YPCA, then the delegation should include two people under 30 years of age.

A simple procedure to follow—but no. In York-Forest Hill riding the local party executive drew up a slate and persuaded the association members to approve it en bloc. In Lambton riding, on the shores of Lake Huron, the local Tory MPP, Lorne Henderson, held the meeting to pick the delegates privately in his home. In Mitch Hepburn's old riding of Elgin, then held by Conservative Ron McNeil, the delegates were picked by the riding executive. In Simcoe Centre, held by Conservative Arthur Evans, the delegates were picked by a small group of the riding executive. In the Tory riding of Northumberland, held by Russell Rowe, the executive met without prior announcement in the home of the riding president and chose the delegates.

If these were not embarrassing enough to party president Alan Eagleson, who had repeated loud and long that this was going to be the most open, above-board convention in the party's history, it became apparent that there had been quite widespread neglect of the requirement about YPC representation. The youth-wing president, a strident teenager from Hamilton by the name of Sean O'Sullivan, began a campaign for justice which was not finally resolved until it was debated by the whole convention, and settled to O'Sullivan's satisfaction.

On January 19 the candidates sped to Sudbury for the second all-candidates meeting. There, at the Sheraton-Caswell Hotel, one of the numerous Tory hotels of the province (a situation which probably has nothing to do with the fact that the province dispenses liquor licences), the five men made their pitch for the northern vote. But it was obvious that Allan Lawrence's time as Minister of Mines and Northern Affairs had earned him solid support north of the French River. He was clapped and cheered almost to the exclusion of the other candidates, even though there was fundamentally little difference in their confessions that the north was economically and culturally hard done by, and in their promises that a new day was dawning.

By the middle of January Allan Lawrence's campaign was developing such visible strength and momentum that a first-ballot victory for Davis was no longer generally considered to be a possibility. The question everyone was now considering was whether Davis would get enough votes on the first ballot to win at all. Playing the numbers game became the passion of the campaign, and there were a vast number of possible permutations.

The voting system for the convention was that the low man after each ballot would be dropped from the next vote, and this procedure would continue until one man had a clear majority. There would be 1,748 delegates in all, comprising 1,170 delegates from the ridings, 255 ex-officio delegates, 265 representatives from district associations, and 58 delegates at large. For Davis to win he would have to have at least 600 votes on the first ballot and have a clear lead over Allan Lawrence. That, at least, was the popular wisdom. If Lawrence was too close, he might get a bandwagon going which would draw support and victory. Alternatively, if either Welch or McKeough were well placed in third position, they might start drawing votes as the convention sought a compromise candidate. Everything depended on the relative positions of the candidates on the first ballot.

Some people were worried that events would move too

swiftly after the first ballot and there would be a stampede to elect a leader without consideration of the possible manoeuvres. There was also concern that the thing might be over so quickly that the advantages of being broadcast live in prime television viewing hours would be lost. (A few months previously, the NDP had held up announcing the results of their leadership vote for almost half an hour after the ballots had been counted, in order to keep themselves on TV.) Among the Conservatives with these concerns was Arthur Harnett, the executive director of the party. Late on the night of the Sudbury all-candidates meeting Harnett was relaxing with reporters and party workers in the party's hospitality suite at the hotel, when he commented, "We have got to have a sixth candidate." The idea was that a sixth candidate at the bottom of the slate would give the delegates in effect a free vote to begin with, so that they could see the way the land lay before committing themselves. Harnett's wish was fulfilled promptly. A few days later a young student from Carleton University, Robert Pharand, announced that he would be a candidate and that he would campaign on the issue of the lack of facilities and rights for French-speaking Ontarians.

The campaign program was getting heavier. On January 22 there was an all-candidates meeting in Windsor; this meeting was unremarkable except that, as a portent of things to come, Davis was picketed by Catholic school students demanding the extension of provincial government aid to grade 13. Another all-candidates meeting was planned for January 26 in London, but early in the afternoon there was a snow storm which made driving or flying impossible, and stranded the candidates all over southwestern Ontario. Davis, making up for his non-appearance in Ottawa, was the only one to get through. Asked how he managed it, Westcott said, "Sheer talent, and you can quote me."

The importance of luck in politics should never be underestimated, and Allan Lawrence was having a run of luck. He was snowed in at a service centre on highway 401 at Ingersoll, which wasn't very lucky, except that among the other people forced to seek shelter at the centre overnight were John Robarts and a number of delegates who had been on their way to the London meeting. Lawrence was able to telephone newspapers and radio and television stations and tell them of his delightful dilemma. Lawrence may have wanted to politic the night away, but Robarts wanted some sleep, so he moved into an ambulance in the parking lot.

The weather was better three days later when the candidates met at Thunder Bay for another area meeting. The efforts by the Davis organization to get as many delegates as possible committed to them had shown them the strength of Allan Lawrence's support, and now they were scared. Davis could no longer afford the luxury of ignoring the jabs and criticisms of other candidates. What had started out as a procession to the coronation, with the other contestants as bit players giving the celebration a little class, had become a bitter fight. Norman Atkins and friends were putting their hearts and souls into the campaign and their work was showing.

Before the Thunder Bay meeting the Davis group hurriedly hired a speech writer named Bill Gold. Gold was a former newspaperman who worked for Hopkins Hedlin Ltd., a public relations company contracting mainly to governments. His first assignment for Davis was to write a defence for the Education Minister to deliver at Thunder Bay. It was a good speech, and but for it Davis might have been unable to hold on to the basis of support necessary for his victory. Coming out fighting for the first time Davis chastised the other candidates for espousing instant policies in the hope of winning the leadership. "Right now it's more important to know the man and his principles than to seek comfort in the bearers of instant policies which–let's face it–may or may not work at some future time," Davis said.

What was worrying the Davis organization was the amorphous nature of Davis's support. Over the previous weeks members of the Cabinet had been publicly stating their conviction that Davis should be the next leader, so that he now had 13 of the 23 Ministers behind him, and he had a good majority of the Conservative caucus with him, too. But what puzzled his organization, and gave hope to the other contenders, was that all this political muscle hadn't been translated into enthusiastic grass-roots support. They felt that if delegates were supporting Davis only out of loyalty to their local political overlords, or because their arms had been twisted, this was not a power base that could be trusted. If Davis had to fight through 2 or 3 ballots, his support could start shifting to a more attractive candidate.

Davis was also suffering from a whispering campaign (sometimes outspoken) that said that though he might win the leadership, he could easily lose the next provincial election, because of his personal unattractiveness and his liabilities as Education Minister. The defensive, lacklustre character of Davis's campaign up to the Thunder Bay speech gave delegates cause to consider this judgment.

Meanwhile, although Allan Lawrence's aggressive campaign had been magnetic, he hadn't quite shaken the volatile maverick image. He was widely mistrusted, which gave hope to McKeough and Welch, who were engaged in a little sub-war of their own. Each of their organizations believed that their man had to finish a strong third on the first ballot. If Davis's support faltered and the Lawrence bandwagon stalled, then there could well be a drift towards the man in the third spot. The McKeough and Welch camps were both selling their men as the candidates with the least political liabilities who would make fine compromise candidates. In this sales campaign McKeough appeared to be ahead of Welch. The Municipal Affairs Minister had good support from his home area and from eastern Ontario, with a reasonable scattering around the province, while Welch's support appeared to be mainly from the Niagara Peninsula. But Welch's organizers claimed that their man was the second choice of a large number of delegates. That put him in a good position—but that second choice vote would only be any good to him if he could overtake McKeough.

On February 4 a Los Angeles warlock, Louis Huebner, proclaimed that Davis and Allan Lawrence were neck and neck and that Davis had something interesting coming up for him at the end of the year.

The same day *The Toronto Telegram* published a poll which claimed that 392 delegates were committed to Davis, 197 to Allan Lawrence, 187 to Welch, 146 to McKeough and 81 to Bert Lawrence. The newspaper said the other 745 delegates appeared to be genuinely undecided. The poll was probably somewhere in the ball park, but not much more. It agreed with what individual candidates' campaigns had found, that there was a very large number of delegates who were still undecided. That large number of uncommitted votes was of great joy to McKeough and Welch in particular, who felt that the thing wasn't over yet if there were still that many votes to be garnered.

The poll was a setback for Davis, and he soon had another one. A farm newspaper conducted a poll of its subscribers and discovered that Davis as leader would be unacceptable to the farming community. This added strength to the view that Davis might win the leadership but lose the election, and Welch's campaign was quick to have copies of the article made and distributed among the delegates.

On February 9 the scene shifted from out in the province, where the candidates had been charming and cajoling the delegates in hotel rooms from Cornwall to Kenora, to the stuffy rooms of the Royal York Hotel in Toronto. Even though the final act would be played in the Maple Leaf Gardens, the Royal York was to be the centre of events for the next three days. The hotel, which somehow made seediness chic, was at once transformed into the brightest, most hectic spot in town. Its dull, third-rate art nouveau decor was plastered with garish multi-coloured signs extolling the merits of the candidates. Hundreds of pretty young girls in the uniforms of the five campaigns roamed the corridors and lobbies handing out buttons, pamphlets, and smiles. Round the next corner might come a band of any shape, size, type or expertise, or a carefully rehearsed spontaneous demonstration of affection for any of the candidates. The candidate himself might be in the middle of it all, being borne joyfully along amid waves to the faithful to deliver a speech, greet an incoming group of delegates, or have himself filmed and photographed while smilingly registering as a delegate. At the top of the escalator to the mezzanine floor a television set (placed there by the wizard Atkins to catch the eyes of rising delegates) played hour after hour of videotapes of Allan Lawrence answering questions from a patsy interviewer, and demonstrating just how dynamic he was on the screen.

The large bank of elevators, a tribute to the mechanical

standards of the 1920s, refused to be seduced into activity by the great events going on around them and in them, and stuck to their plodding, wholly inadequate routine. Once a delegate had finally beaten the elevator system and attained an upper floor, a whole new world was there to greet him. Here stretched an endless concourse of hospitality suites—an item without which Canadian politics could not function—where the candidates and their teams vied with one another to pour booze down the throats of the delegates. It is only a mild overstatement to say that you could travel the length, breadth, and height of the Royal York without being out of ordering distance of some campaign worker who was keeping bar and devoutly pursuing the belief that a filled glass was a vote captured. The greatest single expense of all the campaigns—with the exception of Robert Pharand's—was booze and entertaining. Rental of campaign headquarters, printing, travel, the bands, and the colourful demonstrations on nomination day were expensive items, but they didn't compare with the cost of the spirituous liquors guzzled in those three hectic days and nights at the Royal York.

The booze expenses are available to us because in the end the five campaigns grudgingly gave out figures of the cost of their operations; but the figures were not notably reliable. McKeough admitted to spending at least $100,000, and Davis about the same, although $150,000 would be a more realistic figure for the cost of Davis's campaign. Both Welch and Allan Lawrence admitted to spending $70,000, which would seem to be low. Bert Lawrence stated that he spent $65,000, the most accurate accounting.

It was during those heady days at the Royal York that the interest and excitement that Allan Lawrence had generated when touring the province was solidified into voting strength. This section of the campaign was Norman Atkins' own special department. He called all Lawrence's supporters to Toronto a day early and they met in a large room at the Westbury Hotel, just behind the Maple Leaf Gardens. Even Atkins had not truly appreciated Lawrence's strength until he looked over that packed room and saw that not only did they have numerous followers, but also that these were dedicated people who wanted to show the ability and vitality of the neglected grass-roots Tories. It was not hard to fill this group with enthusiasm, to draw them into the organization and to send them out to proselytize at the Royal York.

While the Davis group were attempting to use the heavy-handed authority of their backbench and Cabinet support to keep their followers in line, the Atkins web was constantly growing as new, enthusiastic people joined and were spun into the fabric of the campaign structure.

As the days were ticked off on the calendar, the excitement and the mutual mistrust of the two leading campaigns grew. The anger the Lawrence people felt when their overture to Davis was rebuffed had turned into a consuming desire to beat him and the authoritarian concept of party management that his campaign represented. Meanwhile, the Davis campaign men, horrified at the power of Lawrence's forces, were suspicious that underhand tactics were being used to undermine the Education Minister. Even three years later, some of Davis's men still believed that party president Alan Eagleson and executive director Arthur Harnett were actively working for Lawrence. How was it, they questioned, that Lawrence got all the delegate lists and other material about the arrangements for the convention ahead of the Davis organization if Eagleson and Harnett were not feeding them the information in advance? Getting this material early was certainly a help to Lawrence because it allowed his group more time to identify its support, and its potential support, and to map strategy for the final drive before voting. But the Lawrence people denied that they received any preferential treatment from party headquarters; they were, they said, just better organized, and thus anticipated when lists and programs would be available and made sure they got them as soon as possible.

It may shock the idealistic reader to learn that not all votes were won by the exercise of sweet reason. For the candidates and their organizations the days at the Royal York were taken up with meetings with groups of delegates and individuals behind closed doors, in the hospitality suites, in the corridors, and at special functions such as the huge dances and parties which some of the campaigns put on. But votes were gained in other ways, too. One backbench MPP, who had the task of looking after a group of ridings for Davis and keeping the delegates committed to the Education Minister, later recalled that it was no easy job. According to him, the delegates were selling their votes for the prices of their rooms—quite an expensive item for delegates—for quantities of liquor, and even for more personal services. Certainly some votes were gathered in return for the services of prostitutes, but the campaign workers who collected pledges from delegates by agreeing to supply these services undoubtedly did it without the knowledge or consent of senior campaign officials. Although it happened, it was not an extensive practice, and had no effect on the outcome of the leadership election. But it certainly added to the mounting excitement of the atmosphere.

Some attempt was made by the party to lessen the marketplace atmosphere at the Royal York and give the affair some semblance of being an intellectual political event. For this reason, policy debates were organized, where the candidates could speak on issues of their choice selected from a list drawn up by the party hierarchy. But these debates were a failure. The candidates went (generally taking along with them a crowd of supporters who clapped and cheered at appropriate moments), reporters were there in great number, but there was a noticeable absence of delegates, who apparently had a clearer idea of what the convention was all about. Leadership, not policy, was the issue of the convention. Policy was really only of great interest to reporters and editors—and particularly the latter, who found it difficult to understand that it was possible to choose a new leader without the benefit of a detailed accounting of his beliefs.

Much more important to the delegates as they made their decisions were instinct, loyalties, the tenor of the approaches made to them by the campaigns, and simply whether or not they liked the cut of a particular candidate's jib. With a large number of candidates on the ballot it was also important for the delegate to have some feeling of the direction in which the contestants were moving (everyone likes to back a winner), and so the Royal York hummed to the sound of rumours being passed around by the campaigns in the hope of increasing the feeling that *their* man was moving up. There was one gallant man working for Bert Lawrence who appeared to do nothing for three days but patrol the corridors button-holing anyone who would stop long enough for him to grab them; he would then loudly pass on a highly inflated figure of how many delegates his man had committed to vote for him on the first ballot. It was so amateurish an attempt at creating reality that no one appeared to take it seriously. But there he was, day and night, winning the campaign for Bert Lawrence.

On Wednesday night, February 10, the party bade an emotional farewell to John Robarts. Some 2,000 delegates paid $10 each to attend the dinner in the Royal York ballroom to honour the departing Premier. It was a family affair with much applause and cheering, words catching in throats and damp eyes. Robarts' career was briefly summarized in a film made up of news clips and party footage which showed the Premier striding purposefully into buildings, out of buildings, cutting ribbons, and so forth; but it was affectionately done. Everyone was very careful not to mention the contest for the succession. That would have been crass bad manners. Again it was "John's day". In his farewell speech Robarts said of the candidates, "I am proud of them. They are my boys. They present a picture of strength and vitality to the people of this province and what the Progressive Conservative party is and what it can offer to the people."

9. *Forty-four Votes*

The candidates were nominated on Thursday night, February 11, at the Maple Leaf Gardens and each in turn got his chance to make a final personal appeal to the delegates en masse. The ice surface had been boarded over and at the west end of the arena was a vast podium covered with royal blue cloth and backed by a tall montage featuring the blue and white circular symbol of the convention. Around the symbol were large photographs of Ontario and anonymous but happy and healthy Ontarians. On the right-hand side of the montage was a photograph of a young girl which had been constructed so that it swivelled round. On the back of the photograph was a score board. The score board wouldn't be used until the next day, so tonight the young girl faced the audience. Tonight was meant to be an evening of fun and noise and display. But for many delegates it would be the time when they made their decision on whom to support.

Hundreds of chairs had been set out on the ice area for the delegates. More delegates, campaign workers, and curious members of the public crowded the stands. In the corridors underneath the stands there was a colourful and excited press of brass bands, pipe bands, silver bands, flag bearers, sign bearers, baton twirlers, dance troops—the whole elaborate cast of those carefully-planned spontaneous demonstrations so beloved of North American politics. Alan Eagleson called for nominations, and the proposer and seconder of a candidate climbed to the podium to speak their piece of praise and honour. Then, at the appropriate moment, the candidate's bands, dancers and sign wavers broke loose from the underground passageway to jam the floor with a seething mass of colour and fill the arena with noise so loud and dominating that it became almost tangible. It made the Gardens' regular fare, the bellows of jubilant hockey fans, seem like feeble cheeping by comparison. Their allotted time over, the demonstrators would ebb back into their caverns under the stands and leave their candidate standing triumphantly on the dais. It was the same pattern for each candidate, one after another.

All the candidates considered the speeches they were to make of extreme importance, since a bad speech might well harm them. But there is no concrete evidence that any of them won votes that night. Some Conservatives maintain that large numbers of votes were won, particularly by Allan Lawrence, but even several years later it is still a matter of dispute.

Davis took much the same tack as he had in his Thunder Bay speech, strongly defending his actions as Education Minister and trying to show himself as a resolute man, decisive and steadfast on any course he felt to be right. "It's not been easy. It's been a tough job," he told them. "And I don't think I have shirked my responsibility. I say to you categorically that our two million young people are going to do a better job of running our government and our country than we are doing."

The speech read well, but it was delivered in Davis's usual monotone, which washed out much of its impact.

McKeough, still seeking to establish himself in that third spot ahead of Welch, tried yet again to cast himself in the role of the compromise candidate. His victory, he told the delegates, would be a victory neither for the party establishment, nor for the dissidents. Welch dramatically threw away his text and made an impassioned speech—which became slightly too impassioned and squeakily strident towards the end—in which he pledged himself to the creation of an open party where everyone would be involved.

Allan Lawrence struck a completely new note. He forgot all about the costs of education and government, ignoring the subject completely. Instead he envisaged himself as the natural successor to John Robarts as a preserver of Canadian unity and Ontario's greatness. It was a speech which some observers (and the other candidates) felt to be cheeky and presumptuous, but the Lawrence organization was convinced that it won him many votes.

Bert Lawrence's speech reflected his dejection. He knew that he was well behind McKeough and Welch. His disappointment at not having done better in the campaigning showed on his face and his final speech to the delegates was the work of a man who knew that there was nothing much to hope for. He said that all the candidates had recognized the problems, but he was the only one committed to specific solutions. He promised to improve the relationship between the government and the people, reform the structure of the Cabinet, enlarge the role of the backbencher in the policy-making process and more closely coordinate the work of the government and the Civil Service. He did not mention that in December, 1969, Robarts had established a committee to think about most of these matters, or that the committee's first report was already in the government's hands.

The next morning, Friday, was cold and cloudy with forecasts of heavy snow that night. In hotel rooms the candidates held last-minute meetings with delegates and the campaign organizations. Shortly after noon people began arriving at the Gardens, and by one o'clock it was thronging with people—candidates, delegates, alternates, campaign workers, reporters, supporters, and about 4,000 members of the public.

The chairs set out on the covered ice the night before had been removed, and in their place now stood fifteen large voting machines, in two lines facing one another. Around the edges of the rink were dozens of people in the uniforms of the various campaigns, all of them either wearing headphones which were plugged into a spaghetti network of wire that laced every passage and aisleway, or else talking earnestly into small two-way radio sets. These were the communications links of the campaigns which would keep the top organizers holed up in offices under the stands in touch with what was happening on the floor.

Each candidate had been allotted an area of seats on the north side of the arena, and each candidate was equipped with telephones which enabled them to speak to their headquarters offices under the stands, even to talk to each other if the need arose. Ranged behind the candidates in the stands were their leading delegate supporters, placed there as a show of strength, while in the upper tiers sat alternates and non-voting supporters. All around the other sides of the ice were more sections allotted to each candidate; these were filled with badge-wearing followers waving signs under the watchful eyes of trusted campaign workers who had been placed there to lead the cheering and keep the delegates in line.

Allan Lawrence's communications system, devised by Norman Atkins, was the most sophisticated. Its nerve centre was in a balcony high above the floor of the arena; there Tom Wells, then Minister of Health and the only Cabinet member to support Lawrence, managed a team of people equipped with a bank of phones and transmitter-receivers. Not only did they have the advantage of a finely-tuned system; their visual control was excellent, too, since with the aid of binoculars they could pick out anyone in the crush of people on the floor.

As the minutes passed excitement increased and there were great bouts of shouting and cheering in the cause of each candidate. Campaign songs were sung—Allan Lawrence's "Winning Is Just The Beginning" and "Davis Is The Man For Leader". Finally, when everything seemed ready, Alan Eagleson explained in his oddly high-pitched voice how the voting machines worked. They were large metal boxes about six feet tall and about two feet six inches wide. On a rail extending out in front of each box was a curtain. Once behind the curtain, the voter would find himself facing a screen on which the names of the candidates had been placed. Beside each name was a button, and underneath the screen was a handle. All the delegate had to do was walk up to the screen, swing the lever, which closed the curtain behind him and armed the machine, press the button next to the name of the candidate of his choice, and swing the lever back. When the handle was swung back, it registered the vote and opened the curtains ready for the next voter.

The Conservatives had decided to use the machines because they were believed to be much faster than paper ballots. No counting was necessary. After each ballot the scrutineers simply had to read off the number of votes for each candidate on the back of the machines and compare the total with their lists of how many delegates had registered at each machine before voting.

These ingenious voting machines were rented from an American company, the Shoupe Voting Machines Corp., of Philadelphia, and the arrangement for their use had been made through Thomas ("Windy") O'Neill, a well-known Liberal, who held the Canadian franchise for the company.

Voting finally began at 3:15 and the delegates joyfully trooped out onto the floor. About an hour later the first ballot was complete. Tensely, everyone in the building waited for the results. But as distinguished-looking men began to scuttle to and fro carrying whispered messages and looking worried, it became apparent to everyone that something was wrong.

Eventually Eagleson climbed on to the podium and announced that the machines had failed to work (or to be operated) properly. Chaos. Groans. Laughter. But there was no laughter from the candidates and their campaign leaders, whose already taut nerves were now close to snapping. Eagleson said that only three out of the fifteen machines had registered the vote correctly; altogether, there were about a hundred votes less on the other machines than registered on the scrutineers' lists.

Although it now seemed likely that the first ballot would be scrapped, news of the result soon spread. Although it was unofficial and, obviously, inaccurate, it gave an indication of the standing of the candidates: Davis had polled 502 votes, Allan Lawrence 379, McKeough 251, Welch 239, Bert Lawrence 152 and Robert Pharand 13. That said a lot to the delegates and campaign workers. It showed that Davis was not strong enough to get a second- or even third-ballot victory, as he hadn't got what was considered the magical 600 votes necessary for a quick kill. Allan Lawrence was close to Davis, but not close enough to overtake him swiftly. And there was no clear compromise candidate. McKeough and Welch only had 12 votes between them, and they were too far behind Allan Lawrence to have a real chance of sneaking through. Bert Lawrence's vote was about what was expected, as was Robert Pharand's.

Eagleson called all the candidates up to the podium and conferred with them quietly and briefly. The candidates, campaign managers, and scrutineers then went off with Eagleson to the plush Maple Leaf Gardens board room at the west end of the arena behind the podium. Secrecy was imposed on what was going on. Leslie Frost, who had been sitting with Robarts, Drew, and other party notables in a special section of the stands, calmly walked into the room saying that he was looking for a drink–and was promptly ejected by a provincial policeman.

Inside that board room the bitterness and rivalry that had been building up between the Davis and Allan Lawrence camps was reaching its peak. The suspicion and paranoia (to use the words of one of the men there) had reached the point where the two groups looked at each other over the table top and seriously considered whether the other had fixed the machines so that they would not work properly.

Politicians of the same party do not easily harbour thoughts that their opponents are cheats, but the thoughts were there in that room, and they were to make the drawing together of the party in the following days a difficult process. Allan Lawrence's people, in particular, could see a clear motive for the Davis organization to tamper with the machines. Much of Lawrence's strength came from northern Ontario, and these delegates had mostly arranged to leave on the long journey home that evening. If things had gone as scheduled, the voting would have been over late in the afternoon, in plenty of time for the northern delegates to catch planes, and trains or to start out in their cars. With the northern strength gone, Lawrence's chances on the final ballots would be cut.

These thoughts were not put into words. There were just suspicious stares across the table as they listened to a representative from the makers of the machines give an impassioned endorsement of the firm's product. It was *impossible* for the machines not to work properly, he said. The company had been making them for fifty years without this kind of trouble occurring. He suggested the trouble was that they weren't being used properly. The meeting lasted fifty-five minutes and most of it was taken up with listening to the company representative. It took only a few moments for Eagleson to get a unanimous agreement from the candidates and their campaign managers that the first ballot must be scrapped and they must start again with traditional paper ballots.

It was all incredibly embarrassing for the Tories. Here they were, live on television and radio on a cold February Friday with millions watching for want of anything better to do, with months of organization behind them geared to showing the people of Ontario that here was not a 28-year-old dynasty, but a young vibrant party—and they had fallen flat on their faces. A telegram arrived for Eagleson from some New Democrats offering their assistance if he needed to be shown how to operate the machines properly. When well known Tory Senator David Walker was cornered by a roving television camera team, he spluttered into the microphone that what with the political affiliations of the supplier of the machines he wouldn't be surprised if the whole thing wasn't a Liberal plot to make the Conservatives look stupid. That remark nearly led to a lawsuit and in the end the senator had to apologize and withdraw the remark. But certainly somebody, perhaps not an outside agent, had made the Conservatives look stupid, all right.

The voting machines affair went on for months after the convention was over. At first the Tories refused to pay the $6,000 rental on them because they claimed the machines didn't work properly. Then an internal report for the party showed that it was not the machines that had erred, but the delegates, who hadn't used them correctly. So the party paid. It didn't pay the full $6,000 rental; O'Neill agreed to settle for something less than the full amount.

At 6:15 Eagleson officially announced that the results of the first ballot were being scrapped and there would be a delay of an hour or so while the party officials ran off ballot papers and collected ballot boxes from the offices downtown. As he spoke, Harnett and a bevy of assistants were buzzing about in a make-shift office behind the stands, urging on copy machines to churn out ballot papers as fast as possible.

The initial excitement so obvious five hours before had been doused by the foul-up and only exasperation remained. Many delegates had sidled off down to the Royal York and other hotels around town for drinks and food. Sensing that they would soon lose their grip on their supporters, campaign officials despatched taxis to the hotels to round up the dispirited Tories.

At 7:40 p.m., four and a half hours after they had first started, the delegates began the whole process again. Now everyone was the worse for wear. The only food available in the Gardens was the dubious offerings of the hot dog stands. The Hot Stove Lounge, however, was doing a roaring trade in drinks, which probably helped tattered nerves and dejected spirits, but which certainly did little for the decorum of the proceedings. The cheering and singing had become hoarse and sporadic. The heat generated by all those bodies under the bright television lights was painful, and everyone was tired and sweaty. Meg, Davis's youngest daughter, who had been the hit of the afternoon as she brandished a sign saying "Vote for Daddy", was almost asleep. Roy McMurtry, who had made it to the convention despite not being fully recovered from his back injury, was laid out on a couch in the now vacant board room and was being ministered to by John Robarts from the contents of the directors' bar, which the owners of the Gardens had thoughtfully left stocked for the use of important Conservatives.

Finally, the results of the new first ballot came through. Bruno Bragolli, a chubby chartered accountant from Hamilton, clambered up a tall, swaying ladder behind the podium. Hidden behind the smiling girl's face, he fixed numbers on to the score board, and then swung it round so everyone could see. It said Davis 548, Allan Lawrence 431, McKeough 273, Welch 270, Bert Lawrence 128, Pharand 7.

The results of the scrapped ballot had obviously had some effect. Davis had gained somewhat, but Allan Lawrence had gained more. McKeough and Welch had both gained, but they were now closer together than they had been before, which made the chances of a shift to the third man even less likely. Bert Lawrence had been the big loser, as his supporters saw from the voting machine results that the game for him was over.

According to the rules, Pharand, the lowest man on the ballot had to drop out at this point, but Bert Lawrence told Eagleson that he also would quit. When this news was broadcast by the party president, workers from the other campaigns immediately rushed towards Bert Lawrence's section to try and get his supporters to wear their buttons. Lawrence sat there stone-faced and refused to throw his support to any of the other candidates; the followers that remained loyally followed his example and turned aside the requests that they put on other buttons. When Davis walked over, shook hands with Lawrence, and offered him a "Davis" button, Lawrence waved it away and sat down. Allan Lawrence's section was the closest to his name-sake's, and instead of using persuasion, Allan Lawrence supporters simply mixed with those of the resigned candidate and waved their signs. To everyone in the arena it looked as though Bert Lawrence's people had thrown their support to Allan Lawrence.

The second ballot didn't get under way until 10:00. When the score board was eventually swung around again it showed

Davis 595, Allan Lawrence 498, McKeough 288, Welch 271. Davis had picked up 47 votes while Lawrence had gained 67. McKeough had won 15 more and Welch had only got one more than on the first ballot. Excitement in the Lawrence camp became intense. They had been consistently gaining at a faster rate than Davis (if you included the scrapped first ballot, which everybody did), and there seemed to be a good chance that they might catch the Education Minister.

The question for McKeough now was whether he could do a deal with Welch and get enough of his support to put McKeough right up with the leaders. He and Welch made their way towards one another through the jam of reporters crowding the aisle in front of the stands. They met and agreed to talk in Welch's headquarters office under the stands. McKeough arrived first and strode in. Welch made it through the crowd a few minutes later, and then Don Martyn, Welch's campaign manager, arrived. After a few seconds, McKeough came out looking furious. A McKeough aide, asked shortly afterwards what had happened, said, "Welch still has the same problem. He only entered the race because he didn't know who to support, and he still can't make up his mind."

That wasn't quite how it went. Welch had campaigned on a pledge for "an open party", and as he walked to his room he came to the conclusion that he would be going against all he had talked about if he attempted to throw his support to anyone. This was the message McKeough was given. When McKeough left the room the jam of people–mostly reporters and cameramen–in the narrow corridor outside had become so thick as to be dangerous. The Welch people, now debating in their office, had posted a girl outside the door to keep everyone out. Her role was a necessary one. Allan Lawrence had come over from his seat and was waiting by the door, hoping to get a word with Welch. Just up the corridor Davis was waiting with similar intentions. Inside the room Welch told his crew about his feelings, and each one of them had their say before Welch told them that they were all free, as were the rest of his supporters, to vote for whomever they chose on the next ballot. With that Welch left and made his way up the passage past Davis who extended a hand—but Welch either didn't see it or ignored it, and moved on. No words were exchanged.

McKeough was bitter, because if the situation had been reversed, he would have supported Welch and Welch knew it. After leaving Welch's office with this feeling, McKeough went off to have a morose drink in the directors' bar where there was a television. The sight of his wife, Joyce, being interviewed and making optimistic comments decided him to go back down to his seat. When he arrived there, voting on the third ballot was under way. He telephoned Davis and told him that if he was knocked off on that ballot he would throw his support to Davis. There were no deals, just that statement.

McKeough's decision was not entirely unexpected. In the breathing space before voting began on the third ballot the people working in the Davis communications centre had come out into the corridor which happened to be beside McKeough's section. Among them was Dalton Bales, Davis's organizer in Metro Toronto, who was wearing one of Davis's campaign favours, a yellow bib over his chest and back which had the name Davis stencilled on in blue paint. Senator David Walker, McKeough's father-in-law, came over to Bales, tapped him on the chest with a finger, and said, "That's the way we'll go."

The result of the third ballot was Davis 669, Lawrence 606, McKeough 346. Davis had picked up only 74 votes, while Lawrence had gained 108 and was now only 63 votes behind Davis, breathing hotly down his neck. They had started out with over a hundred votes between them; the Lawrence bandwagon was rolling steadily.

As soon as the results were up, McKeough barked "Let's go" to his aides and burst out of his front row seat with a brave smile on his face, intending to go and shake Davis's hand. But he moved so quickly that in the confused press of people in the aisle he was carried right past the Education Minister and had to do an about-face. They eventually met, smiled at one another and shook hands.

McKeough's decision wasn't to everyone's liking. He got spat on by one of his supporters on his way back to his seat.

The Lawrence people only made a half-hearted try for

McKeough's backing, since they knew the Municipal Affairs Minister didn't like their man. After the third ballot Lawrence started out to see McKeough, but turned back and sent off John McLean instead. McLean, Lawrence's floor manager, was president of the Halton West riding association, and George Kerr, the MPP for Halton West, was working with McKeough. McLean went up to Kerr and said, "Who do you want to see, Al [Lawrence] or Tom [Wells]?"

"I don't particularly want to see either," Kerr replied. It was not the reply McLean wanted.

A short while before, McKeough had told Kerr of his decision to support Davis. Kerr had said, "I guess I will, too, although I will have half my riding executive against me."

It was now the early hours of Saturday morning, February 13. They had been in the Gardens for about twelve hours. But now that the final showdown was coming, the tiredness and exasperation of a few hours before had gone. There was a last frantic effort by the Lawrence and Davis camps to secure those few votes that would mean victory for one of them.

The voting on the last ballot was finally done, and the ballots were counted. Before the result was announced, a great cheer went up from the Lawrence group. Like all the candidates they had been getting results from their scrutineers, but because of better organization they had been getting them more quickly than the other candidates. They had got results and they thought they had won. At the dreadful sound of that cheer, the stands full of Davis supporters visibly sagged. But though they were quickly delivered, the Lawrence party's results were wrong. Bruno Bragolli made his last climb up that tottery ladder and swung the smiling girl round to reveal the score board. Davis 812, Lawrence 768, it said. It was 2:00 a.m.

Pandemonium broke out briefly, but wasn't sustained. The adrenalin was all used up, and all that was left was an aching exhaustion and the realization that there had been only 44 votes in it at the end. Davis had picked up 143 of McKeough's votes, but Lawrence had gained 161. Was it a victory or a marginal staving off of defeat? Lawrence made his way to the podium, and with Davis by his side and the smile that had looked so good on television on his face, asked the convention to make it unanimous. The delegates and workers, grey-faced and in shirt sleeves, said yes. They didn't stand in groups on the floor below the dais, they stood singly. They had had enough of people for one day.

Davis said a few words of thanks and then Robarts was handed the microphone. Expansive, brimming with good humour from his encounter with the directors' liquor store, Robarts beamed at his audience. "I've achieved my objective. I'm a has-been," he said. Then, turning to the candidates gathered on the stage, "My boys. I love you all."

Down on the floor a dapper dark-suited man with silver hair, also in high good humour, passed among the dissolving crowd. "Hullo, my name's Leslie Frost," he said, and extended that large bony hand. He didn't add, as he had once, "I work for the government," but then that was no longer true.

Stragglers were still drifting towards the doors when a corps of workmen began dismantling and clearing away. A hockey game between the Toronto Maple Leafs and the Los Angeles Kings was scheduled for that night. As one workman came through the door into the arena and saw the shambles of discarded paper, signs and coffee cups, he stopped dead. "What's been happening here?" he asked in amazement.

Outside, the promised snow had fallen thick on the ground. Late night revellers in their cars slid and skidded up Yonge Street on their way home. In the Westbury Hotel McKeough and his followers guzzled down beer and cheered themselves up by putting new words to Allan Lawrence's campaign song. "Losing is so confusing," they sang. Winning, however, was not everything. Davis and his men went up to the Ports of Call restaurant for a victory party. But it would have been happier if they had been able to forget those 44 votes.

10. *Picking Up the Pieces*

William Davis, leader of the Ontario Conservative party, soon to be sworn in as Premier of the province, was in a difficult position.

The leadership contest had been planned as a Friday evening television spectacular with just enough drama to catch the public interest and show them the virility of the Tory party. But what was meant to be Davis's natural triumph had gone wrong and had almost become a total disaster. He was not leader of a new wave of progressive conservatism, but of an aging faction of the party that was self-satisfied, flabby, and out of touch with contemporary political realities and techniques. The faction had achieved power and authority in the 1960s and had used that power to make Davis leader.

It was partly Davis's own fault. He had believed his own billing. He had believed that he was anointed and that the race would be run as planned, with him standing back and letting the old guard work its magic. Although for some years he had had private criticisms and reservations about the things done and the way of doing them in the Robarts era, he mentioned them only to close friends. In the campaign he accepted the old guard's support and allowed it to direct him. But in so doing, he became one of them. He even looked the part. There was no doubt that Davis looked smug, comfortable, and dull.

Davis was now the dull-looking leader of only half of a party—the dull half—and he was profoundly disturbed by the situation. To be the man who led the Conservatives out of power was an idea appalling to his self-esteem and his deep feelings of political loyalty.

Enter Dalton Camp. Throughout the leadership campaign Camp had kept very much in the background. He had attended the meeting at Don Guthrie's house in the summer of 1970 when it was decided to approach Davis with an offer of support, but when that offer was refused by Westcott, Camp had assumed a role of strict neutrality. As former national

Conservative party president, he was an ex-officio delegate at the convention, but that was all. The role of onlooker was not an easy part for a born politician like Camp to play, especially when his friends and associates were energetically hammering away at Davis and the party establishment; but he managed it. When Camp did again step forward it was under circumstances that made the Davis people wonder if a reconciliation with the Atkins group was possible.

Camp chose to reappear late in the morning of February 13, only hours after the final ballot. The setting was the features page of *The Toronto Telegram* which regularly printed a column of political commentary written by Camp. In this particular article Camp began by confessing his high regard for Davis as a man and a politician and said that Davis was the right choice for leader. But with mounting anger he went on to explain why he had voted for Allan Lawrence on every ballot. The story he told was that a federal Conservative delegate to the convention (no admirer of the engineer of Diefenbaker's downfall) had telephoned the Camp home and spoken to Camp's youngest daughter. The MP, presenting himself as a friend of her father's, had asked the girl whom Camp was supporting in the leadership. He suggested her father's choice might be Allan Lawrence; the daughter, knowing that her uncle Norman Atkins was working for Lawrence, agreed that this was probably so. Armed with this knowledge, the MP then rushed to the side of Davis. Camp made it plain that this business of pumping a young girl for information was completely repugnant to him, and that it in some part typified the kind of politicians who supported Davis. He wrote:

> Counting the Senators coming out of the booths with their Davis stickers hanging from their lapels, one reckoned that nothing kept them there during the long day, and the longer night, so much as the urgent need they felt to repel this invader [Lawrence] of their comfortable dreams. Bill Davis had to have them to win the convention, but he will need a hell of a lot more to win anything else.

Camp made it clear that Davis needed the support of the Lawrence organization, and especially the support of the people who had voted for Lawrence on the last ballot. In his opinion the Lawrence campaign had won a strong moral victory, and if the Atkins group were to be drawn into the party they would have to be wooed.

The article worried and perplexed Davis and his men. The same kind of loyalty to family that had provoked Camp's anger at the tricking of his daughter also existed between him and his brother-in-law Atkins. The article was therefore considered an authoritative announcement from the opposing forces about how they felt, and there could be no doubt that they felt angry.

Well, the Davis people felt angry too, angry and humiliated. Some of Davis's people were also offended by Camp's public display of bravado. Not only did the column make them feel that a reconciliation would be damned difficult, it also made the Davis people think that it was the last thing in the world they wanted. To open their arms immediately to the Atkins group would be to admit that they had in fact been defeated in the Maple Leaf Gardens, and that Davis had won the leadership under conditions that made his defeat in an election inevitable unless he could draw the fractured party together.

The new leader's feelings were as strong as those of his aides. He would not forgive or forget easily some of the personal attacks made on him by the Lawrence organization in the heat of the campaign. In fact, it took Davis two or three years to pardon some of the Lawrence people for their vigour in labelling him a loser and the candidate of an encrusted establishment.

So when Roy McMurtry came on the scene a few days after the convention, preaching the need for a union, his first reception was not encouraging. Clare Westcott and Hugh Macaulay, in particular, were not yet ready to accept the necessity of shaking hands with the Atkins group. Davis was the first to bite back his instincts and to admit that McMurtry and Camp were right, he had to become leader of all the party. He had to win over the people who had voted for Lawrence, and he could not do that quickly without the support of the Atkins group. The decision to accept McMurtry's offer of immediate mediation was Davis's, and Westcott and Macaulay fell into line.

The weekend after the convention Davis took a five-day holiday. He went down to Florida, where his friend, developer Gerhard Moog, had an apartment which was at Davis's disposal, and lay soaking up the sun, contemplating the immediate decisions that must be made. It was now his party and his government and he had a natural inclination to make it visibly so.

Robarts had left the government in reasonable shape for the new man. Programs to be incorporated in the Speech from the Throne outlining the government's legislative intentions were already being put together, and work had begun on the Budget some months before. Both statements had been conceived with a 1971 election in mind, and Davis's job now was to take the reins of a vehicle that was already in motion on a satisfactory course. But Robarts had left two important decisions to be made which could be used as election bait. For months there had been rising clamour in southern Ontario for an end to logging in Quetico Provincial Park, west of Thunder Bay. According to the protestors, it was vital that the park be preserved as one of the last truly wilderness areas in Ontario. It was a highly emotional topic, especially in Toronto, and a decision to end logging could give the government an image of sensitivity towards the issues of ecology and the environment. That image would gather votes in the urban areas.

The second major decision to be made concerned the province's Catholic Separate Schools. Under the British North America Act there had to be public financial support of Separate Schools up to the end of grade eight. This was later extended to grade ten, but in the late sixties the Separate Schools requested that the aid be extended to the end of grade thirteen. No decision on this request had yet been made. Finally, Davis also had to make up his Cabinet before calling the House into session; as he recuperated in the sun he turned some of the names and posts around in his head.

But the state of the party, which had to be made ready to fight an election, remained the most pressing problem. Davis was in sympathy with the philosophy of party organization expounded by Camp and Atkins. He felt that the ordinary member of the party out in the ridings should play a much greater role in the association than Robarts had allowed.

Davis felt that internal structures in the organization should be broken down so that the leaders were accessible to the grass-roots membership. The party should be a constantly active organization, not just something that was mobilized at election times. It was with these feelings uppermost, and injured pride held in check, that Davis and his men attended the reconciliation dinner at the National Club. From that dinner there emerged in the following weeks a new party hierarchy which was later to be called "the Big Blue Machine". What was astounding to many people within the Tory party was the way Davis completely capitulated to Atkins and his associates as a result of the dinner meeting. Initially they were all concerned with planning the election campaign. But they received their rewards afterwards when a number of them got full-time senior positions in the party.

Frost and Drew had A. D. McKenzie, Robarts had Ernie Jackson. Like them, Davis needed someone close to him to do the jobs that the Premier either didn't have the time—or the desire—to do. The business of government in the early 1970s was a time-consuming occupation. Davis didn't have the hours at his disposal to keep an eye on what was happening in the party as well. And then politics sometimes gets a little messy. Heads have to roll; arrangements have to be made which might soil the hands of a Premier. The leader needs an agent for these things. It quickly became apparent after the convention that the new Ernie Jackson was Hugh Macaulay. Within weeks a confidential message went out to party workers around the province saying simply: "If you have problems see Hugh Macaulay."

Macaulay was Davis's check on what was happening down at party headquarters, and his power was considerable. "When Hugh talks, you'd better listen because it's really Bill speaking," said Arthur Harnett in an interview at the time. Macaulay's understanding of what Davis wanted—and the Premier's confidence in him—was such that Macaulay was left to make most of the day-to-day decisions himself.

From Davis's point of view Macaulay was almost an ideal man for the job. The men had known each other for ten years, and got along well. Davis respected Macaulay's unusually sharp political instincts, which allowed him to cut through the extraneous material in any political problem and come up with the right answer. Macaulay got on well with Conservatives at Queen's Park and around the province. He was cheerful and helpful to those within the fold, but retained the toughness that enabled him to deal with painful or messy situations when they arose. He was a man on whom Davis could rely without fear that Macaulay would use the association for his own aggrandizement. At 46 Macaulay had been retired for two years, after making a fortune from the sale of the York Mills Pontiac Buick dealership. He had the money and the leisure to work full time for Davis. He didn't need money and he didn't want prestige. Davis could do nothing for him.

Macaulay had most of the advantages that life in Canada could bestow on a man. He came from a well-established, well-placed family. His father, Leopold, had been a Minister in the pre-Hepburn Conservative governments of the 1930s. The war interrupted Hugh's education and he joined the navy. On his return he enrolled as a student in journalism at the University of Western Ontario, where he and his fellow veterans cultivated worldly ways that seemed intolerably arrogant to their younger, non-veteran fellow students, who hadn't spent four years being shot at.

But on graduation, instead of pursuing journalism Macaulay went into the car sales business where he worked so effectively that in 1969, at the age of 44, he was able to retire and devote himself to politics. The concept of duty to the community through political activity had been instilled in him from an early age by his father. He once recalled that his first political involvement came when he was nine years old. "I remember reaching as high as I could to hold a sign so my brother could nail it to a telephone pole." As a youngster he worked in all the campaigns during Hepburn's term until Leopold Macaulay retired in 1942. He missed the 1943 election because he was away at the war and again became active in 1951 when his brother Robert ran successfully for a seat in the Legislature. Political work became a habit, and he volunteered for every campaign during the Frost and Robarts years. Macaulay met Davis at the time of the 1961 leadership convention, when Davis ran Robert Macaulay's campaign.

A friendship grew and Davis, as Education Minister, later appointed Macaulay to the board of directors of Ryerson Polytechnic.

To the outside world Macaulay shows the figure of an aristocratic patriarch for whom the exercise of government is a duty. "It's something useful. It's something for somebody else. I don't want to run for office. I don't have any objectives. You just try to do things that you consider to be useful," he said once, which did nothing much to dispel the haughty impression of his clean features, sharp, clear eyes and crisply curled grey hair. But, like McKenzie and Jackson, Macaulay carefully preserved his anonymity because he considered it impossible for him to do the job Davis wanted if he were constantly in the spotlight of public scrutiny. Within the Conservative party Macaulay was seen as a likeable, approachable man with a very down-to-earth sense of politics, unaffected, hard working, and perhaps the most politically sane of Davis's advisers.

Since time immemorial political reporters have believed that those who have the leader's ear also have the power to sway his judgments. That is sometimes true, but not always. Macaulay certainly had the authority to speak as with Davis's voice in some areas regarding the conduct of the party. In other areas, and ultimately even in the area of party administration, he was only an adviser whose thoughts may or may not have been followed. On a number of occasions Macaulay's advice on political matters was not followed by Davis, or was only partly followed. The power of decision-making rested with only one man, Davis. He knew it, and attempted to ensure that the advice he received was diverse by surrounding himself with a fairly large coterie of people. Sometimes this approach worked, sometimes it didn't.

Ernie Jackson had been both Robarts' proconsul at party headquarters and party fund raiser. Davis split up these functions and appointed William M. Kelly party bagman. Kelly resigned from his job as a vice-president of the Consumers' Gas Company to revolutionize the art of collecting political donations in Ontario. In fact he became both an embarrassment to the Tory party and a terror to the party's financial supporters. The czars of industry and commerce came to regard a visit from Mr. Kelly as an event to be anticipated with foreboding. He took the joy out of giving. Kelly did his job well, too well for everyone to feel entirely comfortable.

In March of 1971, within days of the famous National Club dinner, work began on developing a general outline of the election campaign. These meetings were often held over breakfast; at first these were held in the Royal Hunt Room, at the Sutton Place Hotel, a lavish, dimly-lit room, all walnut panels and English hunting prints, and plentifully supplied with corners. Later the venue was Theodore's Restaurant, an unostentatious steak house on Yonge Street.

Theodore's was not the kind of place where one would expect to find Ontario's most powerful political clique plotting its campaign. But that was one of its advantages. No one would look for them there. The position of the restaurant, just south of Eglinton Avenue, was important too. Just around the corner on Eglinton East was Norman Atkins' office. Over the road, in a new building constructed over the subway station by William Davis's friend Gerhard Moog, Hugh Macaulay had his office. In an apartment block on Eglinton Avenue a few paces west of Yonge Street William Kelly received donors to the Tory cause. Dalton Camp lived a few blocks to the northeast on Daneswood Road, and Roy McMurtry down the road on Lascelles Boulevard.

Over a series of these meetings, the bones of the campaign were put together. The picture that developed was that the kind of campaign Atkins had in mind, with massive use of television and advertising, was going to cost about $4.5 million. It was an astounding figure to all concerned. The most expensive provincial campaign to that time had been Robarts' last election in 1967 which cost $1.7 million. Undaunted, Kelly set about raising the money. The Conservative coffers were already healthily heavy because of Jackson's parsimony —and because of the business community's nervous reaction to Stephen Lewis's election as leader of the NDP. But there was still a great deal for Kelly to do.

Kelly firmly believed that political parties could not operate without being comfortably solvent, and this philosophy was almost a passion with him. Voting for the Conservatives and giving them money assumed the same (grave) importance in his eyes. He had been introduced to the art of political fund raising by his boss, the president of Consumers' Gas, Oakah Jones, who collected money for the Tories. Kelly didn't become well known in Tory circles as a bagman until the 1971 leadership convention when he worked for Davis, a friend for many years. Now, at 46, Kelly looked somewhat older. His sparse dark hair was always brushed neatly back from a large forehead which slightly dwarfed the rest of his face. There was a slim moustache on his upper lip and his clothes were always impeccably tailored, without the hint of a rumple or a fold out of place. When he spoke there was an uncanny resemblance in his voice and phraseology to William Davis. He had a stubby, finely-worked holder for the cigars he smoked continually. Not quite Claude Rains, but not far off.

The basis of his fund-raising system was to mobilize as many subordinate bagmen as possible throughout the province. He liked particularly to enlist men to work for him who were leaders in various businesses and industries. Thus a respected developer might collect among developers, a leading engineer among engineers, and so forth; it was a United Appeal approach to fund raising. Kelly took on the large or difficult contributors himself, and soon earned himself the nick-name "the Assessor". He operated mostly out of the apartment close to Eglinton Avenue and Yonge Street, where those who wished to give were invited to call.

Those who made the trip to the apartment generally had a good idea of what they considered a generous offering to the Conservative party—but they were astounded to find that Kelly's idea of what was generous exceeded their own thoughts by many thousands of dollars. Moreover, they found that he did not consider that generosity was something to be bargained about. If they were going to give, then they should give what he felt to be appropriate, and most of them did. There was a reluctance in the business community to incur the displeasure of the Conservative party by not being open-handed when the hat was passed round. Most of the people approached for funds did business with the government in one way or another, and, rightly or wrongly, most of them felt that the smoothness of their dealings depended on how they got along with Kelly. It was such an ingrained belief in the business world that Kelly never had to make threats or promises, he simply had to sit there and tell them what he wanted.

Kelly's assessment of what a company should pay was reached in one of two ways. It was based either on a percentage of the amount of business the company had done with the government in the past year, or on the amount it gave the party at the time of the previous election–multiplied two or three times. Kelly himself has denied this method of operation, but a junior bagman who was responsible at the time for collecting from about 250 Ontario companies once produced the lists from which he worked. The lists were given him by senior Tories working with Kelly. Down the left-hand side of the lists were the names of the companies. Down the centre of the pages was a column headed "business record" and there were entries after about 15 per cent of the company names. The fund raiser explained that this referred to the amount of government business the companies had received. Most of the amounts set out were below $10,000. On the right-hand side of the pages was another column headed "donation record" and there were entries for nearly all the companies. The entries in this column were in code, but they set out what the company had given at the last election, and what it was expected to give this time.

Kelly was very good at his job. He had been asked to collect $4.5 million and he brought home something over $5 million. At the beginning of the election campaign most candidates were guaranteed $7,000 from party headquarters. As the campaign progressed this was upped to $10,000, and finally $12,000.

From Davis's first day as party leader most of what he did was geared to the demands of the forthcoming election. He had the party under control. He had Camp and Atkins working on preliminary approaches. He had Kelly raising money. Much of what they were all doing was dictated by the work of a man who dropped in to visit Toronto every two weeks. He was an American in his early thirties named Robert Teetor, and he headed the political division of a company called Market Opinion Research of Detroit. Teetor had been working for the Tories since the late 1960s. His services were expensive—between $10,000 and $15,000 a poll—but his work was so accurate and sophisticated that it was a good buy. The company's accuracy in predicting results for the Republican party in the U.S. was so outstanding that MOR came to the attention of John Robarts, who first hired it. Teetor conducted a poll for Davis immediately after the leadership convention, the results of which were to set the Tories on their course for the election.

Teetor found that 75 to 80 per cent of the people of Ontario could name their new Premier unaided—which showed that the convention had not been in vain. But the poll also showed that while people knew who Davis was, they didn't know anything much about him. He had little public personality, and Ontarians didn't have much feeling for him. Teetor felt that if people didn't have any perception of Davis then the first perception they received was going to be very, very important. If they got the wrong idea of the man it would be extremely difficult to change it. The first step, Teetor felt, was to let the people get a better feel of who and what Davis was. He recommended a lot of travelling for the new Premier, generating a lot of local press coverage, feature stories about Davis and his family. His basic advice was that Davis should show himself in a lot of different situations around the province.

Davis and his men took the advice to heart. Davis's itinerary for the spring and summer of 1971 read like a directory of Ontario. At the end of April he went up to Ottawa to talk to Prime Minister Pierre Trudeau about tax sharing, and then borrowed Trudeau's jet aircraft to wing down to Windsor for two days of showing himself to the public. He was met at Windsor airport by a group of about 250 Catholic school students demanding increased aid for their schools. After a moment's conference with his aides Davis, ringed by policemen, walked into the middle of the chanting crowd and talked with them for a while before leaving. It was an important moment. The province's television screens that night were full of pictures of Davis striding into the mob and telling them there was little hope that their demands would be met. Obviously this guy Davis was tough. But he had his lighter side, as the province saw a couple of days later when they opened their newspapers to see a picture of him riding a tandem bicycle and wearing a flaming orange wig in a cycle-for-charity drive in Windsor.

In the following weeks the people of Ontario saw Davis piloting a tug boat in Hamilton harbour, riding in a helicopter, and visiting the CNE boat show. They read stories about his visits to Waterloo, Bracebridge, Kitchener, and Peterborough. They saw him drinking beer in the bar of the Steelworkers Hall in Sudbury, and talking to crowds in London, Timmins, and Niagara. He toured steel mills in Port Colborne, and wineries near St. Catharines. The whole effect was of action, of a new man on the move getting to know his province, making himself available to his people, interested in what they had to say.

Davis *looked* different too. At his first press conference after the leadership convention, on February 24, he turned up in a natty double-breasted brown pin-stripe suit with flared trousers. The outfit was set off by a vivid brown and yellow striped tie. He looked rather uncomfortable in the ensemble, and excused it by saying his wife had always wanted him to have a brown suit. But the old baggy blue was gone for good, and he soon settled down to the wide lapels, the richer patterned materials, and his hair lapping over his collar.

Not all the activity was around the breakfast table at Theodore's Restaurant or out in the highways and byways of the province. Back at the second floor offices at Queen's Park, Davis had a province to run. He picked March 1 as swearing-in day for himself and his Cabinet. For the first time, he decided, the ceremony should not be conducted in the privacy of the Lieutenant-Governor's suite, but in the Legislative Chamber where many more guests, and even members of the public, could be accommodated. But before he could have a swearing-in ceremony he had to pick a Cabinet, and this proved to be a laborious task.

Even before the leadership convention Davis began turning names and portfolios around in his head, but he didn't complete the list until an hour or so before they were all due to meet in the House. Observers predicted that there would be a massive house-cleaning, with many of the Robarts veterans being axed and a new crop of younger backbenchers being brought in. Some of the Robarts Cabinet thought that would happen, too. Four days before the swearing-in ceremony the Attorney-General, Arthur Wishart, announced his resignation from the Cabinet so Davis could feel he had a free hand in selecting the new men. The following day, Friday, February 26, Davis called Wishart to his office and told him he wanted the Attorney-General in his Cabinet.

Wishart was unwilling. He was in his seventies and had been a member of the Legislature for a long time. He wanted nothing so much as to be able to retire to his home and cottage near Sault Ste. Marie. But Davis was persistent, and Wishart finally agreed to be re-appointed a Minister. However, Wishart wasn't told what post he would be getting. He went north for the weekend and returned Sunday night and stayed in his suite at the Park Plaza Hotel. On Monday morning he was getting ready to leave for the 10:00 swearing-in ceremony when the telephone rang and he was told he would be Minister of Financial and Commercial Affairs.

The make-up of Davis's first Cabinet was unremarkable. He dropped Robarts and 5 of his Ministers who had already indicated that they did not intend to run again in the next election. In their place he brought in 7 new people, increasing the size of the Cabinet from 23 to 24. Davis's leadership rivals were given plum jobs. McKeough went from being Minister of Municipal Affairs to the number two spot of Treasurer. Allan Lawrence was given the prestigious post of Attorney-General. Bert Lawrence was given the high-profile and sensitive job of Minister of Health. Welch took over Davis's old job as Minister of Education; but the department was split, and responsibility for Colleges and Universities was given to John White. Otherwise, Davis simply stirred the pot. Truth to tell, there was little in the way of radical changes that he could make, because the backbenches at that time were so devoid of talent. For the time being he was going to have to make do with John Robarts' leftovers.

Davis felt no need to make a clean sweep. He was learning the ropes of being Premier, and he needed people around him who had experience and whom he could trust to be competent administrators until he felt sure enough to assert himself as master in his house. Even in his own office Davis did not shovel out all Robarts' men along with Robarts' mementos. He kept on the Deputy Minister in the office of the Premier, Dr. Keith Reynolds, he kept on Robarts' press aide, Don Beeney, and some of the senior administrative staff remained.

Otherwise, the whole complexion of the office changed. It became a political office once more. When Robarts left he had a total staff of 42 to deal with both his own office and Cabinet affairs. Of those only one had daily political responsibilities. Davis quickly increased the payroll to over 60, and Clare Westcott, as Davis's special assistant, had 9 people working with him on "politically sensitive" matters.

Westcott, the high school dropout from Seaforth, appeared to have arrived. He had always wanted to be behind someone's throne—and now there he was. Reynolds, by contrast, was an apolitical career civil servant who "wouldn't know how to win a vote from his mother," and would obviously be no match for Westcott in any intra-office power plays. A collision between Reynolds, who had the title, but no pull, and Westcott, who had pull, but no title, was expected daily. But it never happened. They both went their own ways and did their own work and tried to keep out of each other's hair as much as possible. Reynolds watched in a rather bemused way as all these mysterious political things were done by Westcott, and even though he felt that as the senior administrator of the office he should know something about them, he didn't press the point.

Westcott was seen by many as being the quintessential political hack of the late 1960s and early 1970s. It was a characterization that annoyed him intensely. "It makes me mad when you're looked on by most people as a sort of backroom fixer who can't work without putting a candle in a whisky bottle and turning the lights out," he said once. A lot of people forgot the achievement of which he was most proud: winning the Greer Award in 1970 for having, in the mind of the Ontario Education Association, made a greater contribution than anyone else to education in the province that year. Not bad for a guy who dropped out of high school after grade eleven and became a hydro lineman.

Westcott was the son of a jewellery store owner in Seaforth, who was also one of the few Tories in the place at the time. This bizarre loyalty was one that the young Westcott adopted, even though it made him something of an outcast in his home town. Westcott's career as a hydro lineman ended in 1946 when a sliver of steel hit his left eye and blinded it. For a few years he worked on a local newspaper and in 1950 came to Toronto. In the evenings he took a journalism course at Ryerson, and during the day he worked at Dominion Securities Corporation. He had been active in the Young Conservatives, and in 1952 was elected a provincial vice-president. This brought him to the notice of the party mandarins, and in 1954 A. D. McKenzie asked him to become a full-time organizer. He did the job for five years, and not only learned a lot about the province and its politics, but also about himself. He discovered that someone who hadn't been to the right schools and didn't have the right family connections had to work twice as hard as anyone else in order to get anywhere. "If you go to General Motors, everybody works. But here, if you really want to hustle, it's funny how the guy who works hard is the guy who gets the breaks," he said. In politics "you must somehow cut the mustard. If someone phones you up and wants something, you find a goddam way to get it done. You never say no."

Westcott's reputation for being able to get things done, for solving problems however great they might seem, was unchallenged, and it led to his being regarded as literally addicted to work. "I guess it's mainly ego, and my drive is often mistaken for ego," he said. "That's partly true, but the other part is that I don't have any alternative."

Westcott and the others may have been working away in the back rooms in those first weeks, but in public the new regime showed little sparkle. So concerned was Davis with the demands of the party and election planning that the administration of government received something less than his full attention. Davis's first opportunity to demonstrate what brand of government his was to be was on March 30 when the Lieutenant-Governor read the Speech from the Throne outlining the government's plans and intended legislation for the spring session of the House.

It was an unexciting document. With one exception it contained little that had not been thought of or promised months or even years before. The senior civil service and Cabinet had begun writing the Speech in January and it eventually was disgorged without any apparent recognition of the fact that the leadership of the government had changed in the midst of the process. The one exception to its list of moth-eaten promises was an announcement of a tremendous house-building and job-creation drive. It was to be, in the words of Trade and Development Minister Allan Grossman, a "fantastic program" involving the spending of $500 million to build 30,000 new housing units and creating 132,000 new jobs. The project was presented in terms designed to excite the public imagination and demonstrate that its government was doing something about the housing problem and also the high levels of unemployment. The public was excited for all of twenty-four hours. The press pounced on the statement, and discovered that there was no evidence that the program would create any more housing starts than were expected before any announcement took place. Moreover, it transpired that the government was being almost dishonestly lavish in its estimate of the number of new jobs that the project would create. Three days in a row Grossman was forced into the embarrassing position of having to stand up in the Legislature and make statements clarifying the true meaning and impact of the program; statements which diluted its impact and revealed it as a flashy, but basically empty, public relations man's dream.

The error of believing that the public and the Opposition would unquestioningly accept anything that was foisted on them was repeated when the budget was announced on April 26. McKeough, pleased as punch with his new job as Treasurer, proclaimed a "full employment" budget. It envisaged spending $4.26 billion and included a deficit of $415 million. But again, when it was scrutinized by the Opposition, it transpired that the estimates of how many jobs would be created by corporate tax cuts and incentives were wild exaggerations. The rest of the budget did nothing to distract attention from this fumbling attempt at grandstanding. It was a dull document with none of the innovative measures the press in particular were looking for. Reporters reluctantly had to admit to themselves that they couldn't call it "an election budget".

So far the first impressions of Davis that Teetor was concerned about had not been advantageous. Every day in the House his government had been under the gun and beset from all sides by opponents who seemed about to overwhelm it at any moment; it appeared disoriented, demoralized, and waiting to collapse. Davis himself did not perform well in the House. As Education Minister he had maintained his position by a superior knowledge of his department; now he was unsure, and he became flustered easily. The contrast between the performances of Robarts and Davis in the Legislature was complete. Robarts was self-assured and always polite to the Opposition, but he managed to be polite in a painstaking way that implied that he felt his time was being wasted. Whenever Robarts walked into the House the atmosphere changed. He had presence, and when he was in his seat all 117 members recognized that they were under his control. While Robarts regarded the House as a nuisance to be steamrolled into inconsequence, Davis did not have the authority to do that, and he simply appeared confused and inept.

There were attempts to regain the initiative. In the middle of April Davis announced that he was accepting the recommendation of an interim report of the Royal Commission on Book Publishing which said that the government should loan the Canadian publishing house of McClelland and Stewart $1 million to stop it being sold to an American company. In May he decided that logging would be stopped in the 1,750-square-mile Quetico Park and that it would be retained as a wilderness area. But even these and other moves failed to gain him any momentum in the Legislature.

Davis's public stature was further damaged early in May when three provincial daily newspapers, *The London Free Press*, *The Windsor Star*, and *The Ottawa Citizen*, working together, produced a series of stories examining the whole question of government land purchases in the picturesque Niagara Escarpment area. There were many facets to the stories, but the one most easily grasped by the public was that the government had bought 506 acres for a park at the Forks of the Credit from a company called Caledon Mountain Estates Ltd., a company with several prominent Tories on its board of directors. The company acquired the land in May and August 1969 for $805 an acre and sold it to the province twenty-two months later for $1,450 an acre.

The entire Ontario Press Gallery got on the trail and found that the government had not followed the recommendations of an unpublished report it had commissioned some years before, which urged massive and swift purchases of land in the area. Details of the report were finally discovered by reporters, and it showed that what land the government *had* bought had been purchased at exorbitantly high prices, and that the vendors had made colossal profits. Generally, it was shown that the government had made no real effort to draw into public ownership that unique part of Ontario's landscape; it was clear that the area was now a gold mine for speculators and was becoming despoiled by unplanned, unregulated cottage and housing development.

Davis was not helped in riding out the affair by his Cabinet Ministers, three of whom contradicted each other in House and were so ineffectual in answering questions from the Opposition that the seriousness of the government's position could not be ignored any longer. On May 21 Davis, visibly angry, announced that a judicial inquiry would be set up to try and discover whether there had been any improper disclosure of the contents of government reports and purchasing intentions to developers and speculators. Davis was not a man who easily lost his temper or showed it when he did, but on that day he cornered one of the reporters responsible for the revelations and gave him a dressing down which neither of them forgot for several years.

The judge who presided over the inquiry decided that the government had not been involved in anything improper over the affair, but John Zaritsky, the reporter who had been the object of Davis's temper, was less fortunate. Zaritsky, of *The Globe and Mail*, was fined $500 for refusing to answer questions at the inquiry about where he obtained some government documents pertaining to the affair.

Not only was the performance of Davis and the government spotted by these embarrassments during those first months, it lacked substance too. The legislative record was so meagre that it seemed the Tories had little hope of winning re-election. But in June that all changed. In the two months before the House rose at the end of July the Davis government introduced nearly twice as many bills as it had in the previous four months, and this flurry of activity gave it the appearance of vigour and initiative which had been so obviously lacking. The voting and drinking age was lowered to 18 years, the sale of crown land was stopped and preference given to Canadians in a leasing system, preference was given to Canadian firms seeking government loans and grants, foreign ownership of Canadian-owned paperback book distributors and investments dealerships was curbed, legislative control of pit and quarry operations was brought in, greater civil rights were given to those appearing before boards and commissions, a detoxification centre program was instituted to help chronic drunks, and a $25 million lawsuit was launched against Dow Chemical Company for alleged mercury pollution of Lake St. Clair and parts of Lake Erie.

By the time Davis called the election he had established a considerable legislative record to put before the people, and had wiped out the stumbling, fumbling image of his first months in office. The turning point, the day when he moved from the defensive to the offensive, was June 3. On that day he announced that the government would not give money for completion of the Spadina Expressway from the northwestern suburbs into downtown Toronto.

11. Stopping Spadina, & Separate School Supplicants

I think one of the things that is very important in public life today, anywhere, in perception of a leader or a premier, is style.

And by that I don't just mean clothes or manners of speech. I mean style of leadership, in the way you make decisions and the way you appear to administer your office. That's why a decision like Spadina, even maybe more than separate schools, is so much more important than just the decision. I think it gives people an idea of what kind of guy he is who would make that kind of decision.

Robert Teetor was giving his interpretation of the poll he conducted for the Tories just after the leadership convention, the poll that indicated that Davis lacked a public personality and must establish himself in the minds of the voters before he called an election. Teetor's analysis did not come before the public until the election was all but won, and it helped to create a school of thought which held Davis to be the most crass and callous of contemporary politicians.

Davis, the thinking went, made the Spadina decision because the poll indicated that would be the popular thing to do. Davis, according to this thinking, refused to extend aid to the senior levels of separate schools because that gathered in the old, bigoted Orange vote. Teetor's polls told Davis that the people wanted decisiveness, and so he masked himself in grim-lipped guise and marketed himself in the package they would most readily buy. The Tories had the money to buy Teetor, the best market analyst around, and they sold Davis in exactly the same way that a supermarket would sell a can of tomatoes. The tomatoes were only of average quality, but the can was irresistible. Five million dollars will buy you Ontario.

This train of thought found many devotees and became a current mythology. Its adherents included cynical reporters, opportunist Opposition politicians, sceptical Tories and a host of politically aware people who were exposed to this thinking. In view of Teetor's pronouncement and the involvement in the Spadina decision of Dalton Camp, the weaver of political Jacob's ladders, the Machiavellian analysis is understandable. But it is not true. Davis as a decision maker is not so easily defined; and the Spadina and Catholic schools decisions are not necessarily typical of his thought processes or methods as a leader.

Davis is not a particularly clever man, not a great analytical thinker. "He's not very bright," was the blunt conclusion of one of his cohorts. Davis's strength as a leader is the ability to grope his way to a decision based not on pure thought, but on his feelings. He has a good sense of what needs to be done in any particular circumstance. His failing in many instances is that he likes to see himself as a fist-on-forehead finder of truth in the balance of logic. The result of this misconception about himself has often been failure. That is not to say that when Davis relies on his feelings about a situation, his decision is invaribly right and widely seen as such; but when he does bring his experience and sense of his constituency, Ontario, to bear on a problem, he has less often been condemned.

Even before the question of the Spadina Expressway was technically his to consider, Davis had come to the conclusion that he would like to stop it if he could. He had been captured by the symbolism of the six-mile strip of roadway that was planned to swoop from Toronto's northwest suburban residential areas down into the centre of the city. Many popular groups rose to oppose the Expressway. Their hard work, organization, and imagination persuaded many people that the Spadina Expressway was not a transportation corridor that should be constructed for the aid of all, but a viper that would kill Toronto. It would engulf parks and cosy neighbourhoods as it rippled south, and once its fangs firmly held the city centre it would daily inject a poisonous stream of cars and trucks that would clog arteries and emit their own venomous gases.

It was a compelling picture that won many converts, the new Premier among them. It was hard to avoid comparing Toronto with the cities of the United States, many of which had become unpleasant places to live, largely because of their planners' subservience to the needs of the motor car. After many, many years of greyness, Toronto had become a place full of life and colour to many of the people who lived there, particularly the intelligent well-to-do. The city had developed into a precious place that deserved affection and protection, and the plans for the Spadina Expressway represented a threat to the only fully-developed yet safe and pressureless city in North America.

Stopping Spadina...

Early disciples of the anti-Spadina cause came largely from the chic areas around the planned terminal point of the Expressway, but the movement grew to include thousands of people from all over the city who saw in their opposition to the road a personal positive statement about the kind of city in which they wanted to live.

The pro-Spadina faction was found among senior Metropolitan Toronto politicians and civil servants, and among people who lived either in the northwest quadrant of the city or on the residential streets along which the northwesterners drove each day to and from the city.

In the 1950s it was widely held that the way to move people about was in cars, on roads. Metro Council's original idea, back in December, 1953, was to extend Spadina Road, which was a north-south road ending well within the limits of the city of Toronto, right up into the suburban borough of North York to a point on Wilson Avenue, north of Highway 401. The estimated cost at that time was $11.5 million. What they were talking about was the construction of a simple, regular road, but by the end of 1957 the scheme had developed to the point where there would be a subway track down the median strip, and the road would have interchanges instead of intersections. In 1962 Spadina was presented as a full-fledged expressway, and gained all the necessary planning approvals. Work began on the interchange with Highway 401. Spadina began moving south the following year when work began on the stretch between Wilson Avenue, its northern limit, and Lawrence Avenue. This was completed three years later, and the work party moved south to prepare the ditch and roadbed for the section between Lawrence and Eglinton avenues.

In February, 1969, the Metro Transportation Committee decided to step up construction of the remaining portion of the freeway and aim to have it completed down to its southern terminal, Bloor Street, in 1975 instead of by 1981. However, in September that year construction was stopped because costs had risen beyond all speculation—and because of growing opposition. The transportation committee held public hearings early in 1970 and was presented with over 200 briefs, mainly from people who were opposed to completion of the expressway. But the committee nevertheless recommended to Metro Council that work be restarted, and in June 1970 the council approved the plan. However, Metro first had to go to the Ontario Municipal Board (popularly known as the OMB) to get planning permission for the final stages of the scheme—as well as permission to spend more money, much of which was to come from the province. What had been a $11.5 million road-building scheme in 1953 had become a mammoth undertaking involving the spending of $143 million on the expressway and $95 million on the rapid transit line down the median strip. At the end of 1970, the multitude of groups and individuals that had been battling singly and together to stop Spadina gathered under one umbrella organization, the Spadina Review Group, to fight against completion before the OMB.

The OMB, with chairman J. A. Kennedy sitting with two other board members, began its hearings on January 4, 1971. Within a month all the arguments which had become so familiar to Torontonians over the previous few years had been presented to them. They weighed projected carbon monoxide levels presented with prophecies of doom by an American expert against the projected figures from Metro Council's experts of how many thousands of people would soon want to drive downtown. They heard appeals ranging from the coolly well-informed to the purely emotional. In the end, the three judges disagreed. Kennedy recommended against completion of the expressway, but his two co-jurors said it should be finished; it was a two-to-one decision in favour of Spadina.

The fact that Kennedy voted against completion was a great fillip to the anti-Spadina faction. Kennedy had become something of a folk hero in recent years because of his tendency to decide planning cases in favour of citizens' groups and against development interests. It was an image Kennedy was to destroy overnight a few years later when he left the OMB and immediately became a developers' lawyer, but at that time he was widely respected, and his vote gave the anti-Spadina group its first mark of official acceptance. Neverthless, their case had been turned down by the board as a whole. There was one final recourse, appeal to the

Ontario Cabinet. This was done promptly, and thus within a few days of becoming leader Davis was handed the job of deciding what should be done about Spadina.

Stopping Spadina . . .

Davis began his consideration believing in "the ultimate futility of giving priority to the passenger car as a means of transportation into and out of the cities," to quote a phrase he was to use later. It was a philosophical position he had come to over a period of time, partly as a result of conversations with Toronto Conservatives, among them Roy McMurtry. But having said (privately) that he would *like* to stop Spadina, Davis considered it politically impossible to actually do so. Close to $70 million had already been spent on the completed portion of the expressway between Wilson and Lawrence avenues and on the preparation of the roadbed from Lawrence to Eglinton avenues. Davis knew that he would be open to severe criticisms of wasting taxpayers' money if he stopped further construction.

And then what would a negative decision do to his relationships with Metro Toronto Council? Metro—as opposed to the City of Toronto council—was behind Spadina all the way. If Davis stopped the expressway, he would appear to be usurping Metro's planning responsibilities and telling them they didn't know how to run their own affairs. Not only that, the picture of the province using a heavy hand on the largest and most sophisticated municipal government in the province might well give the lesser municipalities around Ontario cause to ponder what *their* fate might be. But still he wanted to stop completion of Spadina.

Davis called in Dalton Camp, told him of his feelings about the expressway and asked for Camp's opinion. Camp went away and returned with the view that it would be political suicide. Davis would not only get his teeth kicked in for money-wasting and despotism over the municipalities, Camp said, he would also be bludgeoned for having nothing to offer in place of the expressway. In the privacy of those meetings Camp foresaw phrases such as "the Davis ditch" being used, phrases which did months later become part of the pro-Spadina and/or anti-Davis vocabulary. Camp was adamant that the expressway should be approved.

Within Cabinet, things were no easier for Davis. Charles

MacNaughton, now Minister of Transportation, a ministry which saw transportation primarily in terms of roads, pushed for completion of Spadina. He was joined by a number of the out-of-town Ministers like Darcy McKeough. The anti-Spadina faction was led by Allan Grossman, in whose riding Spadina would end, and Allan Lawrence, who had a goodly proportion of those vocally against the expressway living in his constituency. While Cabinet might thrash the matter back and forth, it was apparent that Davis was not going to get consensus for the decision he wanted around that table.

In the meantime Davis was besieged by Metro politicians pressing the case for the expressway. Albert Campbell, the Metro chairman, after one meeting with the Premier came away convinced that Davis would allow the expressway to be completed; but that seems to have been a false impression probably formed because Davis said little during the interview. Davis has always been a good listener and not at all open with his own thoughts. Many petitioners have left meetings with Davis convinced that the Premier saw the veracity of their arguments, only to be surprised when his decision was announced. In fact, Davis was not impressed with Campbell's case.

Davis's conversations with his political advisers continued. It was pointed out to him that people are very selfish about their own convenience and weren't worried about whose backyard they went through to get downtown quickly; stopping Spadina could not ultimately be a popular decision. Camp pointed out that no alternative to the expressway could be found quickly and that Davis would have to live with the anger of commuters from northwestern Toronto through at least two elections. Davis replied that he would rather live with that than with the expressway creeping further and further into the city as each election came along.

Camp furrowed his high-domed brow and set to thinking. There were many disadvantages to stopping the expressway, but what were the advantages, if any? The most obvious was its appeal to the vociferous groups who had forced the decision on Davis. Saying no to Spadina could establish Davis as someone sensitive to the desires of the aesthetes of urban life, not only in Toronto, but in towns and cities across the province. It could establish him as someone concerned with the quality of environment and life, someone concerned about the future. Davis had come to power as the creature of the party establishment, the heir of John Robarts, crippled at his birth as party leader by near defeat. Saying no would be a break with the past, a break with Robarts, since Robarts had been willing to fork up the province's share of Spadina's rocketing construction costs. Saying no would establish Davis as his own man.

And then there were Teetor's polls. What people wanted, Teetor said, was a decisive leader, a man unafraid to face the tough decisions and come down hard on the side he believed to be right. This was such a situation; the decision to stop Spadina would undoubtedly establish Davis as his own man, firmly in command of his own and the province's future. It was a formula that Davis and the rest of the group felt might well work; so Camp set about writing a statement for Davis to read announcing the decision that the province would not give any financial support for the completion of Spadina.

Davis and his political advisers had resolved the problem in their own minds, but the conflict within Cabinet was as strong as ever. Charles MacNaughton and Darcy McKeough (who, as a former Municipal Affairs Minister, upheld the principle of municipal autonomy) were still ranged against Allan Lawrence, University Affairs Minister John White, Allan Grossman, and John Yaremko. In the end Davis walked into Cabinet the day before he was to make the announcement. He showed them a draft copy of Camp's speech and told them he had decided to refuse to give any more provincial money for completion of the expressway. In practice this was the same thing as refusing to allow the road to be finished.

The statement that Davis read to the Legislature on the afternoon of June 3, 1971, was Camp's first effort at speech writing for Davis. He was later to write other speeches for the Premier, but they didn't come up to the standard of that first effort. It was brief, only nine pages long, but it deftly touched all bases. The statement began by establishing the difficulty of the question, the emotionalism of the subject, the money, the work that had been put into it. The Cabinet, the speech stressed, had also put a great deal of work into studying the problem. "As a new Government, and without prejudice to the past, it is our responsibility to do so," wrote Camp, beginning the theme of a break with the Robarts years. "We are fully aware that our decision will represent not a judgment upon the past, but a decision upon which policies for the future will be built."

A little more rhetoric about the importance of the decision, and then the body blow. "Mr. Speaker, the Government of Ontario does not propose to proceed in support of the plan for the Spadina Expressway."

There was tumult in the House. Tories thumped their desk lids till their palms ached, and laughed at the New Democrats who were doing the same and trying not to look self-conscious about it. For the most part the Liberals sat there impassively, though some thumped along with the rest. Up in the public galleries, which were filled with opponents of the expressway, there were hoots and cheers of joy. Eventually the noise died down, but there was still an excited low buzz of conversation as Davis continued.

He said the province intended to co-operate with municipal authorities in the development of alternative transportation methods, and to increase its financial assistance for rapid transit services. "We must make a decision as to whether we are trying to build a transportation system to serve the automobile, or one which will best serve people. If we are building a transportation system to serve the automobile, the Spadina Expressway would be a good place to start. But if we are building a transportation system to serve people, the Spadina Expressway is a good place to stop," he said.

Next to try and placate the municipalities. "I am well aware—and sensitive to the fact—that we are reversing a decision which was taken by the majority of the elected representatives of Metropolitan Toronto. But the Government and Legislature of Ontario have their responsibilities as well. We can do no less than discharge them in the light of present-day circumstances."

The Premier spent little time discussing the philosophy of his decision. He noted the escalating cost of the project, but said that more important "has been the growing evidence and accumulative experience gathered elsewhere on this continent which demonstrates the ultimate futility of giving priority to the passenger car as a means of transportation into and out of the cities.

"This Government cannot help but heed the rising public anxiety and concern in questions relating to pollution and environmental control. I trust that our decision will give further assurance of our determination to respond to those concerns."

Lest anyone should imagine that the decision was made simply as a vote-getter, Camp wrote, "Over the past seven years the numbers of the general public opposed to the undertaking have multiplied many times over. Whether such would constitute a majority or not I cannot say, but it is at least a substantial and significant minority, including, I might add, vast numbers of those who will inherit the cities and the environment we are now creating."

The speech ended with one of the battle cries of the anti-Spadina movement—"the streets belong to the people"—and further assurance that an alternative would be found that would satisfy the needs of everyone concerned.

There were many questions left unanswered. What kind of alternative did Davis have in mind? How would the immediate problems of the people living in the northwest suburbs be dealt with? What did this statement do to Metro's plans for other major roadways such as the Crosstown and Scarborough expressways? What kind of and how much additional funding did he intend to give municipalities for rapid transit systems? What was going to happen to the unpaved ditch between Lawrence and Eglinton avenues?

But Davis's luck had begun to change. NDP leader Stephen Lewis rose to congratulate the government on the decision on behalf of his party. No questions were going to be raised from that quarter. Liberal leader Robert Nixon was not so happy. Why was the government wasting the $70 million that had already been spent on the project? Why didn't they complete the prepared section of roadbed down to Eglinton Avenue? There were jeers and catcalls from the Tories. But any momentum that Nixon's questioning might have developed was quickly stopped. His deputy leader, Vernon

Singer, whose suburban constituents in Downsview strongly supported the expressway, got up and condemned the Davis decision, arguing that the expressway should be built not merely to Eglinton but all the way. The Tories found it funny enough that there should be two policies coming out of the Liberal party. Their joy was complete a few minutes later when Tim Reid, the young Liberal member for Scarborough East, told the House that he was in entire agreement with the government's decision.

For Davis it was all an unexpected and delightful bonus. The NDP agreed with his decision, and the Liberals were so internally split that their criticism appeared to be of no consequence. The Liberals' dithering performance only served to emphasize the decisive stand Davis had taken. The affair had exposed one of Nixon's great weaknesses as a leader: his inability or unwillingness to impose any discipline on his caucus. There is no doubt that both the Tory and NDP caucuses were as equally divided on the decision as were the Liberals. The difference was that Davis and Lewis made sure that all the fights were held in the privacy of caucus meetings and did not become public spectacles. Nixon attempted to justify what had happened by saying that the Liberal party believed that each member should be free to express his own views on important issues. That may have been a worthy sentiment, but it didn't wipe out the memory of the look of embarrassment and anguish on his face when Singer and Reid said their pieces. It did nothing to appeal to the voters of Ontario who wanted leadership. It made him and his party a laughing-stock in the House and effectively silenced for the time being their attempts at criticism of the decision.

There was an amusing postscript to this phase of the Spadina debate. On June 7, four days after Davis's announcement, Dalton Camp wrote about the decision in his column in *The Toronto Telegram.* When he penned the piece it had apparently slipped Camp's mind that he had played a large part in the shaping of the terms of the decision and had actually written Davis's speech, for in this article he neglected to mention it. Instead Camp wrote with breathless wonder and surprise about the courage and determination of this man Davis who had blossomed so unexpectedly since the leadership convention.

Camp described himself as a late convert to the anti-Spadina cause and continued: "None of us expected to win, because none of us had the prescience to foresee Bill Davis coming to office, much less to know what the measure of the man truly was. We know better now, and whether or not you approve of his decisions in these early months of his premiership, there can't be much doubt that he has the guts to make tough decisions and he has his own view of social priorities.

Stopping Spadina...

"Personally I doubt that Mr. Davis will gain, in net terms, any more votes on the expressway issue than he lost on it. What he does gain is the recognition that he is his own man, that he is not bound by the policies of past administrations and that he has the leadership qualities to reconcile conflicting opinion in his Cabinet."

Camp, of course, was in the happy position of being able to indulge his enthusiasms and be sure of his interpretations. Not many political columnists are in the confidence-building situation of having developed and written in private the policy about which they comment in public. It was not until a year later that Camp's role in the affair was discovered by reporters, and by that time it had little political significance.

While the Spadina decision was clearly a boost for Davis in the way Teetor described it–it established him in the public eye as a firm character–the exact results of his decision on the request by the province's Catholic schools for more money are less clear. No doubt his conclusion reinforced the picture in the public eye of a man unafraid to make the tough decisions.

But what else did it do? One Toronto newspaper executive said that as soon as he heard Davis's separate school announcement, he knew the Conservatives would win the election. His view was that there remained a very strong undercurrent of pro-Orange, anti-Catholic sentiment in Ontario to which Davis's decision would appeal. That feeling was not restricted to professional questioners of government such as newspapermen. A large number of Conservatives, Cabinet Ministers among them, believed that Davis was at his most crassly political when he decided against the Catholics, and then saved his announcement until a few days before he called the election. The inclination was to see the 1971 provincial election as a mammoth replay of the 1936 Hastings by-election, with historic Protestant-Catholic animosities playing the most significant part in the campaign and the outcome.

But there is very little evidence to support the contention that the 1971 election was won and lost on the separate school issue. Indeed, what evidence there is suggests that the issue had remarkably little effect on the election, which is surprising considering how long and with what determination it had been held before the public eye. So far as the timing of the announcement was concerned, Davis seems to have been culpable not of the worst kind of heartless politicking, but simply of indecision. What makes this especially ironic is the fact that this decision helped forge an image of decisiveness.

The question of public financial support for Catholic separate schools has been a recurring one in Ontario's history ever since the British North America Act. The BNA Act guaranteed public support of separate schools, but at that time the education system ended after grade eight. This was later extended to the end of grade ten. Over the years there had been numerous attempts to deal with the inequalities of funding between the separate and public school systems, but the situation became serious in the 1960s when John Robarts and his Education Minister William Davis began to revolutionize the public school system. In their efforts to improve and equalize educational standards and opportunities in the public schools, they increased the inequalities between the public and separate school systems. The Catholic schools just didn't have the money available to them to keep step with the plunge into technical and vocational training at the secondary level. If the Catholic schools were to stay abreast of the others, the money would have to come from somewhere. So parents and the Catholic community had had to pay quite substantial amounts in addition to regular fees for children to go through grades eleven, twelve, and thirteen. Even so, the standard of education, particularly in the vocational and technical areas, was nowhere near the standard in the public schools, and many students transferred for either financial or academic reasons. This led to problems within Catholic families and communities.

In 1964 the Foundation Plan was introduced. This assisted elementary schools, both public and separate, by giving grants to schools in areas where the amount they were allotted from property taxes was low. Even so, in 1969 there was only $577 a year in grants and taxes to educate a child in a separate elementary school compared with $641 for a child in a public school. Students in the two publicly financed senior grades at separate schools, grades nine and ten, were only supported at the elementary school rate. So while in 1969 secondary separate school pupils were being supported by $577 a year, there was over $1,000 a year available to the public secondary schools for each student.

The separate school teachers and trustees and the Catholic community began a campaign to win full public financial support for their school system. They saw that the watchword of educational reform in the late sixties was "equality" and assumed that by making their plight known to all involved they could gain what they wanted through negotiation. In May of 1969 the separate school trustees presented a brief to the government asking for the extension of financial aid to the end of grade thirteen. It was this request that Davis was answering over two years later when he said no.

When their brief failed to bring any response from the government within a few months, the separate school supporters took their campaign to the public and the backbench politicians. They still wanted a quiet campaign, but there was a rising tide of militancy among teachers and students that the leaders of the campaign could not easily control. The marches and demonstrations began. In the fall of 1969 both the NDP and the Liberals announced their policies on the issue. The NDP favoured extension of aid, so long as it did not result in the unnecessary duplication of facilities. The Liberals came out in full support of the separate school trustees' position.

In the spring of 1970 opposition to the separate school supporters began to appear. There were a number of briefs submitted to the government by religious groups, but perhaps the most important brief came from the Ontario Public School Trustees' Association. This document came out strongly against a segregated school system, and even recommended that existing grants should be *reduced.* Although this brief was uncompromisingly negative in its response to the Catholic trustees' request, it contained the basic argument of most of those who questioned whether there should be further support for separate schools. Would not this result in a divided society? Would it not make it impossible for the government to refuse support for *all* religious and private schools? Should the province not be moving towards a more unified education system, rather than a more divided one?

The separate school supporters' campaign reached its peak at the end of 1970 when 15,000 Catholics gathered at the Maple Leaf Gardens for a mass rally to appeal for justice and equality. But the Conservative government was caught up in its own campaign to elect a new leader. During that campaign, whenever Davis was asked about the extension of aid, he usually replied that it was the policy of the government not to increase support. He was a member of that government and was in agreement with that policy, he said. Moreover, he could not hold out any hope to separate school supporters that if he became Premier he would change that policy. Davis, more than most people, did not want to see the Ontario education system Balkanized after his years of work trying to unify it.

But when he became Premier, Davis's perspective changed. It was no longer simply an educational problem for him, but a social and political one as well. Close to half the population of Ontario was Roman Catholic, and there were about 400,000 students in separate schools. While those figures showed that the majority of Catholics did not send their children to separate schools, any decision that could be seen as an attack on the separate system might well draw together the province's Catholic population into an anti-government voting force. Davis and his advisers had the depressing picture of renewed bloody violence in Northern Ireland before them, and so they were hesitant to make any swift pronouncement that might set off religious strife in Ontario. This fear might not seem very realistic, since the situations in Northern Ireland and Ontario were not comparable. While the separate school supporters might feel hard done by, they were certainly not subject to the extremes of inequality suffered by

Catholics in Northern Ireland. Nor was the social and religious discipline among Catholics in Ontario as strong as in Ireland. Nevertheless, putting the possibility of violence aside, there was the danger of stirring up old Protestant-Catholic feuds, and—anathema to any government—there was the threat of creating lasting bitterness against the government in a large section of the population.

Over the period of the Conservative leadership campaign the Ontario Separate School Teachers' Association commissioned a poll of public opinion regarding extension of aid. The poll showed that there was not strong opposition among non-Catholics to public funding of grades eleven, twelve, and thirteen. In May of 1971 Teetor's poll for the Tories revealed a similar lack of interest in the subject. Given a list of 11 issues, Teetor's sample rated the separate school issue eleventh in importance. Even Catholics on average rated it tenth in importance. When asked their opinion about the question, nearly 56 per cent of the total survey said they opposed extension of aid and 38 per cent approved. Nearly 72 per cent of Catholics were in favour of more funds, but 25 per cent of them were opposed.

But even though it was apparent to Davis that the separate school issue was not anywhere near as important in the minds of the voters as employment and the economy, he was still nervous about it. His new Minister of Education, Robert Welch, was delegated to draw up a report on possible compromises. Welch produced a list of about a dozen alternatives to straight agreement to or refusal of the separate school trustees' request, and these were debated long and hard in Cabinet. But always they came back to the incredible cost of maintaining two parallel education systems, the way this would tend to fragment the system, and the fact that it would open the door for other religious denominations and private schools to demand public funding.

Some Cabinet Ministers watched with growing exasperation as Davis twisted and turned away from what, to them, seemed to be the inescapable answer: there could be no extension of aid. Davis had resolved the Spadina conflict within his Cabinet by walking in and telling them what the decision was to be. On the Catholic schools issue he held meeting after meeting not only with Cabinet, but also with the Conservative caucus, discussing the issue from every angle. His indecision seems to have been genuine. It was not simply a ploy to leave a polarizing issue such as this until the last minute before the election.

Finally Davis interrupted a meet-the-people trip into the Niagara Peninsula to return to Toronto on August 31 and announce that his government would not give aid to the top three grades of separate high schools. "There has been no issue since I've been head of the Government that has received a more exhaustive analysis, where there has been any greater probing of conscience than on this issue," he declared. The decision had been made "as much as humanly possible without regard to any political consideration, advantage or disadvantage."

Davis believed the decision would be to his disadvantage politically, and he remained jittery about it. The polls had said that the Catholic school question was not an issue of major importance to the voters, but Davis felt differently. He was not such a firm disciple of polls as some of those around him. They were fine as guides for general directions, but he didn't like them as final arbiters of his fate. In fact throughout the election campaign Davis went through spells of being convinced that he would lose the election because of the separate school decision. Even on election night, as he and his cronies sat in the basement television room of his house at Brampton waiting for the first results, Davis told his friends that if the Conservatives lost it would be because of this decision.

It is impossible to assess just how important the separate school decision was in the election result. Rabid Orange Tories, or those cynical about the way old political ways live on in Ontario, said it was of great importance; that it appealed to age-old Protestant intolerance, particularly in rural southern Ontario. They claimed it smoothed over rural discontent about regional governments and the centralization of schools and social services. If Teetor's polls are to be believed that is not true. Not only was the extension of aid not a major issue in the minds of the electorate, but Davis was in a commanding position well before the separate school decision was made. Moreover, there was never any strong indication that the Tories were in danger of losing those 34 ridings in southern Ontario which were the basis of their power and which were, historically, the ridings where a call to religious intolerance might be thought to have some meaning.

Davis believed that the decision had a significant effect on the outcome of the election, but for sound reasons. He thought that people saw the logic of his arguments against extending aid, and against fragmentation of the school system, and that they supported him for those reasons. That is a more likely explanation, but even then it was probably the decision rather than the content that was important. As an apparently firm stand on a contentious issue it reinforced the impression that he had given at the time of the Spadina decision. The vague picture of Davis as a hazy but basically acceptable character that the people of Ontario had had in March had been completely changed. Bland Bill had become decisive Davis. While the Tories had worked hard at creating a strong image of their leader by wheeling him around the province and showing him to the people, the two decisions that firmly established him in the minds of the electorate were not made with gaze firmly fixed on Teetor's polls. Davis was certainly packaged and sold, as will be shown in discussion of the election campaign, but not in the context of Spadina or the separate schools.

12. The Opposition

The improvement in the public perception of Davis, the party and the government that the Conservatives achieved in the summer of 1971 was spectacular; but it was not quite as remarkable as appearances indicated. Despite Davis's initially dull image, despite the Tories' twenty-eight years of accumulated liabilities, the basic strength of the party was never seriously affected. In May, with Davis's personal popularity still at a low ebb and with the Opposition parties running rings around the Tories in the House, Robert Teetor found that the government had a significant lead in the public's mind. According to Teetor, if an election had been held in the spring, 32.9 per cent of the voters would have voted for the Conservatives, 26.5 per cent for the Liberals, 19.3 per cent for the New Democrats. Twenty-one per cent of the respondents were undecided and if they were divided up in the same proportion as those who gave a definite answer, the Conservatives would have won nearly 42 per cent of the popular vote. The Liberals would have won 33.6 per cent and the NDP 24.5 per cent. As it happened, those standings were very close to the results of the 1967 election. Thus, short of falling flat on their faces or being badly outmanoeuvred, in the course of the hypothetical election campaign, the Conservatives would certainly have been returned with a comfortable majority.

The figure that nagged away in their heads was that 21 per cent of the voters who were undecided; a large proportion of that group was made up of people whose voting history identified them as people who might vote either Conservative or Liberal. What was worse, most of those "switchers" liked Davis less than they liked the Liberal leader Robert Nixon. And worse still, they rated Davis less able to deal with the current economic issues than Nixon or Stephen Lewis. The economic issues of unemployment and the effects on Canadian industry of domestic American unemployment policies were, according to Teetor, the major concerns of the voters.

That, however, was back in May. With the aid of Teetor's polls, Kelly's money and the tremendous opportunity to affect events that being the government gives, the Tories had worked away during the summer to eradicate their uneasy feelings about that 21 per cent group of undecided voters. By mid-August senior Conservatives were showing optimism. They were saying openly that the worst they could do was be returned with the same number of seats, 68, that they held before. There was now, they felt, a strong possibility that they could gain from 5 to 10 seats. The depressing thought of a Conservative minority government, which even top Tories had admitted as a possibility early in the spring, had now gone from their consideration.

Throughout this time the Tories had been gathering cards to improve their hand, but what Teetor's May poll showed was that they still held the ace of trumps that had been in their hand ever since Drew won his majority in 1945. That card was the general weakness of the Opposition parties. Without the prospect of any one party being able to make heavy inroads into that great block of 34 safe Conservative seats, the Tories were not really threatened. Their great fear was being driven into minority because of antipathy (or even apathy) towards Davis, and that had been dealt with.

The Conservatives, by myth and magic, had developed over 28 years a style for keeping themselves in power. What is astonishing is that over that same period the Opposition parties had developed nothing. Late in the summer of 1971 the Liberals and the NDP were in the same position they had been in in 1945 and all the subsequent election years—about to be badly beaten. The weaknesses of the Liberals and NDP fell into two major categories: leadership, and their inability to appeal to a wide and diverse section of voters.

In Robert Nixon the Liberals had a leader who had a highly idealized view of politics as a formal gentleman's game whose ultimate purpose was the discussion of issues before the public. With this precept he failed to respond to the real issues of the campaign, shrank from presenting himself to the public as a strong leader, and made excuses for not disciplining his caucus and his party into a political force.

Stephen Lewis, on the other hand, was a strong party leader, exerting his influence over a party that, unlike the Liberals and Conservatives, required grass-roots approval for all the major stances taken by the caucus. Lewis had built his political reputation as an organizer and had maintained it by being able to hold together all the disparate groups within the NDP. In the Legislature he was far and away the most effective member of the Opposition. Instinct for the jugular was what it was called, and he certainly had it. Tory backs stiffened at the sight of those hawkish eyes and jutting chin, but even the most red-necked, time-serving backbencher would be in the House to hear him speak. He was without doubt the finest speaker in the Legislature. That clipped enunciation and those flowing phrases scared the Tories like nothing else. But they scared a lot of other people, too—voters—and that was Lewis's downfall. He looked too hungry, he sounded "too clever by half".

Unlike Nixon, Lewis had built a strong and efficient organization, to fight the campaign on traditional NDP lines. They planned to take door-to-door politics right across the province. The NDP campaign method of canvassing every household in a riding two or three times before voting day had worked well in by-elections, and Lewis had hopes that it would be equally successful on a province-wide scale. Nixon, on the other hand, leaned towards the Tory way of doing things, with a tour of the province by the leader, lots of advertising, rallies and so forth. But both of the Opposition parties had the fundamental weakness of being unable to expand their basic support from the traditional areas of their power. The NDP proved unable to break out from their power base among trade unionists and engender any wide acceptance. The Liberals were, if anything, being pushed further back into their traditional area of support among the farming communities of southwestern Ontario.

For the "old line parties", the Liberals and the Tories, the quality of their leadership is far more important than it is to the NDP. Ever since the arrival of "presidential politics" the New Democrats have maintained a situation where the strength of the party resides in the membership. But for the Tories or the Liberals it is the leader who must bind the membership together, set the goals, and be the personal manifestation of his followers' hopes. If having such a man was important for the Tories in power, it was doubly so for the Liberals in opposition. It is much more difficult for the leader of an Opposition party to keep up morale and the sense of movement than it is for a premier. But the Liberals had been racked by an almost continual leadership crisis since the departure of Mitch Hepburn.

For years the problems of the provincial wing of the Ontario Liberal party were put down to a "Messiah complex". The only Liberal for two generations who had beaten the Tories was Mitch, and he did it by the force of his personality and embracing oratory. That, reasoned the Liberals, was the kind of man they needed again to bring them to power. And so when they cast about for new leaders, as they did nine times in the intervening years, they hunted for someone with a touch of glamour, a trace of Mitch. So besotted were they that they found Mitch in the most unlikely guises. One emotion-charged speech from a candidate was all it needed for the Liberals to believe that this man would take them back to glory. Never mind the candidate's other qualities or lack of them, if he could bring an audience to its feet at the right moment and however briefly, he was the man. It was all incredibly inept and stupid. The blind search for a new Hepburn obscured many things, not least Hepburn's true qualities. As an administrator he certainly was not someone to emulate; he had been a total failure there. But he had been extremely tough with the party, his caucus and Cabinet, demanding loyalty and a toed line. There was a great deal of ruthlessness and muscle behind Hepburn's sharp wit and dynamic personality, but in the 1950s and 1960s the Liberals failed to realize that those qualities of toughness were as essential to the Hepburn make-up as the glamour.

So while Drew, Frost, and A. D. McKenzie built an organization, the Liberals constantly rejected men who might have done the same thing for them. As the messiah complex became more ingrained, the chances of ever finding the right man decreased. Even messiahs are dubious about leading lost causes. Increasingly, too, the provincial wing was rejected by the federal party, which *did* have organization and the ability to win. The federal rejection was initiated by Hepburn's battle with King, but it survived the passing of those two men. The total lack of interest or commitment by federal Liberals to the provincial cause was partly a result of the way the party was organized. There was one Liberal party in Ontario, encompassing both federal and provincial wings. The result was that anyone with potential who worked his or her way up through the party naturally gravitated and was encouraged by the hierarchy towards the federal arena. This was where the power was, this was where the party bosses wanted the talent.

The provincial Liberals, therefore, became poor cousins, to be patted on the head now and then, but never taken seriously. The political make-up of Ontario was such that the federal Liberals could count on enough voters in the province to support them to maintain a healthy showing, so why bother to expend all the effort required to defeat the provincial Tories. The extraordinary fact that the same people who voted for the Liberals in federal elections generally supported the Tories in provincial elections (one of the scenic wonders of Ontario to outsiders, a Niagara Falls of the political world) was of no significance and less interest to the national party.

The provincial Liberals pursued their dream alone. After Hepburn's brief return to the leadership from 1943 until his final defeat in 1945, the Liberals turned to Farquhar Oliver. Oliver, a Grey County farmer, was a ponderous man with none of Hepburn's dynamic qualities, but he was something of an orator and in the 1945 leadership convention he made a particularly rousing speech that got him the job. That 1945 Liberal leadership convention was a strange one. Oliver's campaign manager was a former Hepburn Minister named Colin Campbell. But on the day of the voting Oliver got a surprise about as rude as possible in the political world. He came downstairs in the King Edward Hotel to find that his campaign manager Campbell was running against him. To make matters more intolerable, Campbell still had the keys to Oliver's headquarters, where all the campaign literature was stored. After Oliver won the leadership, Campbell was no longer among his trusted advisers.

Oliver fought the 1948 election without success and resigned immediately after. He was succeeded by Walter Thomson, a Toronto lawyer who was also an orator and who showed some of Hepburn's impetuous thinking. But he took the Liberals to their lowest point in all the 30 years—7 seats in the Legislature. Thomson ran a one-man show, and from outside the Legislature at that. He never sought to win a seat at Queen's Park before the 1951 election, and indeed only visited the Legislature once or twice. He resigned after the 1951 election and Farquhar Oliver returned to lead the party through the next election, in which the Liberals picked up a few seats.

By the 1959 election John Wintermeyer was leader after beating former federal Finance Minister Walter Harris in a leadership convention a couple of years before. Wintermeyer was perhaps the most likely prospect the Liberals had in the entire 30 years. He too was an orator, but politically was a babe-in-arms compared with the Tories led by Leslie Frost.

Wintermeyer was beaten personally in the 1963 election and resigned the leadership. The convention to replace him was in September, 1964, and one of the leading candidates was a 36-year-old farmer and science teacher named Robert Nixon. Nixon had inherited (it's the only word) Brant riding in a by-election in 1962 which was called after the death of his father, who had held it since 1919. Although he was expected to do great things, he didn't make much of an impact in the House initially. He didn't engage in any of the big debates in the early sixties, particularly the furore over Bill 99, the police state bill, and those who saw him as the natural successor to Wintermeyer were disappointed. In the spring of 1964 Nixon announced that he would be a candidate for the leadership, and he appeared to be the front runner. But he again failed to shine in the House during the spring session, and victory went to an idealistic social worker named Andrew Thompson. Thompson's Irish accent and stirring prose revived old dreams, and even the press called him "a new Mitch".

Having started out as front runner, young gangling Bob Nixon ended up third. He was knocked off on the fifth ballot and Thompson defeated broadcaster Charles Templeton on the sixth. Templeton, a former hell-raising preacher, was another white hope of the Liberals, but his stock declined when in 1964 he failed to win a by-election in Toronto's Riverdale riding. Nevertheless, when Andy Thompson resigned late in 1966 for health reasons, Templeton was the leading candidate. At first Nixon said his inclination was not to run, and he declared his support for Templeton. But a few days later Templeton said he would not be a candidate. His reasons, he said, were his family, his personal finances (he had ended up $20,000 in debt after the 1964 leadership), he was not a member of the Legislature, and there was strong opposition to him in the caucus. The strongest opposition came from Elmer Sopha, the MPP for Sudbury, who even held press conferences to voice his feelings. Sopha's misgivings were too strong to be purely political, and they apparently originated with a dispute over money Sopha had raised for Templeton in 1964, which Templeton never acknowledged receiving.

Two weeks after Templeton's statement Nixon announced his candidacy, and within hours senior party officials were calling for his election by acclamation. On January 6, 1967, Nixon was elected leader unopposed.

Had the Liberals elected the defeated candidates at each convention since 1943 they might have done better than they did. Campbell, Oliver's manager-cum-adversary, was a mining engineer with a good knowledge of finance and experience in party organizing. Walter Thomson's opponent, John Brown, was a chartered accountant, quiet but intelligent and determined. Leslie Frost just scoffed at Thomson's blusterings; he might not have found Brown such easy prey. Even Harris, a former federal Cabinet Minister with a great deal of political experience, could well have had more telling effect than Wintermeyer. But the Hepburn syndrome won through on each occasion. Liberals even saw Mitch in Bob Nixon. "If Nixon isn't an orator, he is a farmer–and Mitch was a farmer, wasn't he?" The thinking had become as obtuse as that by 1967.

"Something in a dapper lounge suit with a smidgen of good old Ontario dirt in the cuffs," was the way one reporter described Bob Nixon in 1967. It was a pretty apt description. At home on the farm as a boy he had ingested both farming and the big city politics. His father had been in politics since well before he was born, and that fact had marked their relationship. "He was just the man who brought the coloured comics home on the weekend, looking white and tired," Nixon recalled once. Mackenzie King and other contemporary Liberal big-wigs were visitors to the Nixon farm, and the tousle-haired young boy was allowed to sit in on some social conversations in the farm drawing room. To begin with, Bob Nixon was somewhat overshadowed by his elder brother Jackson. But after his brother was killed piloting a bomber over Frankfort in 1942 Harry Nixon leaned towards his younger son. In fact while Harry was off campaigning in 1943 Bob, 15 years old at the time, was back running the farm with the help of a hired man. Bob Nixon was hay-making the day the news of the Liberals' defeat by Drew came through.

Nixon went to high school in Brantford and then on to McMaster University and the Ontario College of Education. He taught in Toronto and Sault Ste. Marie before getting a job in the science department at Brantford Collegiate Institute shortly before his father's death. There was never any question that he would run in the by-election that followed his father's death, and he won easily.

Nixon had learned from his father a deep and abiding respect for the institutions of parliament. It was one of his personal strengths–and a political weakness. Time and again, both as backbencher and leader, he pulled his political punches through reverence for the form of parliamentary manners and procedure. He didn't take any part in the debate on Bill 99, and allowed Andy Thompson all the glory and the subsequent leadership, because it would have upset the balance of speakers from each party had he insisted on having his say. "He's just like his father, ploughs a straight furrow, but he's colourless," was the sour comment of one old-time caucus member when Nixon won the leadership.

The new Liberal leader didn't get off to a good start. Robarts called the 1967 election shortly after Nixon took over, and he had time neither to establish his position in the party nor to prepare for the contest. The Liberals increased their number of seats in the election–they went from 24 to 28–but their share of the popular vote dropped from 35 to 32 per cent. Liberals looked nervously at the NDP, who had increased their seats from 7 to 20 and their share of the vote from 16 to 26 per cent. Obviously it was the NDP that was profiting by the Tories' malaise and not the Liberals. There were mutterings within the party and a dump-Nixon campaign sprang up, but it never got moving; instead the grumblers went underground.

Nixon now found himself faced with the situation that

had helped paralyse every Liberal leader since Hepburn. He could not count on the total support of his party or his caucus. There was a large section of Liberals who didn't like him, for various reasons. Many, yearning for Hepburn, saw nothing in this tall bespectacled figure to conjure up memories. Others found Nixon unable to build the organization or the broad base of support they felt necessary if the party was to out-run the NDP and defeat the Tories. Nixon had an easy and effective speaking style and a friendly manner, but he kept himself very much apart. Even his close advisers had no real feeling that they were playing a part in the running of the party. More often than not they knew darned well they weren't.

The question in the minds of many Liberals after the 1967 election was whether they could break out of their traditional area of strength, the rural ridings of southwestern Ontario, and establish themselves as an urban party as well. Many Liberals were involved in the blossoming world of city politics (Stephen Clarkson, for example, ran for Mayor of the City of Toronto in 1969 as a Liberal candidate) and there were high hopes that this might be translated into seats at Queen's Park. But Nixon was not of much assistance to that faction of the party. He felt uncomfortable with urban audiences, and it showed. He realized that he had little understanding of the problems and needs of urban Ontario, but he tried hard to play a role that would attract urban voters. In time Nixon was to become more comfortable with urban issues, but he was never very convincing. He once said, "Sometimes I just want to go back to the farm and roll up the driveway behind me." His roots and commitments were in the country.

Nixon himself could be forceful and effective in the House as an opponent of the Tories, but the picture was spoiled by the individually unruly and collectively flaccid group he had around him. The ineptness of the caucus was partly Nixon's fault. In any case, he had to take responsibility for it. There was talent there which, properly channelled, could have done a much better job of providing cogent and forceful criticism of the Conservative government. But they didn't. Morale within the caucus was bad because of the gulf between Nixon and his men. He expected nothing from them, and they gave him nothing. Laziness was one of their chief vices. As well as not pushing them into putting their backs into their job, Nixon gave little or no encouragement to that handful of talented men that he had. They were shunned even in such trivial things as the seating plan in the house, where Nixon arranged the seats largely in terms of seniority. The more elderly and tired veterans were right down there in the front seats while the younger, hungrier and more effective members were in the back rows. It may seem a small thing, but it had a real effect on internal morale, which in turn had an effect on the perception of the party from outside, particularly from the Press Gallery, which in turn further affected morale by writing the Liberals off.

Despite these problems the Liberals had a good record for bringing up issues in the House, but they lacked the ability to follow through or, indeed, to establish at once that what they had said was important. In 1970 Lewis made an issue out of the sale of crown land to foreigners and hammered away at it until the government changed the policy. In fact Nixon had brought up the same question four months before in a press release, and it had gone unremarked. The same happened with questioning of why hydro rates were increasing and who had made the decision, the government or Ontario Hydro. Lewis burst into the headlines with this issue a month after Nixon had brought it up.

This situation caused the Liberals to feel that they were being hard done by by the reporters in the Press Gallery. The average reporter was characterized by the Liberals as being a staunch NDPer with eyes only for what Lewis and his band were doing. While that was not true, it could certainly be said that the Liberals were to quite a large degree being ignored by the press. This was partly the fault of the reporters, who mistakenly sensed that the New Democrats were on the move and were the act to watch. It was also the fault of the Liberals, who did not know how to get their message across either in the House or to the reporters outside. They were constantly out-manoeuvred by the NDP and should not have been surprised that this made an impression on reporters.

In that context the Liberals were in a difficult position

when presenting their case on any issue. The problem was that their case often was so nice in its definition, so tortuous in its search for a pathway between the left-wing Tories and the right-wing NDP, that its impact was lost. It is hard to base a party philosophy on the merits of a few subordinate clauses. This lack of room to move was a great problem for the Liberals, which was why they were as pleased as the Tories when Stephen Lewis was elected to the NDP leadership. It seemed to them that he would move the New Democrats several paces to the left, and thus give the Liberals room to breathe and be identified.

But Nixon had other problems. "The problem with Bob is that he really isn't sure that he can do a better job as Premier than Robarts can," was the comment of one caucus member. This lack of confidence on Nixon's part showed itself in an unwillingness to push himself forward as leader and to become the embodiment of the party. This distaste for "presidential politics" might not have been a hindrance had he concentrated on building up the Liberal organization and the abilities of the caucus. But he didn't do that, either. Instead he maintained that elections should be fought on issues, and that if the voters could see that the Liberals had a clearly-stated and carefully-evolved policy program, then the people would see them as a logical alternative to the Tories. So at the end of 1970 he called a policy conference which was held in Toronto at the end of January, 1971. It was not Nixon's fault that the Conservatives decided to hold their leadership convention over the same period, and that the public found the choosing of a Premier more engaging than the drawing together of 32 pages of policy resolutions. Nixon, however, felt happier with that document tucked in his hip pocket, and he called it "Blueprint for Government".

The production of that document at three days of frolic and interminable policy sessions at the Royal York Hotel raised the spirits of the party as well as comforting Nixon. The election of Davis to the leadership of the Tories a few days later added to their self-confidence. Their hopes soared in the following months as the Conservatives fumbled their way through the spring session. The Liberals considered themselves the obvious choice for voters who could not stomach the New Democrats and who felt that the Tory dynasty had finally wasted away.

It has been a feature of Ontario provincial Liberalism that self-satisfaction sets in early, as soon as anything goes right for them. It is a function of the messiah complex, the belief that the apocalypse arrives without warning and is instantly fulfilled. So it was that spring. The sight of the Davis Cabinet wriggling in discomfort was enough to make the Liberals lounge back in their seats and wait for plums to drop from the trees. There was even talk of them winning 60 seats in the election. When the Tory counter-attack came, they were completely unprepared and their deficiencies were immediately exposed. The Spadina statement shattered not only their united public image, but also set off internal bickering and back-biting. Nixon sighed, gritted his teeth and said such things as: "There is something much healthier and more fun in the approach that 'I'm an individual and by Jesus I think I can do well in politics.' It's very difficult for someone with this attitude to fit himself into a highly organized, doctrinaire position under a strong leadership."

These feelings of dedication to the rights of the individual in politics were genuinely and strongly held by Nixon. He had an idealized view of what political life ought to be, which went right back to nineteenth-century reform politics. He recognized that politics was not (and probably never had been) the way he thought of it, but he found it very difficult to compromise his ideals. They were more important to him than his desire to form the government of Ontario. This made Nixon more engaging and likeable as a man than the other leaders, but did not equip him to do what it took to win the election.

One of the things that made Nixon likeable was his coarse dismissal of this "nice guy" image he had among those who knew him, but who didn't have to put up with the frustration of working for him. He found it rather sickening to be thought of as a pleasant, amiable character, and he put down any moves by his advisers or the party to market him in this or any other way. "I have a basic mistrust of image politics," he said once. "I still believe that politicians have got to talk about issues and that the people should vote on issues." So his refusal to cater to the needs of the situation didn't stop with his dealings with fellow politicians, it also included the voters. If the voters did not choose to respond to his philosophized view of politics, then hard luck. Hard luck on everyone.

Even so, Nixon was ambitious, but his chosen battleground was the Legislature, not the province. That for him was where it all happened. It was in the Legislature that the issues were developed, it was in that sober atmosphere that debating points were won. That was where the Tories were, and that was where he chose to attack them. It was a very personal battle. Nixon spent a great deal of time in the House, spoke often and well, extemporizing generally cogent criticisms of government legislation.

But he neglected the party organization, which was weak both in the calibre of the people involved and in its knowledge of what was happening in the province. Nixon didn't travel around the province much, either, thus cutting himself off from the voters and from an essential element of provincial campaigning, the small-town newspapers, and radio and television stations. In terms of the numbers of ridings they influenced, these were of considerably more importance to the politicians than the big urban dailies.

It is strange that after 28 years the Liberals showed many more of the classic signs of dynastic rot than did the Tories. Factious, out of touch, completely possessed by themselves, they displayed all the qualities that herald collapse. But had not the collapse come and gone in 1943? Not quite. The Liberals were still the official Opposition party, a title which may be of no significance at all to anyone whose life is not influenced daily by the courtly goings-on of the Legislative Chamber. But within that milieu the title has its opulence, and some importance.

The parliamentary system was not designed to be a two-party system; it pre-dates such things as parties. Rather, parliamentary democracy has *encouraged* a two-party system. It is an adversary system, with the government and the loyal opposition facing one another, and the two parties are now assumed to be interchangeable; if the opposition becomes the government, then the government smoothly becomes the opposition. With the development of political parties, there was a natural tendency for them to develop into two main blocks in any particular parliament. And such is the regional nature of Canada that the two ascendant parties have differed from area to area.

Where the situation becomes complex is with the emergence of a strong third party. Some political scientists claim that in this situation the tendency is towards the disappearance of one of the parties as a major force and the return to the two-party system. This case is made despite the fact that through the 1950s and 1960s in election after election the three parties in Ontario were holding to percentages of the popular vote that didn't change all that much. The Conservatives maintained a level around 40 per cent, the Liberals, with all their inadequacies, held on to about 30 per cent, and the NDP, the rising party, took a few points here and there to climb to over 20 per cent.

The question that arises is whether Ontario has established a three-party system, or whether this is a transitional phase before a return to a two-party system. What keenly interests those involved is which party is going to get the chop if the two-party system does return. The statistical evidence favours the growth of the NDP and the demise of the Liberals. Up to the summer of 1971 the shifts in support of the 28 years had seen the Liberals depending on an ever-declining range of voters, while the NDP had diversified from their roots among the Toronto working class, gained support and seats in other urban areas and even in less populated ridings. The process of growth had been slow, but New Democrats felt it had been sure and stable, a firm base on which one day to build a government.

It nearly formed the government in 1943. With 34 seats it was only 4 short of Drew's minority government, and with 32 per cent of the popular vote only 4 less than the Tories. In 1945 it was knocked right back to 8 seats and 22 per cent of the popular vote, but the precedent that the voters were prepared to heavily support the socialists had been established. In 1948 they again formed the official Opposition party, but were slaughtered in 1951 when they only won 2 seats. In 1953 Ted Jolliffe stepped down from the leadership and Donald MacDonald, the CCF national organizer, was elected in his place.

MacDonald, a teacher and former journalist, nursed the party through the fifties and sixties, gradually building and extending the organization. The breakthrough came in 1967 when for the first time since 1948 the party, now the NDP, got more than 10 seats. They won 20 seats, only 8 less than the Liberals. During the fifties and sixties the party had maintained between 15 and 20 per cent of the popular vote, but this had been translated into few seats because the party's strength was concentrated in the industrial centres of Toronto and Hamilton. In 1963 nearly half of all the votes cast for the NDP came from Toronto, but this situation represented only 7 seats. In 1967 they got 26 per cent of the vote and 20 seats. The difference was that the NDP had established itself in a number of other urbanized areas, Oshawa, Sudbury, Windsor, and Peterborough. They had successfully identified themselves as a working class party and their support had been gathered partly from the Conservatives but mainly from the Liberals.

While the party had shown no great signs of going anywhere, no one had exhibited any desire to supplant the solid, pipe-smoking MacDonald, but after the 1967 election the crown had become something worth coveting. Stephen Lewis was ready. By 1970 he had been in the Legislature for 7 years, and at 33 years old had established a reputation as a powerful parliamentary force as well as a fine organizer out in the province. The son of federal NDP member David Lewis (who became the national NDP leader in 1971) he took in his politics with his pablum. In 1959, after getting a degree in history at the University of Toronto, he went to Britain to work for the Socialist International, a meeting point for socialist parties of all strains from around the world. The war in the Congo erupted that year, sparking his interest in Africa. Lewis and a friend went to a youth congress in Ghana. They had intended to stay in Accra for 10 days, but Africa and its problems became an obsession with Lewis and he ended up spending 2 years teaching English and history in Ghana, Kenya, and Uganda. In 1961 he returned to Canada and was appointed the newly-formed New Democratic Party's federal director of organization. In 1963, at the age of 27, he was elected MPP for the riding of Scarborough West.

Lewis quickly was labelled as "a boy wonder" and "one of the brightest lights to appear on the Ontario provincial scene in years". The records of his first years in the Legislature are full of Lewis's succinct and merciless attacks on the Robarts government, particularly over its health and welfare policies. His razor-sharp invective could bring the Tories to boiling rage; they quickly adopted the slight man with the deep-set eyes and jutting chin as their personal bête noire. But Lewis the circling hawk, Lewis the swift destroyer, was possessed of a very cool head. As a result of his work in a series of by-elections he gained a reputation in the party as a fine organizer, even invincible. He was credited with securing James Renwick's victory in Toronto's Riverdale riding in 1964, and the win for Max Saltsman in the federal by-election in Waterloo North. Lewis's leap towards the leadership began in 1969 with his work on the NDP's successful campaign in the provincial Middlesex South by-election.

As an organizer Lewis emphasized the need to canvass door to door in search of votes. He maintained that it was the only way the New Democrats could counteract the effect of the money that the Conservatives and Liberals had to fight campaigns. The NDP could come to power in Ontario only by mobilizing a huge work force of supporters and sending them out in the ridings. Canvassers for the party would call on each household two or three times before election day. The canvasser would become, ideally, almost a part of the family, so that people in the riding were voting really for their canvasser rather than the candidate. The tactic worked well in by-elections.

In 1968 Lewis got caught in a situation of potential conflict of interest. He was a director of Brown Camps Ltd., drawing a salary of between $12,000 and $15,000 a year. A new NDP member, John Brown, was president of the company, which provided treatment for wards of Children's Aid Societies who were emotionally disturbed. The Societies paid the company for looking after and treating the children. Whatever the philanthropic intent of the two men, the fact remained that 80 per cent of the Children's Aid Societies' money came from the provincial government. Robert Nixon brought the matter up in the Legislature and questioned whether Brown and Lewis should vote on the estimates of the Department of Social and Family Services, which financed the Societies. He called for an investigation by the standing committee on privileges. But the Speaker ruled that there would be no conflict of interest until either of the men voted on the estimates of the Department, which so far, as participants in the company, they had not done. Lewis and Brown avoided the conflict by getting out of the company.

The affair delighted the Tories. The enemy who painted with such unremitting precision their own warts had his own blemishes, it appeared, and they were slow to drop this agreeable topic. Even years later, when they were having their own problems with conflicts of interest, the Conservatives would mutter darkly that there was more to the Brown Camps situation than ever came out. When pressed for details they would primly say that it was not for them to spread unfavourable information about an opponent. Outside the Tory party Lewis's reputation was not tainted by the affair.

Lewis won the leadership of the NDP in the fall of 1970 with the overwhelming support of the powerful unions affiliated to the party, and the Conservatives quickly moved to use this against him. They took every opportunity to ask whether Ontario wanted to be governed by a front man for the unions, and American unions at that. Lewis tried to defuse the issue by taking little notice of it. When he did respond, he would insist: "We're not beholden to the unions the way the Tories are beholden to the corporations." Nevertheless, many people failed to understand the difference between companies giving financial support to the Conservatives, and unions and union members giving money and the time of union officials to the New Democrats. If one were to accept that companies did not donate to the Conservatives without hope of gain, why should one believe that the same psychology was not at work in the relationship between the NDP and the unions?

The tie to the unions was not the foremost concern of the NDP strategists as the election approached. More worrisome to them was Lewis's strident, uncompromising image. He came over terribly on television. The evening news each night showed not a diligent Opposition leader revealing the inadequacies of the government, but an arrogant, ruthless fanatic who would have the whole province cutting sugar cane given half the chance.

Part of the problem was Lewis's features. His eyes were too deep-set and close together beside a sharp nose. In person, the effect of the eyes was offset by his easy smile, but on television the smile came over as a sinister grin, made more terrifying by the way he held his head back and pushed forward his jutting chin. The picture might have been less damning had he not been such a superb speaker. That only heightened the sense of arrogance.

Lewis used words as a surgeon wields a scalpel. The sight of the knife going in gives everyone a twinge, even when it's not their flesh. That was the effect Lewis's words had. He was the only politician at Queen's Park who spoke in sentences. Most people, even politicians, do not; they "Um" and "Ah" and grasp their way towards a full stop. Lewis's sentences flowed irresistibly on like a majestic river and he used with precision a profuse vocabulary that sent many listeners scampering for a dictionary. Too clever by half, that was the trouble.

With that image of its leader, with that association with the trade unions, the NDP was widely seen as a devotedly socialist party that would radically change the fabric of life in Ontario. It didn't need much prodding from the Conservatives to get that message home. The New Democrats did indeed want to re-work the political fabric of provincial life, but in reality they were not nearly as left wing as popular imagination felt. Most western European socialists would have had a hard time figuring out exactly where Ontario Tory philosophy ended and NDP philosophy began. The New Democrats had back-pedalled from the old socialist mainstay, nationalization, and now generally talked of public involvement rather than public ownership of major provincial industrial concerns. So far as the introduction of a planned economy was concerned, the Conservatives were right there with them, and the arguments were of quality and quantity rather than the substantive question of free enterprise versus control.

Of the three parties the New Democrats in general had

the best relationship with the Press Gallery. That is not to say that they had the Gallery in their pocket; they didn't. There were certainly reporters who leaned towards the NDP, just as there were reporters whose sympathies rested with the other parties. The NDP members and party officials in general had franker and more open dealings with reporters than did the other parties. As a body reporters like blunt honesty, and the New Democrats seemed prepared to display that quality. Lewis, in particular, and his executive assistant Gerry Caplan, dealt openly with reporters, who in turn responded to their intelligence and their willingness not to play the evasive games that the other parties pursued. Also, reporters had a rather different perception of Lewis than that which appeared on the television screens. They enjoyed his keen humour, which he could use on himself as well as on anyone else, and most found his easy affability engaging.

The upshot of this was that in the late summer of 1971 a number of stories appeared which fairly pointedly stated that Lewis was not the hawk he appeared to be, but in fact a rather shy, sensitive man who was pained by the impression given that he scared old ladies and children. The stories also pointed out just how moderate a party the NDP was, and not the vanguard of the Red Menace. There doesn't appear to have been any connivance between the party and reporters to produce "soft" stories on the NDP. At this period most newspapers were asking their Queen's Park reporters for stories on the mood and preparedness of all the parties as the election approached, and the stories on the NDP were matched by others on the Liberals and Conservatives. While the stories generally got over the message that the NDP believed to be in their best interests, all but one or two were not soft in the sense that they reproduced party pap.

At this time there was a general feeling in the Press Gallery that the NDP was poised to strike for power. In the myopic view of the Gallery, the New Democrats had won the laurels in the House, despite the Conservatives' come-back at the end of the summer. There was much talk of an NDP minority government, and the view was expounded in print and in the more cosy and confidential setting of the Press Gallery bar that at the very least the parties were starting off even in the election campaign.

The press build-up of the NDP finally served the Conservatives, by strengthening their hand when they talked of the threat of socialism. The Queen's Park reporters were badly out of touch with the world outside the pink stone Legislative Building in imagining that a strong performance in the House was indicative of acceptance in the countryside. The press stories may have talked about the moderate tenor of the NDP, but nothing could convince the voters that there was anything moderate about the Waffle faction of the party. The Waffle, an ultra-socialist, ultra-nationalist group made up largely of intellectuals, characterized the party in the public's eye much more than moderates like Walter Pitman, Donald MacDonald, and Stephen Lewis. Waffle leaders such as Mel Watkins and James Laxer received wide and persistent news coverage of their calls for extensive nationalization and a tough line against foreign-owned industries. At a time of relatively high unemployment, Ontarians were in no mood to experiment with philosophies that might cost them their livelihoods. The Waffle presence within the NDP was strong, but the faction did not have the authority in the party that its publicity suggested. It was, however, an acute embarrassment to Lewis, and not entirely to be trusted to respect party discipline or party policy stands.

Over all, the New Democrats felt pretty good about their prospects. They had won the last by-election, Middlesex South, in 1969 by a reasonably respectable margin. Middlesex South was in the heart of Tory country around London and the NDP felt this boded well for them. Robarts, with all his prestige, had done poorly in the 1967 election, and there seemed little reason to suppose that Davis could in a few months establish himself in the minds of the voters as even Robarts' equal. There seemed every reason to suppose that the Conservatives were going to lose seats.

Moreover there was a trend across the country to chuck out long-established provincial governments and replace them with new parties. It had happened in Manitoba, in Quebec, in Nova Scotia, in Saskatchewan, and in New Brunswick. Surely it was Ontario's turn now. Within the NDP they were better organized than ever before. For the first time they were going to run a candidate in every riding, and they had amassed the troops to run a canvass campaign of by-election intensity in almost all ridings. If they could do what they had done in Middlesex South in every riding in the province, then why should they not win the election? They would soon find out.

On the morning of Monday, September 13, Stephen Lewis drove down to Belmont, south of London, with Murray Weppler, David Lewis's executive assistant and a former *Ottawa Citizen* Queen's Park reporter, who was being lent to the provincial leader for the duration of the campaign. It wasn't quite in Middlesex South riding, but close enough. There Lewis spoke to about a hundred local farmers over lunch and got rapturous applause. Lewis's spirits soared; this was indeed a hopeful sign. Meanwhile Weppler was constantly on the telephone in the lobby of the village hall, keeping in touch with Queen's Park. September 13 was the last day at Davis's disposal to call the election if voting day was not to be so late in the fall that the weather would interfere with campaigning.

Time and again Weppler came back from the telephone and shrugged towards Lewis. The only news from Queen's Park was that Davis was holding a Cabinet meeting, although there had been a number of announcements made by the Tories during the morning. The report exonerating the government in the Niagara land deals was released, and it was later announced that the elderly and the poor would no longer have to pay Medicare premiums. Obviously Davis was clearing the decks, but would he announce the election that day or hang on for another week? Lewis was preparing to leave when Weppler finally came back and beckoned excitedly. He had just heard on the phone that Davis had announced that the election would be held on October 21.

Lewis and Weppler piled into their station wagon, and with Weppler at the wheel burned up the road back to Toronto. Lewis reminded Weppler that it would not be a good start to the campaign if the party's leader was nailed for speeding, and then settled back in the front passenger seat. He sat silent for most of the journey, listening to the radio, which was bringing the latest news from Queen's Park. Occasionally Lewis would take a break from gnawing his fingernails to comment, "I feel good–and I feel relieved–

because I don't see that there is anything more we can do internally to prepare the party for the election. I think we are going to do well. The atmosphere for us is good."

13. *A Can of Tomatoes*

The mathematics were against the Opposition parties from the beginning. Whereas the Liberals and New Democrats could muster only about 10 safe seats each, the Conservatives had at least 35 ridings on which they could count. More generous accountings at the time put the Tory haven at around 43 seats. In a House of 117 seats even a backbone of 35 ridings took them a long way along the road to the 59 seats needed for a majority.

Those safe Tory seats stretched like a great blue band across southern Ontario from the Ottawa Valley to Lake St. Clair. At the core were 22 seats the Tories held east of Toronto. Standing on the Scarborough Bluffs and looking towards the dawn there were only two blots on the otherwise true-blue Tory landscape right the way to Ottawa: Peterborough and Oshawa, both of which were held by the NDP. One need look no further than that great swath of blue in searching for Les Frost's bequest to the Tories.

This was Orange Ontario, rural Ontario, basic Ontario. Primarily it was farming country, but not wealthy farming country such as one could find in southwestern Ontario. A family could make a living all right, but the usually rocky land was not generous with its bounty, and demanded unrelieved toil. Despite years of road building by the Conservatives, it remained a relatively isolated area of family farms and small, introspective communities. Compared with the rest of southern Ontario, the southeast was left practically unmarked by the great changes of the fifties and sixties. As the landscape remained the same, so did the politics. With few urban centres to provide them a foothold, the NDP wrote the area off. Asked what his plans were for a campaign in the region, Stephen Lewis replied with a laugh, "We'll fly over and drop hay bales to the animals." It was no less barren ground for the Liberals. Liberals here were still Grits, Reformers, and Catholics.

The other side of Toronto, west, presented a different picture. This was the region that had been subject to massive growth and urbanization. With its burgeoning cities of Hamilton, St. Catharines, Niagara, Kitchener-Waterloo, London, and Windsor it was used to the idea of change, and that could include political change. The NDP had their foot in the door here. They held 3 seats in the Hamilton area, and 2 in Windsor.

In the southwest lay the remnants of the old Liberal empire. No fewer than 14 of their 27 seats were in this region. But many of these ridings were held not as Liberal enclaves from which sorties into neighbouring ridings could be made. Rather, they were personal fiefdoms that depended on loyalty to the individual MPP. Murray Gaunt in Huron-Bruce and James Bullbrook in Sarnia are good examples of this. The burghers of Sarnia would continue to elect Bullbrook, but when it came to matters of patronage they would take their requests to Lorne Henderson, the Conservative backbencher whose riding of Lambton surrounded the town. Such was their liking for Bullbrook that they would support him against all comers, even though they recognized that they would have to trot out into the country if they wanted to get their relatives jobs in government liquor stores in the town. And in Huron-Bruce the electorate had continually returned Gaunt even in the face of suggestions from Tory candidates that their deplorable roads would be brought up to the standard of the neighbouring Conservative ridings if they would have the sense to elect a government member.

Nevertheless, the Conservatives also had a strong hold on southwestern Ontario. Many people had done well out of the boom, some by knowing the right people at Queen's Park, some by being swept along in the tide of development. However it was achieved, everyone knew that the bounty came from the Tories, and the landscape was liberally dotted with Cabinet Ministers to prove it. Anyone leaving Toronto, travelling west, soon found himself in the riding of James Snow, Minister Without Portfolio, then on into the riding of George Kerr, Minister of the Environment. Then there was Robert Welch, Minister of Education, down there in Lincoln riding, then a bit of a gap that marked the Liberal enclave at Kitchener-Waterloo, and then you were in London where there was John White, Minister of University Affairs, and Agriculture Minister William Stewart. A little north of them was Revenue Minister Eric Winkler, while down at the far end of the area were Darcy McKeough, the Treasurer, and Charles MacNaughton, Minister of Highways and Transportation.

In the 15 ridings of northern Ontario, generally defined as that part of the province north of the French River, things were not so sure for the Conservatives. They held 7 seats, with the Liberals and the NDP holding 4 each. But feelings of neglect and alienation were so strong in the north that the Tories had come to accept that there was little they could do to avoid losing some of those seats, probably to the NDP which, because of the hewers-of-wood-drawers-of-water economy, was gaining support through the unions.

There are strange things done 'neath the midnight sun, and in the ridings of Cochrane North and Cochrane South they were very strange. Since Confederation there had been an agreement between the Liberals and Conservatives in those ridings that the Tories would run dummy candidates in federal elections and the Liberals would put up straw men in provincial elections. And so it was. René Brunelle, the Minister of Lands and Forests, faced no opposition in Cochrane North save the NDP candidate who was given long odds against dumping a Minister, while in Cochrane South the NDP member, Bill Ferrier, was seen as the beneficiary of the deal. It made it a straight fight, with no chance of anyone sneaking in on a split vote, and even with a free hand the Tories hadn't managed to come up with much of a candidate.

The great unknown was Toronto. Toronto had 26 ridings, but it could not be considered a block. Each riding had its own peculiarities, its own reasons for voting the way it did; it all depended on the candidate and the make-up of the riding. Thus St. Andrew-St. Patrick riding and its neighbour, Bellwoods, had in the past switched quite happily from voting for Communists to regularly re-electing Conservatives. Staunchly small-"c" conservative High Park had voted for a temperance CCFer rather than George Drew, and had gone on to elect muck-raking NDPer Morton Shulman. Some ridings with a strong ethnic flavour could not be drawn away from an MPP who reflected the cultural heritage of the riding, other ridings could. Some ridings would go for the candidate with glamour, with pizzazz, others would avoid it at all costs. Some ridings were concerned about unemployment, some were mainly concerned with directors' fees. In some ridings the population changed almost entirely in three years; in others many people lived in the houses in which they were born. In some places people thought the decision to stop the Spadina Expressway was the most ridiculous thing they ever heard tell of, in others it was the dogma of the new Renaissance.

Most of the Toronto ridings were large in terms of population and difficult to campaign in, but some were huge. York Mills, Dalton Bales' riding, for example, had more voters than the entire province of Prince Edward Island. This riding had 95,596 people on the voters' list while Bellwoods, the domain of John Yaremko, had only 20,947 voters. Gerrymandering? Not entirely. York Mills had grown enormously since the last redistribution. But most of the Toronto ridings had between 30,000 to 40,000 voters, which made Bellwoods something of a rotten borough, and put it in the same bracket with the province's smallest riding in terms of voters, Algoma, right up there in northern Ontario, which had 16,829 voters.

The Conservatives were strong in Toronto. They held 12 of the seats, the Liberals held 6 and the NDP 8. But everyone agreed that a number of Toronto seats would change hands. Just what the final outcome would be was anyone's guess.

There was some difference of approach among the three party leaders to the issues of the campaign. Premier Davis, facing the television cameras in the Queen's Park press conference studio after announcing the election, said it was "a question of leadership". He asked for a personal mandate to lead Ontario through a period of international political and economic difficulties. "It is especially a time when the people of Ontario require leadership in the management of their affairs and it is also a time when the leader of this province needs to feel that he has the confidence of the people of Ontario," he said.

There was lese-majesty in Nixon's assertion of much the same stand. His party would be campaigning on the theme "A change you can trust", he said. The issues would be the economy and the need for jobs, the decentralization of government, the environment, and Ontario's role in Confederation. Lewis said the NDP would fight the election on the themes of creating jobs, reducing the cost of living, reforming the tax structure, protecting the environment and regaining control of the economy from foreign investors. Having made those statements Nixon and Lewis left Toronto to begin their campaign tours. Both flew off in chartered vintage DC-3 aircraft, Lewis for the north and Nixon for the Ottawa Valley. Davis went home to Brampton for a week's relaxation that was intended to get him in shape for his tour of the province.

For those Queen's Park reporters who had looked at the mathematics, the issue seemed to be whether the Tories would win a majority and how large it would be, and whether the NDP would finally supplant the Liberals as the official Opposition party. This analysis infuriated Nixon who lit into the reporters accompanying him on his tour, accusing them of promoting the NDP. The Liberals were out to *win*, he emphasized, not scrapping for second place. Nixon may not have altered the reporters' minds, but he touched their most sensitive nerves when he accused them of unfairness and partiality. Thereafter the newspapers were deluged with stories about Nixon from their reporters on the tour.

No one was particularly short of money. The Liberals and the New Democrats pleaded poverty in comparison to the Tories' war chest of $5 million, but they were hardly in penury. The Liberals had budgeted $2 million for their campaign. They had already collected a fair amount of it, and aimed to continue collecting through the campaign. Joe Cruden, a Bell Canada executive and the chief fund-raiser for the campaign, had reasonable success. The general practice of the captains of industry and the moguls of commerce was to give 60 per cent of their political donations to the party in power and 40 per cent to the leading Opposition party. But in 1971 the fear of a strong showing by the NDP was such that the percentages had been changed somewhat and the Conservatives got about an extra 10 per cent and the Liberals 10 per cent less than usual. Nevertheless, the Liberals were by no means short of cash.

On the second day of the campaign Lewis released what he said was a detailed accounting of the NDP's planned spending and receipts. It foresaw total spending of about $628,-000, with $228,000 being spent on the central organization, and the remainder in the ridings. What those figures didn't include was the value of the 150 volunteer organizers the NDP had spread around the province. Fourteen of these organizers had been working in the ridings since the spring, and a few had been in the field for a year. Some of these people were given paid leaves of absence from their jobs as union organizers, and others came from New Democratic Parties in other provinces or at the federal level. The cash value of these people took the NDP campaign close to $1 million. In addition the party had recruited 8,000 unpaid volunteer grass-roots canvassers and riding workers. Lewis confidently hoped that these people would number 35,000 by election day. That number wasn't achieved, but the unpaid volunteers significantly added to the hidden value of the NDP campaign.

It was the most elaborate campaign the NDP had ever mounted. Quite apart from the extensive organization at the riding level there were such signs of having joined the mainstream as a chartered airplane for the leader's tour. Previously NDP leaders had bumped around the province in a bus, but Lewis took to the air. It wasn't much of an airplane, a 28-seat DC-3 which looked as though it had fond memories of the Berlin Airlift, but it was the symbolism that counted. The NDP had achieved such stature that they warranted an airplane for their leader to take his message to the people. For those that cared to notice, it might have been remarked that the Liberals had rented a similar DC-3 from the same establishment, Millardair of Malton, which specialized in rescuing these stalwart aircraft from early graves. Even Premier Davis had occasion during the campaign to forsake his 48-seat Viscount turboprop for the robust pleasures of flying in one of Carl Millard's treasures.

If the NDP had achieved some equality in the air, they came nowhere near reaching parity in the war of the advertising campaigns. They budgeted $50,000 for advertising, which was not in the same league as the Liberals, who were themselves mere Lilliputians in the game played by the Tories.

The Tory advertising campaign unfolded by Norman Atkins in the early days of the election campaign was the most spectacular political sales job the country had seen. It was highly sophisticated in its organization and the material it produced, but there was nothing subtle about the message. It was Davis, Davis, Davis. Davis in living, breathing colour. Davis barbecuing hamburgers. Davis, his back to the camera, walking pensively on the beach by his cottage in the evening sunlight. Davis among crowds of supporters. Davis walking through woods with his wife, Kathy. Davis with his family. Davis, Davis, Davis.

The Premier was seen more than heard. He had not yet developed the ability to seem at ease when faced with a camera, and it was decided to have a professional announcer quoting from Davis's speeches rather than to allow the Premier to talk for himself. Noticeably absent from the multitude of ads that besieged Ontarians from their television screens were references to the Conservative party. "Davis is doing things for people," the ads said—and then in print so small and transient on the screen that only an unblinking eagle eye could catch it, "This message sponsored by Ontario PCs." The Liberals and NDP screamed that American presidential politics had arrived and that the Premier was being sold like a can of tomatoes, a phrase that a Tory researcher had once used, to his everlasting regret.

"TV does it. It's not American. It's a product of TV. It's the leader-oriented society." Those were Atkins's comments at the time. "The leader is important. Trudeau proved that was right."

Whatever Davis had, it certainly wasn't the natural ability

to communicate with the nation simply by looking into a television camera that had captured the country for Pierre Trudeau three years before. Davis needed help. The help was Ad Hoc Enterprises and it worked out of cramped, rather seedy offices on the second floor at 461 Church Street, in Toronto. Ad Hoc was the most important of Atkins's innovations. It was known as "the media group" or "the creative group", and was made up of the best advertising and media people that Atkins could get his hands on. His idea was that instead of simply giving the job of planning and producing an advertising campaign to one favoured advertising agency, he would set up his own especially for the election. Atkins believed that all the creative talent the Conservatives required could not be found in one agency. Establishing Ad Hoc enabled him to draw together under one umbrella all the individuals that he wanted, from a number of advertising houses. It also provided a way of assembling a group of committed Conservatives.

There was never much difficulty in getting these people leaves of absence from their firms. It paid to be in with the government. Large amounts of money were spent each year by most of the government Ministries on advertising, and these accounts were seldom tendered for. Awards were made, not on the basis of who could do it most cheaply, but on which firm's approach the Minister liked the best. If a company had a proven ability to work with the Conservatives during an election campaign, then why should they not be equally easy to work with on government business?

Ad Hoc itself and the people involved were not things that the Conservatives liked to talk about much. There was even a mild effort to make it look as though Ad Hoc didn't exist at all. All the films, recordings and newspaper advertisements created by Ad Hoc were placed with newspapers and television and radio stations by another advertising agency called Foster Advertising Ltd. This was the front company, the agency of record, which bought the space and the time, but it had nothing to do with creating the ads. There was also considerable reluctance to name the people involved in Ad Hoc.

During the summer, prior to the start of the campaign, a

leading figure in Ad Hoc was William Straiton, who had his own company, Straiton Market Development Ltd. Straiton's role was to direct much of the filming for the television commercials used early in the campaign. With cameraman Jerry Fijalkowski, a former associate of Polish film director Roman Polanski, Straiton followed Davis around on his "meet the people" tours with camera constantly humming. Straiton also conducted interviews with Davis filmed at the Premier's cottage near Honey Harbour in Georgian Bay. It took a lot of rehearsing and numerous "takes" before Straiton got the kind of inflection and spontaneous warmth that he wanted in the Premier's answers. Despite the hours of work that went into these "interview" sessions, only a small amount of the footage was used—and that was used on free-time television. The bulk of the commercials placed by the Conservatives used silent footage of the Premier and a series of brief man-on-the-street interviews. The editing of the films and commercials was done by Donald Haig, of Film Arts, a film editing company which operated out of the office underneath Ad Hoc on Church Street.

Haig liked the man-on-the-street technique because people tended to view them in the same way that they do news programs, and hence found the comments of the interviewees believable. To make the message even more forceful, Ad Hoc selected a cross-section of interviews to try and ensure that the viewer would see at least one man-on-the-street with whom they could identify. Thus the commercials contained interviews with very distinct types—young and old, long hair and hard hat, blue collar and white collar, male and female. None of the interviews were phony or staged, but there was an attempt to make them look as much as possible like the kind of man-on-the-street interviews that a television news team would do. But the questions asked were designed to elicit a favourable response. "What do you think of Bill Davis? Is he doing a good job?"

William Straiton bowed out of the picture at the start of the campaign, his job done. In came Malcolm Wickson, a former national director of the Conservative Party, as Ad Hoc's administrative co-ordinator. Wickson was a real estate developer in British Columbia and an old friend of Norman

Atkins'. It was in conversations with Wickson over a number of years that Atkins developed his unique concept of campaign organization. The concept involved a much more systematic approach to campaigning than had previously been practised. Individual tasks were narrowly defined, and planned and assigned in a way that made it relatively simple to ensure that they were done. One of the great weaknesses of many campaigns had been that too much tended to be left to too few people, with the result that too little was done. With a systematic approach Wickson's job of co-ordinator was essential to the success of Ad Hoc's work.

A very real effort was made to surround the Davis campaign with a festival atmosphere. The bright red, white, and blue campaign colours appeared everywhere: on buttons, lapel stickers, posters, cheerleaders' uniforms, hat bands, everywhere. But the main attempt to unleash the kind of patriotic exuberance that had marked Centennial year was made in the music of the Davis campaign. Composer-arranger Ben McPeek got a call from Ad Hoc the day the election was announced. "They wanted some music. Something to sell the man. They said 'We want to sell Davis'." The Conservatives, according to McPeek, wanted something like a cross between Ontario's Centennial song, "A Place to Stand", and the song that stirred many American hearts, "The Ballad of the Green Berets".

Undeterred, the gallant McPeek called in advertising copywriter Dawn Thompson, and in two days they wrote the words and music for the Tory campaign song "Keep on Goin' ". The song was all the Conservatives could have asked for. Not only did it focus on Davis—the climactic lines were "Davis will make it go, go Ontario, Davis will make it grow, come on Ontario"—the tune lent itself to a variety of interpretations and arrangements. Thus McPeek arranged and directed a recording studio band in a number of versions of the music. There was a straightforward version which was the background for most of the radio and television commercials. There was a hotted-up version for use on pop radio stations. For rallies there was a marching version with emphasis on the brass section. McPeek called the Dixieland arrangement the "let's-get-drunk" version. For the less Rabelaisian there was a folk song arrangement in both English and French, and for the country music radio stations there was an arrangement which emphasized harmonica and guitar. The version for classical music stations featured classical guitar and was, according to McPeek, "humble but proud". Finally there was a version that featured mandolin for use on radio stations that catered to ethnic audiences. "They're out to present the man in the many guises he'll be in," explained McPeek. Yes indeed.

The problem with selling Davis and Davis only was that there were a lot of people around the province who weren't going to have a chance to vote for him, only the citizens of Peel North could do that. At the same time there were 116 other Conservative candidates who needed to pick up those votes intended for Davis. Ad Hoc were enticing the voters into the store with only one of the products of a particular brand when in reality they wanted to sell the whole line. Davis was the "loss leader". A number of Tory candidates, understandably, figured that they had a few selling points of their own, and were philosophically unwilling to tie themselves irrevocably to Davis's market appeal.

But Ad Hoc had its own ideas about that. To persuade local riding associations to go along with the Davis campaign the Candidate Service Centre was set up. It was run by Richard Canney, an advertising executive with Roberts/Fenton/McConnell Ltd., who worked just down the road from Atkins' Camp Associates. The stated purpose of the centre was to upgrade the advertising material developed by the riding campaign organizations. The riding organizations were encouraged to send in their proposed material for Canney and an assistant to assess and "upgrade". In reality these services were something of a come-on. Canney's group had a wealth of material developed by Ad Hoc to send to the ridings and it all featured the red and blue on white central campaign colours, and yes, it all featured Davis. There were all kinds of campaign knick-knacks: buttons, pins, posters, pamphlets, calling cards, "vote at" cards, the whole range of campaign paraphernalia. And if a local candidate wanted a few billboard posters the Candidate Service Centre could furnish those, too, though the candidate might be somewhat surprised when he saw one pasted up in his riding saying "Fred Bloggs is for Bill Davis". Even at billboard dimensions Fred Bloggs would have a hard time reading the fine print which assured him that he was also for the Conservative party.

The local organizations didn't have to accept Canney's hand-outs, but most of them did. For one thing they were hand-outs, free, and even though most of the local campaigns were pretty well financed, any campaign manager worthy of the name will accept whatever free help is going. Then the party's regional organizers, who worked out of head office in Toronto, pushed the riding organizations in their areas to make use of the centre, and the massive television advertising campaign was organized from Toronto. A local candidate therefore found that all the major advertising in his area ignored him and promoted Davis. He had little choice but to become a Davis candidate.

While Ben McPeek was at the RCA recording studios with his band and his choir of six adults and five children putting all the various renditions of "Keep on Goin' " on tape, down the hall in another studio Jerry Goodis and his assistant Charles Dunbar were taping the soundtrack for the Liberal television and radio advertisements. Goodis, a 42-year-old plump, trendy advertising executive with *chutzpah*, chuckled to himself. There were the Tories down the hall with what sounded like a symphony orchestra, and there was he with one cellist scratching out a tortuous melody that he hoped would be a requiem for the Conservative government. But Goodis revelled in the underdog role. In the recording studio he and Dunbar were putting the finishing touches to an ad campaign that had taken them 10 days to produce—and which they had only been asked to do 16 days before. Goodis, Goldberg, Soren Ltd., whose reputation for excellence rested on their proven ability to send people rushing to buy the products of Speedy Muffler King and Wonder Bra, was taking its first shot at political advertising. Goodis had got the opportunity because of a foul-up in the Liberal campaign.

The Liberals' advertising agency for some years had been Ronalds-Reynolds, whose senior vice-president, Hank Karpus, was a loyal Liberal and a member of the campaign committee. But when Karpus produced his ideas for the campaign for the other senior Liberal organizers they were turned down; they just didn't have what the Liberals wanted. So the Liberals did what Liberals usually do (Trudeau would do the same thing two years later) when they don't know where to turn next. They sent for Senator Keith ("the rainmaker") Davey.

The Senator came down from Ottawa and the problem was placed before him. An election was expected any day and the Liberals had no advertising campaign ready. Jerry Goodis was the answer that the Senator produced. Relief, but not immediate relief. Goodis wasn't sure that he wanted to do it. He had met Bob Nixon a few months before when the idea that he should work for the Liberals was first mentioned, and he hadn't been especially impressed. Goodis was a highly emotional man and it carried over into his politics, which had centred on the Committee for an Independent Canada at that time. One of the first questions he asked Nixon was, "When was the last time you cried?"

Nixon was taken aback. Brant County farmers have a somewhat different way of looking at life from cosmopolitan Toronto advertising executives who can make buying mufflers an issue of multi-culturalism. Nixon replied that he couldn't remember when he last cried. "Well, I don't think I can help you then," Goodis said, and that was the end of the interview. But under pressure from Senator Davey, Goodis agreed to try again, and after an extended private interview decided that he could work for Nixon. Goodis came to the conclusion that not being able to remember when he cried last was not necessarily a deficiency in a politician. He found that he liked Nixon and that he had answers for the questions of policy that concerned Goodis. On September 15, two days after the election was called, Goodis said he would prepare the advertising campaign. He and Dunbar worked for ten eighteen-hour days and produced ten thirty-second television advertisements and a sheaf of newspaper ads. The commercials had the Liberals jumping up and down with excitement, and they could hardly wait to unleash them on the voters and the Tories.

Goodis used powerful pictorial techniques to make capsule criticisms of some of the things the Liberals said were wrong with the Conservative government, and he used the soundtrack to put forward the Liberal alternative. All the commercials, both print and television, ended with the catch phrase of the campaign, "Had enough? Vote Liberal." One commercial showed a derelict farm while a commentator talked about Tory agricultural policies forcing farmers to leave the land by the thousands each year. That ad fell particularly flat because only a farmer could tell that the farm was derelict. To the average urban viewer, the farm looked like just the kind of place in the country they had always wanted. Another ad showed an aged couple walking along, painfully slowly, while the narrator talked about the Tories' deplorable treatment of pensioners. One began with a close-up in slow motion of a car travelling through what looked like a grass field. The camera panned back to reveal that the car was in fact driving along the overgrown unpaved roadbed for the unfinished portion of the Spadina Expressway. A newspaper advertisement depicted the Statue of Liberty holding the Ontario flag instead of the torch. The caption asked, "After 28 years of Conservative rule, is Ontario in the right hands?"

Only one of Goodis's ideas was rejected by the Liberals. It was to have been a newspaper advertisement to be used in the last few days of the campaign. For it, Goodis had acquired a photograph taken by a newspaper of Premier Davis. The Premier had a cigar in his mouth, and a self-satisfied grin on his face. The caption was, "The party's over. Had enough? Vote Liberal." But the Liberal hierarchy decided that was in bad taste and never used it.

Non-Liberals criticized the Goodis ads for being too negative. The Liberals responded to this criticism by buying complete pages of newspapers towards the end of the campaign and reprinting verbatim all the policy statements of "The Blueprint for Government". The party hoped that the sheer weight of all those words would convince the electorate that the Liberals were in fact a viable alternative to the Conservatives. Few Liberals expressed any illusions that those great slabs of type would actually be *read* by the voters. They counted on the impact of mass.

The Liberal advertising campaign was entirely different from that of the Tories in approach, content, and political professionalism. The New Democratic Party's aims were surprisingly similar to those of the Conservatives. Like the Tories, the NDP had an image problem on their hands. With Davis the problem was not enough image. With Lewis it was too much.

While Ad Hoc was trying to sell Davis as a leader, the New Democrats were trying to sell Stephen Lewis as a human being, family man, sensitive soul. Film-maker Allan King, a long-time friend of Lewis's and creator of the dramatic documentary feature film "A Married Couple", volunteered his services free. King's problem was to overcome the obstacles presented by Lewis's face and his style of speaking. Lewis's deep-set eyes were a particular problem "because you do a great deal of character reading in the eyes, and if the eyes are deep-set it's a little hard to see them to judge the man. It's a mild form of wearing sunglasses. You're always uncomfortable talking to somebody wearing sunglasses because he's talking to you from behind the blind. You can't see what he's doing. It's a very hostile thing to do. People aren't very comfortable with it." King saw Lewis's clipped articulate speech as a compensation for shyness. "Who wants to vote for a ruthless, manipulative, hawklike, shrewd person?" he said, summing up his problem.

Lewis and his executive assistant Gerry Caplan were initially somewhat fearful of the whole idea of a campaign film based on Lewis. Not only did the NDP, with its professions of being a mass, democratic party, veer away from all blatant leadership rituals, it also had a puritanical streak which was horrified at all notions of political salesmanship through film and advertising. But Lewis and Caplan had every confidence in Allan King's honesty. "Anything he has ever done has had to be real," Lewis said. "So whatever he did with me had to be real. He wouldn't countenance anything else. If I emerged well, then so be it. If I didn't, well, that's tough, but that's real."

While the NDP's sensitivities required that there be no rehearsals, no scripts and no refilming of scenes, King's films did aim to present Lewis in a favourable light, figuratively and actually. The favourable light that King used was strong backlighting behind Lewis's head and soft flat foreground lighting which wiped out the deep shadows around Lewis's eyes. Much of the filming was done with Lewis's right profile to the camera, that side of his face being much less hawklike than the left. At first King followed Lewis around to meetings, filming him in question-and-answer sessions, but the results were not good. The people talking to Lewis were not used to being filmed, and they did not look natural. These clips were not used. King was better pleased with candid shots of the Lewises and their children at the family cottage. "When you see a man with his family and kids, it's the most intimate and spontaneous way of getting a sense of what he's like," King said. Norman Atkins could well have said the same thing about the films of Davis and *his* family at *their* cottage.

The essential part of the NDP film campaign was the product of a three-hour filmed interview. King aimed to get Lewis talking about how he felt about issues rather than simply reciting party policy. He felt he succeeded, and all the 30-second commercials the New Democrats used were clips from this interview. The lighting and the content certainly showed a Stephen Lewis that was new to most people, but there was something unsatisfying about the commercials. They were very obviously clips from a continuing conversation which had begun before the clip began and would end after it had finished. The result was that they lacked wholeness, they didn't leave the viewer with the impression that he had been told the complete message. Whether the viewer found that compelling, a spur to discover more about the NDP, or whether it merely irritated him is impossible to assess. In any case the NDP budget for commercials was so small that relatively few people got to see the commercials.

Much wider distribution was given to a specially produced colour magazine called "The New Democrat". This was the major piece of province-wide promotional material for the NDP. The magazine contained endorsements of the party and Lewis by such notables as Pierre Berton, June Callwood, and Bruno Gerussi. Dalton Camp could not resist twitting the

NDP about the magazine in his column. He pointed out that the magazine was full of pictures of Stephen Lewis and wondered if the NDP were not engaging in the leader-selling tactics for which they were criticizing the Tories. He concluded that they were, and that the only differences between the two campaigns were that the Conservatives were reaching a wider audience and that their advertising was more honest. Davis, Camp said, had people on the street speaking for him in the Tory commercials, while Lewis, in the magazine, only had the "beautiful people" and the social élite.

The Tories' advertising campaign was the most clearly thought out and best organized of the three; but it was also by far the most expensive. The Conservatives always kept well clear of putting any figure on the cost of the campaign. The NDP and Liberals threw figures like $3 or $4 million around without much justification. Atkins scoffed at these estimates, but in view of the fantastic volume of television and radio advertising bought by the Conservatives it is impossible to imagine that they spent anything less than $1 million.

There can be no doubt that the money was well spent. The kind of tidal wave advertising that the Conservatives were doing towards the end of the campaign, especially in a dozen or so keenly contested areas, was bound to have an effect. In some areas, such as London and Peterborough, the Tories ran seventeen radio commercials a day. Advertisers consider eleven spots a day to be saturation advertising.

14. Fear and Loathing

The Tory mandarins had no great faith that free and easy news coverage of their campaign would be to their advantage. The Conservatives preferred to keep control of their campaign by presenting their side through advertising rather than leaving the job to the uncertain interpretations of the news media. Queen's Park reporters had already dubbed them "The Big Blue Machine" and the press had explored with unconcealed suspicion the size and slickness of the Tory campaign. So while Lewis's and Nixon's campaign tours of the province were planned from the start with the press in mind, the Conservatives took a different tack. For them the aim was to present Davis in innocuous situations to as many people as possible. The less the press was given the opportunity to say, the better.

The news coverage generated by the party leaders' campaign tours was one of the few weapons Nixon and Lewis had to counter the Tories' money. Neither of them bothered much about holding rallies or meeting people in the areas they visited. They concentrated instead on the local news media and on providing daily copy for reporters travelling with them. Lewis's tour group was the most efficient at generating pure "news" each day. In fact, it was so efficient that editors back home were in a constant tizzy lest they should be accused of being unfair to the Liberals and Conservatives in the quantity of their coverage. Many stories about Nixon and Davis saw the light of day simply on the grounds of equal time or space and not on newsworthiness.

Lewis was accompanied by a small but efficient team of helpers. Murray Weppler acted as advance man and organizer, Gerry Caplan, Lewis's executive assistant, was political assistant and speechwriter, and Caplan's wife, Barbara, worked on research and press liaison. They were helped no end by a team of workers back in the NDP offices at Queen's Park headed by Ellen Adams with whom they were in constant touch for information. Lewis aimed to produce a new statement of NDP policy almost every day of the campaign, and he kept pretty close to that target. Most of his statements were elaborations of known policy, but he tried to give them a new twist by relating them to situations in the places that he visited. Thus he talked about pollution and the lack of secondary manufacturing industries in Sudbury, and in Thunder Bay he dwelt on the government's public housing record and the stupidity of locating a reconstruction of the Hudson Bay Company's Fort William on a site once occupied by the Bay's great rival, the Northwest Company.

Nixon's tour program was considerably more hectic than either of the other leaders', and was more pointedly aimed at the press. A fairly typical day involved swooping in on five cities. One such day began with a dawn take-off in the DC-3 from Toronto to Peterborough. There was a press conference at Peterborough airport which the local reporters attended. The plane then took off again and went to Hamilton, where everyone jumped into a waiting bus for the trip downtown. There was another press conference in the Hamilton Press Club, a quick lunch, and then back out to the airport. Then on to London, where again a coach was waiting to take everyone downtown for another press conference. On this particular day there was then a bit of a delay because the DC-3 had been shedding parts of one engine between Hamilton and London, and the crew were in favour of replacing them before continuing. With everything apparently back in place the plane went on to Windsor, and again everyone was rushed downtown to a television studio where Nixon taped an interview. Leave the airplane behind and on by bus to Chatham, where there was only a grass strip airport and consequently no certainty that the DC-3 could land. A speech at Chatham to Liberal workers. Back into the bus and out into the country to talk to a meeting of farmers. On to Brant County to drop Nixon at his farm, Cinderella-like, a few moments before midnight struck. But the bus did not turn into a pumpkin and the reporters and Nixon's aides were finally delivered to Toronto in the early hours of the morning.

Nixon generally had a group of four aides with him. Ontario Liberal Party President Jean Richard travelled along with him on much of the campaign. From his office Nixon had his executive assistant John Morritt, a speech writer, and a secretary. Even though Nixon had more people with him than did Lewis, the organization was not as efficient as that of the NDP leader.

In comparison to the other two, Davis's tour was a regal progression through Ontario. Lewis and Nixon made forays out into the province from Toronto. Davis packed bag and baggage, bands, aides, reporters, and photographers into a convoy made up of two coaches and a mobile canteen truck and set off for an extended expedition.

In the first coach travelled the Premier and his wife Kathy. Davis's coach, which had been equipped with a changing room and office space, housed the Premier and his retinue, which was considerable. There was Brian Armstrong, Davis's personal aide and a former assistant to National Conservative Party director Liam O'Brien; Paul Weed, on-the-road tour director; David MacLeod, who worked in Davis's office and who was the son of former Communist MPP Alex MacLeod; Tom Campbell, a senior official in the Cabinet office, who was Davis's liaison man for all government business. There was an OPP bodyguard for the Premier, a few secretaries, a six-piece brass band named "Jalopy", and on various occasions a bevy of young girls who would get off the bus before Davis at any stopping point to whip up enthusiasm in the crowd.

With so many people in the Davis entourage it is not surprising that the reporters were put in a separate bus. The main feature of the press bus was a well-equipped bar which functioned at all hours, in defiance of Ontario's liquor laws. At the beginning of the campaign the Press Gallery asked Davis to make Don Beeney, his press officer, the press aide on the tour. The reason was that Beeney, who had been a Canadian Press reporter, was the only person around the Premier who understood reporters and how they worked. Beeney was a civil servant, but he was given a leave of absence for the duration of the campaign. With Beeney was Doug Caldwell, a Conservative party volunteer whose regular work was in an employment agency that specialized in finding people of executive calibre for industries and businesses. But Caldwell had a function other than assisting Beeney. He was also there to listen to what the reporters were saying about their reactions to Davis and the campaign, and to report back to Paul Weed in the Davis bus.

Despite the panoply surrounding Davis, the Premier said remarkably little to capture the imagination during the campaign. His tour was rigorous in the extreme, but it seemed to consist of movement that had no function other than to present the person of the Premier before remarkably unenthusiastic—and generally small—crowds of people in cities, towns, and villages across the province. Nothing appeared to be happening. Davis made the same speech several times a day, day after day. After a while he seemed to be almost sleepwalking, isolating himself from the monotonous repetitiveness of what he had to do each day. A system had been determined on which the tour and Davis's actions were organized, and he stuck to it to the letter, just putting himself in the hands of the organization and being borne along by its momentum. Davis undoubtedly met and talked with many thousands more voters than did either Lewis or Nixon, which was important, but the major tactical strikes of the Davis campaign were not made out on the tour. Whenever he had something important to announce he flew back to Toronto.

There is a tremendous advantage in an election campaign in being the government party. The Conservatives used that advantage sparingly, but with consummate authority. They used it to demonstrate that they were the government, that they were continuing to govern, that they considered all this business of the other parties being viable alternatives to be hogwash, and that the Liberals and New Democrats were making irresponsible promises.

On October 7 Davis broke into his tour to return to Toronto and present a position paper he intended to put before a federal-provincial conference on the economy that was planned for the fall. It was a fairly tough document that continued Ontario's battle of words with Ottawa over taxes and shared programs. At the same time Davis announced a winter works program aimed at creating 41,800 jobs, at a cost of $93 million. The proposal included personal income tax cuts, grants to municipalities for capital expenditures, stepped-up provincial government public works programs and increased building by the Ontario Housing Corporation. And that wasn't all. Davis said his government was proceeding with plans to create a new 1,500-acre park at Bronte Creek, west of Toronto, which would be linked to the metropolitan centre by the Go Train system.

The advantage of being the government was apparent the next day when the newspapers came out with the stories all over the front pages. Statements by the opposition parties on their plans for employment, federal-provincial relations, and parks could not have had that impact.

Davis's use of this advantage was to be expected. What he did on October 13 was not. On that day he again made a side trip to the press conference studio at Queen's Park and announced that the various promises made by the Liberals and New Democrats during the course of the campaign would cost the provincial taxpayers over $2 billion a year. The Liberals, Davis said, had made campaign promises that would cost $2.165 billion and the NDP's proposals would cost $2.227 billion. In order to pay for their proposals, he said, the Liberals, for example, would have to double personal and corporate taxation, double the retail sales tax and add 3¢ a gallon to the gasoline tax. That was a fairly heavy blow, but apparently acceptable. What was unacceptable about it was that under questioning from reporters Davis admitted that these figures had been prepared, not by the Conservative party, but by the Treasury Board of the government. It had not been party workers who had drawn up this statement, but civil servants paid by the public. When asked how he justified using civil servants for a clearly political purpose Davis's lame reply was that as government leader it was his responsibility to make the public aware of the cost of programs, no matter who proposed them.

Nixon and Lewis squealed with rage at Davis's statement, but it was too late. The public's concern over the Premier's misuse of his office was more than outweighed by concern over unemployment, rising prices, and the threat of increased taxation.

On October 15 Davis announced a cut in the rate of provincial income tax.

The Toronto Star published an opinion poll on October 16, five days before polling day, which showed that the Conservatives with 45 per cent had a commanding lead over the Liberals and New Democrats, who each had 27 per cent of the popular support.

On October 17 Davis announced that a reorganization of the provincial government would take place after the election, to make it more efficient and more responsive to the needs of the people.

The same day *The Star* published the results of another poll which showed that the Conservatives had achieved their objective. Of the three party leaders, Davis had become the voters' favourite.

On October 20, the day before polling day, the province's old age pensioners received confirmation in the post that their Medicare coverage would be free from January 1, 1972. Farmers had already received their property tax rebate cheques. In subsequent years the government has found it impossible to get these cheques out until much later in the year.

The moves made by Davis in the last few days of the campaign were grand full-scale assaults in their overall electoral campaign. But behind the scenes, individual campaigns had been going in the 117 ridings across the province. In many of them what Davis did was of crucial importance; there, by virtue of the strength of the Liberal and NDP candidates and the Davis-oriented material supplied by the Candidate Service Centre, the Tory candidates' fortunes were tied to those of the Premier. But in that sweep of ridings from Toronto east to the Ottawa Valley, and in a number of others dotted here and there, the election was fought in a way that had nothing much to do with Ad Hoc and the slick commercials, the trendy songs, the expensive complex polls.

Those eastern seats were bound to the Conservatives by paternalism as much as history, by jobs as much as philosophy, by the beneficence of the Conservative member as much as his ability as a legislator. Hastings riding was a good example, but the story could have been repeated in Frontenac-Addington, Renfrew South, Lanark, Grenville-Dundas, Glengarry and Prescott-Russell, and other ridings. Clarke Rollins, 59 years old, had been the Conservative member from Hastings riding (which runs north from the Bay of Quinte almost to Madawaska) for over a decade, yet the records of the Legislature noted only an occasional question or speech in the House. Even in the more cosy surroundings of the legislative committees Rollins spoke seldom. The record of his accomplishments was to be found not in *Hansard* but out in Hastings, and it was seen in the miles of paved highways, in the number of people who worked one way or another for the provincial government, in the thousands of voters who relied on Rollins to "fix" things for them, and in the sure bond between the Conservative party and the local municipal governments.

Hastings' early prosperity in timber and minerals was gone and had not been replaced by other industry. There was farming, but only patches of the soil were productive; much of the scrub landscape was pock-marked with the stark grey rocks of the Canadian Shield thrusting through the thin topsoil. Clarke Rollins and his predecessors had moved to find jobs for those for whom there was no other work. Now the provincial government was by far the riding's largest employer, through Ministries like Lands and Forests, and Highways, right down the line to agencies like the school boards and Ontario Hydro. These jobs paid better and offered more security than could be expected elsewhere in the riding. Throughout the riding people said that Clarke Rollins had helped them or a friend of theirs get one of these jobs.

Faith in Rollins' ability to produce was the source of his heroic stature among the people of his riding. Even simple everyday things like truck licences were requested through Clarke Rollins, whose proven dexterity at "fixing" things would doubtless be necessary. The fact that many of the permits and services requested through Rollins were the people's natural right was unimportant. "Clarke" knew how to deal with those people at Queen's Park. "Clarke" would get it done. Which, of course, he did—and in the process put himself in an unassailable position as the riding's member. He had never had another Conservative try to wrest the nomination from him, and the Liberals and New Democrats only put up token candidates against him. Often they had a tough time finding someone in the riding willing to run against him.

So pessimistic were the Liberals about the chances of their candidate, Ian Munro, that they gave him the grand sum of $1,500 to fight the campaign. Munro confessed that he could count on only 20 votes each from the riding's larger towns of Tweed, Deseronto, Bancroft, and Stirling. He was even having difficulty getting enumerators, who were paid 10¢ a name, while Rollins' problem was how to tactfully say "no" to the flood of volunteers going to him for these jobs. Donald Hodgins, owner of a feed mill, was finance chairman for Munro, and found that it was hurting his business. Hodgins joined the Liberals shortly before the election and found it did nothing for his standing in the community. "I even had one fellow tell me I didn't respect the memory of my father," he said. Hodgins' father was an active Conservative.

The power of the mythology was great, but far more pervasive in political terms was the unity between local government and the Conservative party. Rollins' campaign manager was Kenneth Smith, the county warden and president of Hastings Conservative Association. In Deseronto, the reeve, George Lyons, was also president of the town's Conservatives. The reeve of the township of Tyendinaga doubled as president of the township Conservative association. Where the municipal officials and politicians weren't active Conservatives they were certainly supporters of Rollins. William Shannon, clerk-treasurer of the village of Marmora, told a reporter about the $500,000 in special provincial grants the village had received through Rollins' aid. Jack Brown, reeve of Bancroft, talked about how Rollins persuaded the government to change a "silly law" which stopped the school board from paying the costs of hooking into the Bancroft sewer system.

Rollins' control over municipal government was important, partly because it brought to his side all the influential people in each locality, and also because it kept the succession in his hands. Municipal politics in the Tory belt was the breeding ground for provincial politicians. That was where the new Conservative MPPs were going to come from and, of course, the Opposition candidates, if any. Every one of the 34 members of the Hastings County Council signed Rollins' nomination papers for the election.

It may come as no surprise therefore to learn that Rollins' campaign owed little to Ad Hoc or the new election technology. "We don't have interference from headquarters or anywhere. It's always been that way. It's always been an independent Clarke Rollins campaign," Rollins said. So the big event of the campaign in Deseronto was a card party, and in the Clarke Rollins election committee rooms in that town they didn't bother to put in a telephone until the last week of the campaign. Rollins himself just drove around the riding renewing old acquaintances. That was really all that was needed.

Robert Teetor's polls for the Conservatives had indicated that the voters, including that crucial 23 per cent who might vote either Liberal or Conservative, wanted strong leadership that would take the province through the current period of economic turbulence. Making Davis the essence of the Conservative campaign had dealt with the leadership aspect of the problem. The Premier's announcements in the last half of the campaign dealt with the rest. Davis was making concrete proposals to Ottawa about management of the economy. Davis was putting forward schemes to combat anticipated high unemployment levels over the coming winter. Davis was showing how ill equipped the Opposition parties were to take over government. Davis was so adept at economic management that he was able to propose an income tax cut. By October 21 the message had sunk in. Keep on going the way you've been going. Don't get embroiled with those socialists and Stephen Lewis, who has a lean, hungry look and thinks too much. Davis will make it go. Come on Ontario.

There was a heavy turnout at the polls on voting day. Seventy-three per cent of the qualified electors voted, a percentage unmatched since Mitch Hepburn's first victory in 1934. Within an hour of the polls closing in the early evening it was apparent that there was something of a sweep for the Tories. The final results gave them 78 seats, an increase of 10. The Liberals dropped 7 seats to 20. The NDP dropped 2 to 19. The Conservatives had increased their share of the popular vote to 44.5 per cent, more than 2 points up on 1967. The Liberal vote had declined from 32 per cent in 1967 to 27.75 per cent. But the New Democrats vote had increased from 26 per cent to 27.15. Obviously, the Tories had captured that essential Liberal-Conservative switch vote. They had also cut the New Democrats' number of seats, but the NDP had actually increased its base of popular support. In terms of seats, the Tories' anti-NDP drive had worked, but the

New Democrats had continued to build support.

The Liberals were the big losers. Their proportional loss in seats was more than the NDP, and their share of the popular vote dropped to a low point it hadn't touched for nearly fifty years. Whereas in 1967 they had been second in 60 of the seats they didn't win, in this election they were second in only 44.

A look at the map showed just how bad the Liberal position was. The Conservatives won 5 of their 10 additional seats in Metro Toronto. The big losers were the Liberals, whose representation in Toronto was cut from 6 seats to 3. Only Philip Givens, former Mayor of Toronto and an Ottawa MP, was able to stem the tide by beating a strong Tory candidate, Barry Lowes, in a close contest in the Conservative riding of York-Forest Hill. The Liberals lost seats in northern Ontario, too, to both the Tories and the NDP. Otherwise the Liberals' only significant gain was in Ottawa East, where a young lawyer, Albert Roy, defeated the sitting Conservative. But, over all, the Liberals had been driven back into their homeland of agricultural southwestern Ontario. In this region they did well. They didn't gain seats, in fact they lost 2, but their majorities in each of the ridings that they won increased considerably over 1967. The explanation offered by the Liberals for this trend was that where the voters were determined to squash the NDP and the Liberal MPP was strong, they voted for him instead of the Conservative.

Though the NDP had increased its share of the popular vote, they were down on aggregate 2 seats over 1967 and they hadn't supplanted the Liberals as official opposition party. Two of their most notable losses were Peterborough, where Walter Pitman, Lewis's challenger for the leadership, was defeated, and the union town of Oshawa where Clifford Pilkey was defeated by the Conservative candidate. The NDP also lost Middlesex South, outside London, which they had picked up in the 1969 by-election. Again, the Tories won. Up north the signs were better for the NDP. They had held Sudbury East before, but they won another 2 seats in the Sudbury area, one from the Liberals and one from the Conservatives. The mining, heavily unionized Nickel Belt region became an NDP enclave. The New Democrats also picked up a seat at Port Arthur riding in Thunder Bay, this one from a renegade Liberal who two years previously had decided to sit as an independent. They had kept their hold in the Windsor area, despite determined Tory efforts to shove them out. In Toronto they had lost two seats and gained one, though their margins of victory were generally considerably less than some of the massive pluralities chalked up by the Tories. Dalton Bales, in York Mills, for example, won his seat with a plurality of 23,000 votes.

The Conservatives had lost only two sitting members; Gaston Demers lost to the NDP in Nickel Belt riding, and Jules Morin was defeated by the Liberal Albert Roy in Ottawa East. Of the 26 seats in Metro Toronto, the Conservatives won 16, an impressive showing. The Tory Belt stood firm. In the west they gained seats in Niagara, Brantford, Middlesex South, Oxford County. In the east, with the NDP losing Peterborough and Oshawa, the view from the Scarborough Bluffs to Ottawa was now completely uninterrupted by anything but Tory blue.

The victory stunned the Conservatives with joy. The Tory party had again made their new leader victorious at the polls, and they had introduced a new political technology to Ontario politics. Moreover, the system of polls, sophisticated advertising, and complex campaign organization had been cleverly blended with the older electioneering practices in ridings such as Hastings.

They had countered the threat of a massive canvassing campaign by the New Democrats with a hefty canvass of their own in urban ridings. The NDP tenet that everything would fall into their hands if the canvassing campaign were only big enough had been exposed as a myth. But the NDP campaign had been partly defused because the Tories engaged in door-to-door canvassing on a large scale themselves. The belief of Camp, Atkins, and the supporters of Allan Lawrence that the Conservatives must become a popular party that encourages the involvement of its grass-roots members had been proved correct.

The mobilization of large numbers of Conservative party members was the most admirable aspect of the Tories' campaign. Other features were not so laudable. The importation from the United States of massive advertising as a major component of the campaign was perhaps the most nauseating innovation. Pap advertising for commercial reasons is offensive enough. Presenting a bar of soap or a cigarette as a harbinger of Spring, or Love, or Happiness is dishonest and manipulative. Using the same techniques to sell one particular man is equally dishonest. In the United States, under the Presidential system, this procedure may have some faint pretensions to be linked with reality. But it is a denial of all the basic assumptions of the Canadian political system.

The ultimate political authority in Ontario is not the Premier, or even the government; it is the Legislature, the assembly of all the elected representatives of the voters. The Premier holds that post because he leads the party that has the support of the majority of members of the Legislature. In elections there has always been a strong element of voting for party leaders, but even in 1971 a considerable number of seats were won or lost because of the qualities of the candidates in those ridings. Nonetheless, the trend towards adulation of the leader–the all-powerful Presidential figure–was marked, and it was emphasized by advertising.

Advertising cannot, perhaps, change someone's character, but when used in politics it is extremely selective in the qualities it chooses to present to the public. Thus, Stephen Lewis was presented in advantageous lighting. Thus, William Davis hardly said a word on camera because his tongue-tied discomfort would have been obvious, and something of the insularity of the man would have come through. Instead, by songs and showmanship, the good qualities were accentuated and puffed up, and only a partial picture was presented. Political advertising may not be dishonest, but it is certainly open to being badly misleading. Moreover, the men and women who engage in political advertising are generally people from the advertising industry whose trade is selling, whose skill is manipulative subliminal persuasion, and whose tool is appealing to stereotypes.

One of the more serious implications of massive advertising campaigns is the cost involved. The Conservatives' need for money to pay for the campaign led them down a number of roads which were conducive neither to the internal health of the party nor to public confidence that the government acted without favour to those who had shown it friendship by making donations to the party. This was to be one of the most serious problems that Davis would have to contend with in the coming two years.

But for the moment he and the Conservatives were on top of the world. He could now fashion the party and the government to his liking, change personnel, methods, and institutions to his taste. The future was not so rosy for Bob Nixon and Stephen Lewis; uneasy lies the head that fails the crown.

15. To the Victor . . .

The change that came over William Davis after the election was remarkable. Previously, the high pressure sales techniques of the Tory campaign had reduced Davis to the status of a commodity. They removed his personality and his authority, while his control over events seemed negligible. In the eyes of the press and the Opposition Davis still bore the cross of the near-failure at the leadership convention, and the thought that Davis was a surrogate for the party establishment, and barely acceptable to many Conservatives, lingered. But the election result wiped Davis's record clean within the Tory party and the government. He was now the undisputed master, and he quickly set about demonstrating an uncompromising and sometimes ruthless determination to have his house decorated to his liking.

In the months following the election, practically everyone and everything in the Tory party and the government changed. In the party the remaining Robarts warhorses were ousted and Davis's new allies installed. In government the committee investigating productivity and efficiency produced its recommendations for a new organization, which were quickly implemented. Davis's own office grew like Topsy. The only area where there was not an immediate and extensive change of staff was in the Cabinet. Davis needed to keep the experienced Cabinet members on through the turbulent period of the reorganization of the government.

A cynic might be forgiven for curling his lip and remarking that the first months of 1972 were pay-out time for Davis; the time when he repaid his political friends. The number of them who obtained important and often lucrative jobs with the party and the government was certainly impressive. But the cynic might have a better case if all the jobs were sinecures, which they were not.

Ross DeGeer, for example, took over as executive director of the provincial Conservative party on January 1, 1972, replacing Arthur Harnett. DeGeer, a young stockbroker and former president of the Albany Club, was a veteran of the Stanfield federal leadership campaign, and of Allan Lawrence's provincial leadership bid. He had planned and organized Davis's tour during the 1971 election and was more suited to Davis's tastes in party management than was Harnett, who had been the appointee of Alan Eagleson, the party president. (Eagleson had been able to snatch the presidency because Robarts didn't much care what was happening down at party headquarters, and couldn't be bothered to prevent it.) DeGeer was a devout Tory with that Red tinge to his politics which characterized the Camp-Atkins group. He earnestly believed in the need to decentralize the strength of the party and to maintain the activity of the riding associations between elections. While some Conservatives, generally those who had been ousted in the post-election shuffle, felt that DeGeer was too idealistic and lacked political realism, no one tried to suggest he was a time-server.

Equally, Michael Gee, who during the election campaign had worked on preparing and writing press releases for the Tories, was appointed head of the caucus research office at Queen's Park. This office, which prepared speeches and information for the Tory backbenchers, had been markedly non-political. Davis wanted to beef up the quality of the work the office produced and to have close ties between it and party headquarters. Richard Canney, from McConnell Advertising Ltd., who had run the Candidate Service Centre during the election, also got a job in the caucus office, as communications coordinator. But none of these jobs could be considered pay-offs. For one thing, all three men would have commanded higher salaries in business than they received for these jobs. For another, they all worked hard.

The situation was not so clear-cut with some of the other appointments. In April, 1972, Ward Cornell was named Ontario's Agent-General in London, England. Cornell, famous among sports fans as a commentator for "Hockey Night in Canada", had a record of political service to Davis. He worked on publicity for Davis in the leadership campaign and was involved with Michael Gee during the election in preparing and writing press releases. Cornell also managed the election campaign of John White in London, Ontario, Cornell's home town. After the election White was named Minister of Industry and Tourism, which was the department which oversaw the work of the Agent-General and Ontario House in London, England. And, by a striking coincidence, shortly thereafter the government announced that the best person in the whole world for the job of Agent-General was none other than Ward Cornell. Allan Rowan-Legg, the man who inconveniently held the job at the time, was fired, given healthy severance pay of $35,000, and his expenses of $7,000 to return to Toronto were paid by the government. The job of Agent-General was not a particularly arduous one and the pay was reasonable, over $30,000 a year at the time, as well as offering a liberal expense account. The Agent-General was, in point of fact, Ontario's ambassador in Britain, and the emphasis was on his role as an emissary of good will.

There was a certain smack of patronage also to another appointment through the Ministry of Industry and Tourism early in 1972. This Ministry had by far the largest advertising account in the government, which was understandable, since it sought to extol the province's virtues as both a place to work and a place to play. In the past there had been some division of the advertising work among a number of companies, with Baker Lovick BBDO Ltd. having the largest share. It had inherited this work when it took over James Lovick Advertising, an old Tory company with links to Davis since some of the staff had worked for him in the leadership campaign. But the Baker Lovick people had been completely cut out of the election campaign by Norman Atkins, and early in 1972 they were cut out of the Industry and Tourism account also. The account, worth $1.25 million in work, was given to Camp Associates, Atkins' company. The following year the account was worth $2 million in work.

There were two sets of mildly extenuating circumstances for this blatant piece of favouritism. The company that had taken over James Lovick Advertising was American-dominated, which perhaps made it an inappropriate spokesman for Ontario's dreams. Secondly, Camp Associates did have extensive experience in tourism advertising for the province of New Brunswick, whose Premier, Robert Hatfield, was a pal of Camp and Atkins. The Camp Associates offices housed the Toronto New Brunswick tourist office. But the observer might be forgiven for wondering whether the Maritime practice of fighting elections to see who gets the tourism ministry account had not been introduced to Ontario.

Other jobs were taken on for reasons of pure altruism. Fund-raiser William Kelly, for example, became at the beginning of 1972 the full-time unpaid bagman for the Conservatives. But we shall hear more of Mr. Kelly's exploits later.

One of Ross DeGeer's first moves as executive director of the party was to increase the size of the headquarters staff in their offices above the Press Club on Richmond Street. Paul Weed left his debt collection agency to become DeGeer's assistant. Ray Parry, who had directed film crews for much of the advertising footage taken for the election campaign, was taken on as an adviser on the use of film, particularly by the riding associations. There was also an information and research director, a youth director, a provincial organizer, a Toronto organizer, and someone dealing with women's groups in the party. The total complement was twelve, whereas it had varied between four and six at the end of Robarts' time.

Meanwhile much more profound and extensive changes were taking place up the road at Queen's Park. On December 23, 1969, Robarts had established the Committee on Government Productivity, forever thereafter known as COGP. The terms of reference required the committee members to "inquire into all matters pertaining to the management of the government of Ontario and to make such recommendations as in its opinion will improve the efficiency and the effectiveness of the Government of Ontario". Robarts, the management man, had become increasingly concerned that the existing organization of the government was unable to deal with the complex planning that a large and multi-faceted government in the 1970s was going to have to do. There appeared to him to be too little co-ordination, too much vertical structure in the government and not enough horizontal communication, and too much reliance by Ministers on the thinking of senior civil servants. The COGP was made up of five top civil servants and five businessmen. Robarts hoped that the businessmen would tell the government how it ought to be running things and that the civil servants would temper those thoughts with the knowledge of how governments actually have to work.

The committee members made up an impressive collection of public and corporate muscle. To chair the committee Robarts chose John B. Cronyn, senior vice-president of the London brewing company of John Labatt Ltd. Cronyn was also on the board of numerous other companies ranging in their endeavours from selling insurance to constructing buildings. Cronyn, whose home base was Robarts' riding of London North, was a friend of the Premier's and also a good Conservative. The other business executives were C. C. Hay, a director of Gulf Oil; G. R. Heffernan, president of Co-Steel International Ltd.; A. Powis, president of Noranda Mines Ltd.; and R. D. Wolfe, president of the Oshawa Group Ltd. The civil servants were the secretary to the Treasury Board, the secretary to the Cabinet, the deputy Attorney-General, the deputy Treasurer, and the deputy minister in the office of the Premier. To act as executive director to the committee Cronyn hired a young self-made millionaire who was teaching business administration at York University named James Fleck.

Over a period of three years (from 1969 to 1973) the COGP produced ten reports dealing with every facet of government operations. The committee spawned junior committees and task forces which dealt with side issues. It touched everything, and when it had finished nothing remained unchanged. The report on which everything else pivoted was report number three, which dealt with the fundamental organization of the government and the Cabinet. This report was made public by Premier Davis on December 10, 1971, together with a statement that the bulk of the recommendations were being accepted by the government and would be speedily introduced.

In analysing the government organization the committee found essentially what Robarts had suspected. The vertical lines of authority through each Ministry up to Cabinet were inefficient. They did not allow for co-ordinated planning between Ministries with touching interests, such as the Ministries of Health and Social and Family Services, many of whose clientele among the public were obviously the same people. Ministers didn't have sufficient time to give thorough consideration to proposals coming to them from civil servants or presented to them collectively as the Cabinet. They were far too susceptible to the ministrations of forceful civil servants who, if they knew how to get around their Minister, could get practically anything approved.

In this context, the committee did not use this example, but it was obviously thinking of things like Ontario Place, which started off as an $11-million park on Toronto's waterfront with a few added attractions and ended up as a $35-million extravaganza of futuristic fun and frolic. It speedily ran the gauntlet from the reasonable to the absurd, largely because the Minister responsible at the time, Stanley Randall, himself a man of unbridled enthusiasms, was susceptible to the enthusiasm of the civil servant in charge of the project, James Ramsay. And when Randall went to the Cabinet he was able to silver-tongue them into accepting the project because none of them had the time or the information to really question what was being proposed. Once the project had been accepted in principle it developed an irresistible momentum of its own. So the Cabinet ended up with a scheme that cost over three times what they had first imagined—and which would also be unprofitable and require them to fork out from $1.5 million to $2 million each year to keep it going. Such was the price of rubber stamping.

Instead of each Minister going into the Cabinet room each Wednesday morning to push his own pet project, the COGP proposed a rounded organization for communication, policy and program consideration, and planning. The committee said that Ministries with related or overlapping responsibilities should be grouped together in policy fields, and that each policy field should be headed by a Minister whose job would be to consider the overall policy directions of the group. These policy Ministers, called Provincial Secretaries, would chair the weekly policy group meetings and would also be the groups' representatives on the Policy and Priorities Board of Cabinet.

This board, chaired by the Premier, was to be the group that looked furthest into the future and chose general policy directions. The board was to comprise the Premier, the Treasurer, the Provincial Secretary for Resources Development, the Provincial Secretary for Justice Policy, the Provincial Secretary for Social Development, and the chairman of the Management Board. The Management Board was another Cabinet committee whose basic job was to decide whether the province could afford the various program and policy proposals being made.

The Justice Policy field was to include the Attorney-General, the Solicitor-General, the Minister of Correctional Services, and the Minister of Consumer and Corporate Affairs. In the Social Development field were the Ministers of Health, Education, Universities and Colleges, and Social and Family Services. The largest was the Resources Development field which included the Ministers of Agriculture, Environment, Labour, Industry and Tourism, Transportation and Communication, and Natural Resources.

The only point where Davis really fell out with the committee was over the area of finance and intergovernmental affairs. The committee felt that this too should be made into a policy field, including perhaps the Treasurer, Minister of Housing, Revenue Minister, and Minister of Intergovernmental Affairs. Davis said no. Instead, control of the treasury, intergovernmental affairs and planning were all put into one mammoth Ministry. Revenue was kept separate.

This arrangement appeared to be a great improvement over the lack of organization that existed previously. It should have meant, for one thing, that any particular proposal had been considered by most of the Ministers from a number of points of view by the time it came to Cabinet for final approval. The system should have meant that the Ministers were constantly made aware of the broader implications of what they were doing. It should have meant economy, because there was less chance of a flighty program getting through the net. At the time of writing it is still too soon to judge the ultimate success or failure of the system, although Davis has been forced to admit that it had some flaws, particularly with regard to the position of the policy secretaries. The one general criticism that might be levelled at the system is that it lacks political sensitivity. There were, after all, no politicians on the COGP. This deficiency was most evident in the position of the policy secretaries, and it was the role of these men that sparked the most opposition, as well as the most interest among the press and the public at the time.

On January 5, 1972, in a ceremony so anti-climactic that even Davis didn't bother to break into his Florida holiday to turn up, the three provincial secretaries and the Treasurer were sworn in by the Lieutenant-Governor. Davis did talk to them briefly on the telephone before the ceremony, but that was all. As it turned out, the absence of Davis, the lack of feeling that this was a state occasion of some moment, was prophetic. Everyone had guessed after the announcement of the COGP report who the provincial secretaries would be. They were Davis's leadership rivals. Allan Lawrence was the Justice Secretary, Robert Welch was the Social Development Secretary, Bert Lawrence was the Resources Development Secretary, and Darcy McKeough was the Minister of Treasury, Economics and Intergovernmental Affairs. Quickly these men were dubbed "super Ministers". Davis appeared to have abandoned the usual practice of quickly disembowelling the rivals for the throne. The "super Minister" argument said that because these men were on the ostensibly powerful Policy and Priorities Board they would have a great deal to say about the overall planning and direction of government. COGP protested that as chairmen of the policy groups the policy secretaries would only be first among equals and would not have any extra authority, but this was not believed. These men, it was felt, would be directing their groups of ministries with strong hands.

The counter argument, which turned out to be the right one, said that Davis had politically emasculated his leadership rivals by making them policy ministers. They would have no administrative responsibilities, which meant they would never be in the public eye, never feed on the publicity which is a politician's life-blood. The truth of this view became apparent as soon as the new session of the House began. Allan Lawrence, Bert Lawrence, and Robert Welch, previously among the most visible Ministers in question period and out on the speaker's platforms of the province, were never heard. At first the Opposition members tried to ask them questions, but they were told in reply either that the question was too specific and should be re-directed to the line Minister involved, or that the question involved policy which had not yet been determined. After a few weeks no one bothered to ask them anything any more. They just sat there–or didn't bother to go into the House much at all. Within two years Allan Lawrence and Bert Lawrence had disappeared from the scene altogether. Welch survived only by getting out of his job as Policy Secretary and back into a Ministry with administrative responsibility.

Darcy McKeough's new job didn't quite fit into the pattern of the others. There he was, the Minister of Treasury, Economics and Intergovernmental Affairs; COGP had recommended that this be three Ministries and here it was one with McKeough sitting atop it. Welch and the two Lawrences might have gone to their political graves, but McKeough seemed to be in a very powerful position. Some observers saw McKeough's empire as the reward for that moment in the Maple Leaf Gardens on February 12, 1971, when he pinned on a Davis button. Whatever the motives behind the appointment, McKeough was quite clearly the number two man. One or two reporters in the Press Gallery equated McKeough's position with that of Robert Macaulay after the 1961 leadership convention. Macaulay had also managed three Ministries, been the lightning rod of the government—and had burned himself out in the process. Perhaps McKeough also would burn himself out? It didn't quite happen in the Macaulay pattern, but McKeough did come perilously close to self-immolation.

The reorganization of the government troubled the Liberals and the New Democrats. They felt that the integrated, specialized planning and policy development that it envisaged would completely cut the ground away from under the Opposition. They argued that they had no resources to enable them to do their legitimate job of questioning government proposals and producing their own suggestions. They questined whether efficiency and the profit ethic should be the main goals of government. Governments existed to serve people, not to follow the practices of the business world. The COGP had emphasized the need for direct communication between the government and the people. This was to be one of the major tasks of the Policy Secretaries. The aim was a "responsive" government, aware of and flexible enough to cater to the needs of the people. This, the Opposition felt, undermined the role of the Legislature as the assembly of the representatives of the people and the rightful place for discussion of issues. If the government was going to by-pass the Legislature, that, they argued, was a denial of parliamentary democracy.

In order to counter the tremendous advantage in planning and information the reorganization would give the government, the Opposition held that the committees of the Legislature, which consider government proposals, must be given resources of their own. The committees should be able to hire expert staff to help them dissect the legislation and policies put before them. But the government, and Davis especially, showed marked reluctance to give the committees the kind of independence and authority the Liberals and NDP were asking for.

What was not apparent to either the Opposition or the government at the time was that the Conservative backbenchers were looking askance at the reorganization and wondering what it meant to them. If the role of the Opposition member was to be made more difficult by the new system, the role of the government backbencher was going to be doubly so. The backbenchers were already restricted in the effect they could have on government policy. The Opposition could at least argue their criticisms on the floor of the House and in the committees. The Tory backbenchers could speak their piece privately in the Conservative caucus meetings and by button-holing Ministers in the corridors. But in the House or in committees party discipline took over and they had to keep quiet about any reservations they might have about what the government was doing. The reorganization indicated to many of them that the government would look for their advice less and less.

This willingness on the part of the Tory backbenchers to demonstrate to the government that they had something to contribute to what went on at Queen's Park was of great importance in the early spring of 1972. The backbenchers' opportunity to remind the government of their existence came at the end of March when *The Globe and Mail* published a series of articles about the Workmen's Compensation Board. The articles contained reports of some sensational charges. A company liable for a penalty levy (imposed by the Board because it had a poor safety record) had had the levy dropped. This had happened after the company had scuttled a lobby by a number of firms to get certain practices by the Board altered. Another, quite separate, charge was that a member of the three-man governing board of the WCB had been pressured into retiring early and paid off with $60,000.

The government could not ignore the stories, and the matter was sent for investigation to the Committee on Resources Development, whose responsibilities included scrutiny of the Ministry of Labour and the Workmen's Compensation Board. The first meeting of the committee was held simply to decide how they were going to approach the subject and how wide-ranging their inquiry would be. Representation on the committees was always in the same proportion as in the House, so that Conservatives had a good majority. The Opposition members went with the idea of getting a free-wheeling and wide investigation of what was happening down at the Board, but their hopes were not high.

Past experience was that in any investigation of affairs that might be embarrassing to the government, the Tory majority on the committees managed to contain the extent of the investigation and even limit the inquiry. So it was with some surprise at that first meeting that the Opposition members realized that their broad proposals were not going to be restrained by the Conservatives.

The method of procedure accepted by the Conservative backbenchers was so unstructured that when they came to hear evidence, the first meeting was chaotic. Witnesses were allowed to make the most wild and unsubstantiated charges, no transcript was kept, and there was no logical questioning. On top of that, the committee had decided that television film cameras would be allowed into the committee room for the first time, and reporters could use tape-recorders, also a first. That evening the whole mess was shown in living colour in hundreds of thousands of living rooms across the province. But it didn't look like a mess on the television screen. The viewers only saw former Board member Jack Cauley alleging that he had been bought off, that there had been blackmail at the Board, and that false affidavits had been sworn out by Board employees in an effort to incriminate him.

Davis had to step in. But it was too late for him to restrict the committee's chosen path. The charges had been made in open session, and if Davis had tried to get the Conservative members to curtail the investigation it would have looked as though the government was trying to hide its guilt. The only thing Davis could do was agree to the committee's request that they be allowed to hire a lawyer to conduct the questioning of witnesses in an orderly manner, to assemble the evidence, and generally to bring some courtroom decorum and sanity to the proceedings. It was an important precedent. The Legislative Committees could not be as confined again as they had been, and they had established their right to investigate matters before them as extensively as they chose. The committee heard evidence ten hours a day for seven weeks. They found that there was no substance to some of the more sensational charges made by Mr. Cauley, but they did find that conditions at the Workmen's Compensation

Board were deplorable, and that a complete re-assessment of its role and organization was essential.

To the Victor

The establishment that the Tory backbenchers felt the need to challenge was the Premier's office. In the year of Davis's occupancy, it had changed out of all recognition from the compact cluster of rooms maintained by John Robarts. It had become a doughy body that oozed through the whole eastern end of Queen's Park, flopping daily into new rooms. As soon as it was contained it burst out again, rolling down new corridors, up new staircases, through new doors. A new world of busy administration was being created, all to help Davis do his job. While before the election the emphasis in Davis's office had been on politics, in the fall of 1971 the emphasis changed to administration. There was some politics still, but now the administrators had the power. Davis's gaze was fixed on what he was going to do with the government now it was firmly in his hands, and he put politics away on a shelf. With the politics went the need to daily maintain contact with such people as the backbenchers. A period of self-imposed isolation set in for Davis.

The growth of Davis's office was quite astounding. John Robarts, in his last year in office, spent $350,262. The estimate for Davis's first year was nearly double that, $658,000, and in 1972 he asked for $995,000. A month before he stepped down Robarts had a staff of 38 people, of whom 12 were in the executive category. Those people served not only Robarts, but also the Cabinet. The equivalent figure for Davis in the spring of 1972 was 85. Fifty-three of those people were in Davis's own office and 32 served the Cabinet. Robarts had had 12 people at the executive level; Davis had 30 in all.

What is more, those figures for the Cabinet do not include the staff for the provincial secretaries, which were considered part of the Cabinet complement. This would add another 35 people to the list.

Altogether Davis had 120 people at an estimated cost in 1972 of $2,629,000 working in fundamentally the same areas as 38 people at a cost of $559,281 in 1970. The number of staff had increased three times and the cost five times over the two-year period.

Those bald figures aren't entirely fair, however. The introduction of the policy fields had greatly increased the number of things Cabinet was considering. The general increase in size and expense reflected the growth in the province and the greater demands on the Premier and the Cabinet. It may well be that Robarts was operating with less staff than he actually needed. Nonetheless, part of the growth was directly attributable to Davis's way of doing things; his management style. Davis was much more of a delegator than Robarts had been. Robarts felt happiest when working with a small, close-knit group of advisers. Davis needed a wider circle, both because he liked to receive information from a variety of sources and because by not giving his ear exclusively to one group he could maintain his authority.

To run the office, to be his chief executive officer, Davis hired James Fleck, the former executive director of the COGP. Fleck, 40 years old, understood the politics of administration well enough to know how to get his way in that area, but he had no experience and knew nothing about Queen's Park politics. The man who *did* know provincial politics, Clare Westcott, was none too pleased with the appointment of Fleck. Having battled with Davis all the way to the Premier's office, Westcott didn't like having to share the glory, and having to play second fiddle was irking in the extreme. Westcott's title was executive assistant, which anyone could see was something lower than chief executive officer; so a low-key, but persistent, running battle developed between Westcott and Fleck.

It was not that Westcott's influence had waned; it was just that Davis's interests had broadened. Westcott was still an important aide whose thoughts Davis solicited on many topics, and he relied on Westcott's network of contacts at all levels of the civil service and out in the province to provide information from a standpoint different from that which came up the regular pipelines of the civil service. But Fleck was in the more powerful position because he had control of the Premier's time and had a great deal of influence over whom Davis saw, what he did, and how he did it.

Now Davis hardly moved from his office without a bevy of courtiers in his wake. Robarts might on occasion have one or two assistants with him, but then it was only when necessary. When Davis even walked down the hall to the Legislative Chamber it was like a European court on the march, since he was seldom accompanied by fewer than three people. Generally they included one of his bodyguards (amiable young men who look and dress like junior business executives), his appointments secretary Brian Armstrong, and one of his press aides, normally Campbell Macdonald, the communications coordinator. In extreme cases the entourage could be vast, with eight or nine people in the train. The arrival of Davis by car at any function had the impact of an assault by a motorized infantry unit as all the doors of the line of cars opened, spilling out a host of followers. Davis might then be chatty, easy-going, and natural at the gathering, but he did not have the comfortable personality that would allow him to break through the forbidding impression made by his retinue. The sheer numbers of the people around him served to insulate him from the public and his own supporters. He placed himself psychologically apart because he felt most comfortable that way.

In Quebec the people didn't seem to mind their Premier assuming the trappings of royalty, of a head of state. Premier Robert Bourassa could whiz about in his jet plane accompanied by his personal hairdresser, a flamboyant bodyguard wearing a flashy suit and a very obvious revolver, and a host of other attendants. Quebeckers enjoyed seeing their Premier cutting a bit of a dash on the political scene. Ontarians didn't get the same joy from seeing Davis perform similar antics. The flaunting of the perquisites of power made them suspicious.

The decisive election win produced in Davis and some of those around him a dangerous degree of pride and political insensitivity. Even when the dangers of these feelings were shown him it took some time for him to recognize how important they were. It took even longer for him to respond.

The investigation of the Workmen's Compensation Board was the first pin-prick which began to deflate the bubble of pomposity among senior Conservatives after the election. Their arrogance was most often demonstrated in the House when they childishly chose to play what was known as "the numbers game". Ministers would put down serious Opposition criticisms or suggestions by sneering across the floor and reminding the Liberals and NDP that the Tories had 78 seats.

Davis himself displayed a tendency to use these heavy-handed, unpleasant tactics. One example occurred during the debate on the plans for the reorganization of government. Liberal leader Robert Nixon was deploring the effect it would have on the effectiveness of the Legislature, and warned Davis that he was going to have problems with the Opposition and his own backbenchers.

"Don't you wish you had that problem?" Davis jeered.

"I believe I could solve it better than you so far are attempting to solve it," Nixon retorted.

"We are going to solve it, but don't you wish you had it, Bob?" There was a touch of glee in Davis's voice at this point.

"That is one reason why Government should change on occasion—so that the feelings associated with complete confidence and the amiability of that everlasting smile are replaced with the idea that what we have is something less than perfect," Nixon bit back. An unbiased observer of the unpleasant scene would have found it hard to disagree with him.

But to a large degree Davis's Opposition was no longer the 39 Liberal and NDP members on the other side of the House. The large Tory majority had created a new Opposition force which was not so easy for him to deride, not so easy for him to deal with at all. It sat up in the Press Gallery.

16. The Press Gallery

When members of the public crossed the third-floor corridor and climbed the stairs up to the east public gallery at Queen's Park to watch their Legislature in action, they passed a nondescript door bearing a notice forbidding entry. Inside was the oldest blind pig in Ontario. The room was many things. It was most obviously a bar—a bar that operated without a licence for generations until the Speaker of the Legislature ruled that as it was within the precincts of the House it was under his charge, didn't need a licence, and would be exempt from the tribulations of having to get one. By formal title, however, the room was the Press Gallery lounge.

The most eye-catching piece of furniture in the room was a very large long table. It demanded attention not only for its size but also because even the extensive job of restoration that it had undergone could not disguise the fact that it was an aged and very battered table. It was a table that had played a large part in the lives and memories of most political reporters at Queen's Park for at least two generations. Over its broad beer-stained, cigarette-burned surface every political event of the past few decades had been mulled over, speculated about, worried at from this way and that, laughed about, groaned over. Countless Cabinet Ministers had sat with trusted reporters in the semi-privacy of the table's noisy surroundings and let slip tidbits of information which would find their way into the next day's newspapers.

The table was the place to which Minister's executive assistants went if they wanted to get some idea of what the Gallery was thinking. It was the place party hacks rushed to if they wanted to try and con some reporter into writing a story favourable to their party. That table, more than the gallery overlooking the Legislative Chamber, was the place around which the life of the Press Gallery revolved. It was the only place where the Gallery could be seen as a community with a common purpose to discover what was going on in the political world around it.

In the untidy offices around the lounge the reporters worked individually on their own jealously-guarded information, picking out on rickety typewriters their own judgments about what was news, what was important. In no sense did the Gallery present—in newspapers, by radio or television—a unified, common view of what had happened during the past twenty-four hours at Queen's Park. Even so, after the 1971 election a common unease spread through the Press Gallery; everyone there was uneasy about the size of the Conservative majority and about what it foretold.

While there were individual reasons for this common attitude, which ranged from the philosophical to the political, there was a common suspicion that yet another four years of Tory rule was going to be boring. Conflict is the stuff of headlines, of stories that are interesting to read and exciting to write. There was not much prospect of a lively time with a demoralized Opposition and a government so powerful that debate in the House was of no significance. Events in the House would become a daily pantomime. There would be a few tasty snippets, perhaps, but no good red meat. A strongly entrenched government was one that did not have to bother much about the House and, equally, didn't have to bother much about the press.

Politicians are arguers of cases. They stand or fall on how well they present the case to vote for themselves, to support such and such a policy. The prize for the best argument, the object of the debate, is power. Once power is achieved it is something of a nuisance to have to keep the debate going day by day when the election should have been the deciding factor. This was a common attitude among Conservatives, and it was one of the most obvious examples of their arrogance of power. Another was the expression often used by Ministers whenever they were asked when they would make public a certain piece of information or when they intended to pursue a particular policy. "In the fullness of time," they would reply, smile, and sit down.

For many years there had been less sycophancy evident among the reporters at Queen's Park than there was in the Press Gallery in Ottawa. Leslie Frost cuddled the Press into numbness but John Robarts created a generation of sceptics in the Gallery. His disdain for the Press made the reporters adversaries, and despite a quick and continuing turnover in the Gallery, this relationship persisted. When a new wave of reporters hit Queen's Park around 1971 they learned through the example of a handful of men who had been there for some years and whose styles were aggressive and acid. The most influential among the old hands was Harold Greer, columnist for *The Montreal Star*, whose daily thoughts were also sold to newspapers across the province and the rest of the country, but Del Bell of *The London Free Press*, despite his local base, was also a man to be reckoned with. He and Greer and the other old hands such as Don O'Hearn, columnist for Thomson newspapers, set the tone for the newspaper reporters in the Gallery.

At the other end of the scale were the radio and television reporters whose concept of their jobs was to push a microphone in front of a Minister and ask, "What have you got to say about this?" Invariably the Ministers found a lot to say, and most of it had little to do with what the story was really about. Considering the massive audiences that both radio and television attracted, the general poor quality of the electronic media reporters was a major deficiency in the Gallery. Their numbers have been and still are growing rapidly, and in the future they will probably be the power in the Gallery. This will inevitably mean much closer ties between the government and the Press, because in order to do their job, such as it is, the technology of radio and television demands the help of government in setting up studios, providing transmission lines, and the like. It is difficult to believe that this is a healthy trend.

There was a clear division in the Gallery between the newspaper reporters and those from radio and television. With a few exceptions, the electronic reporters were looked down on and mistrusted by the print men. The exceptions were the three CBC men—Bill Casey and Bill Harrington from television, Ken McCreath from radio, and Howard English from CKEY. Apart from them, the electronic media reporters were regarded by the print men as lost souls who managed to make the rest of the Gallery look stupid with their inane questions. On their side the radio and television reporters found the superior attitude of the newspaper reporters distasteful, and they felt that the Gallery failed to take into account the particular problems faced by electronic media reporters. The champion of the electronic media was Bob Carr, who operated a freelance service. The election of Gallery officers each year devolved into an attempt by Carr to win an influential place on the executive and a campaign by the newspaper reporters to stop him.

When *The Toronto Telegram* was still in existence its

reporters and those from *The Star* had engaged daily in fierce battles to be first with the best story. Occasionally *The Globe and Mail* got a punch in, but it preferred to keep out of the squabbles of the other two Toronto papers, addressing itself instead to its province-wide and national audience, however illusory that concept may have been. When *The Telegram* was folded at the end of October, 1971, *The Star* became flabby, and the historic inclination of its editors to spend their days writing ridiculous memos became a frantic addiction. Despite the high quality of the reporters in *The Star*'s Queen's Park bureau, they spent so much time chasing their own tails or the tails of editors downtown that their ability to operate effectively was seriously hampered. Two bureau chiefs, Clare Hoy and Vince Devitt, found the situation so intolerable that they demanded to be re-assigned.

The Globe and Mail bureau was in a more fortunate position. Its reporters were given express orders by *Globe* managing editor Clark Davey that as much as possible they were to keep away from the trivia of the House and of the daily mountains of press releases. Davey maintained that the important stories at Queen's Park were not to be found exclusively in the amateur dramatics of question period, and he ensured that his reporters had the time to ferret around in the wings where the denouement was being orchestrated. It was a highly successful approach which gave *The Globe* numerous successes in 1972 and 1973, and it was a concept that to some degree infected the whole Gallery.

The result was that the government's news management techniques worked less well than they had before. With reporters chained to the activities in the House, by means of the swift corridor interview and the cunning press release the government could maintain reasonable control. Deadlines and the lack of time would ensure that only the skimpiest, most favourable stories would appear. If a press conference were called for 11:00 a.m. the Ministers knew that *The Star* and *The Telegram* would have to rush out with the basic information to get the story in their late-morning editions. There would be no time for their reporters to do much with questioning after the statement. Since *The Globe and Mail* was a morning paper and its reporters had all night, if necessary, to build up their stories, it was much less susceptible to these pressures. In attempting to keep up with *The Globe*, *The Star*, instead of freeing their reporters from many of the daily chores, increased the size of its bureau from three to five reporters.

But the Ontario Conservatives were never as good at news management as the Liberal government in Ottawa. In November, 1972, a tri-level conference on urban affairs was held at the Four Seasons-Sheraton Hotel in Toronto. The new federal Minister of Urban Affairs sat down with the provincial ministry and with representatives of Ontario's municipalities. But it was all done behind closed doors. Reporters were left out in the hallways waiting to pounce on their contacts when the meeting adjourned for a break.

Ontario had provided reporters with a turgid position paper which had been the basic source of information for reporters writing stories for early deadlines. However, with the doors locked and the meeting under way, junior officials from the federal Urban Affairs Ministry began drifting among the crowd of reporters, slipping into their pockets transcripts of what the Minister, Ron Basford, was actually saying inside the meeting room. It was good stuff and Basford captured himself quite a few headlines.

Queen's Park was a relatively small community with common interests in politics and government, with the same people dealing with one another day to day. Inevitably, clubism develops. It was evident among the political parties, and despite the Press Gallery's defence of its purity, it too was in a number of ways part of the Queen's Park club. In the early 1970s the situation was not nearly as bad as it had been in the late 1950s and early sixties. At that time the government had given reporters a stationery allowance of $50 a year and reporters had been paid for acting as secretaries to Legislative Committees. Those practices had been stopped, but still the Gallery was not an entirely independent body. Offices, furniture and telephones were provided gratis. A number of newspapers had tried to pay for their accommodation in the Legislative Building, but were told that there was no way the government accounting system could accept payment for the offices. In all, these hand-outs were worth $75,000 a year.

A constant problem to the Gallery was its lounge and bar.

In 1971 the government redecorated and refurbished the Gallery lounge at great expense. The Gallery president at the time, Peter Jackman of *The Ottawa Journal*, maintained, with some justification, that the redecoration would firmly establish the lounge and surrounding offices as Press Gallery space and make it more difficult for the government to move the reporters out. But what was more worrying was the fact that the government provided, and paid for, two stewards to man the lounge. Their job was primarily to distribute the sea of reports, press releases, and other documents that came into the Press Gallery each day, but one of them was always fully employed dispensing drinks and sandwiches from the bar.

Parties were the main way in which reporters were evident as part of the Queen's Park club. The most exotic was the annual MPP's tour of northern Ontario on the Ontario Northland Railroad. The trip lasted several days, and the Press Gallery was invited. The train chugged around, stopping now and then to allow everyone to gaze at some northern landmark or to take on fresh supplies of booze. The trip was nothing more than a travelling drunk and poker game. Back at Queen's Park, reporters were routinely included in the invitations to most of the social events.

There is little evidence to suggest that being part of the club tainted reporters' news stories. In many cases the social contact opened up channels of information to them that they would not otherwise have found easy to develop. But one of the results of the close association was that over the years there was a steady drift of reporters into government or political jobs. The lists of Ministers' executive assistants and of the staff of Ministry public relations and communications branches were heavy with the names of former reporters.

Peter Jackman, the Gallery president in 1971, later became communications director for the Ministry of Treasury, Economics and Intergovernmental Affairs. The executive assistant to George Kerr, Minister of the Environment, was Gordon Hampson, former Queen's Park reporter for *The Hamilton Spectator*. CKEY's Legislative reporter, Michael O'Rourke, had resigned in 1971 to be a Conservative candidate in the election. When he was defeated he got a job with the Ministry of Industry and Tourism, which he later left to go into a private public relations firm. Robarts' press aide William Kinmond had been a *Globe and Mail* reporter in the Gallery, and the man who did the same job for Davis, Donald Beeney, had been a reporter for Canadian Press. Later, CFRB's man at Queen's Park, Andrew StuParick, got a job managing the press conference studio which was also used by members to record films and tapes to send to their local radio and television stations.

There were in addition many former reporters who had not worked at Queen's Park immediately before joining the government or the service of a particular Minister. James Mackenzie, one of *The Globe and Mail*'s Toronto City Hall reporters, joined the staff of Social Development policy secretary Robert Welch. Mackenzie came from Welch's home territory of St. Catharines. William Morris, a general reporter for *The Globe and Mail*, became executive assistant to Natural Resources Minister Leo Bernier. Davis's speech writer, John Miller, was a writer for *Canadian Magazine* before joining the Premier's staff.

From the government's point of view, ex-reporters were quite a desirable commodity in these jobs. Reporters were generalists who often had wide experience of many facets of society. They were equipped to act as a useful filter between the Minister and the civil service. In communications branches reporters were valuable because they knew how to write press releases in ways that were most likely to get them printed in newspapers, and they were often known by, and on easy terms with, reporters in the Press Gallery.

Money was often a major reason for reporters joining the government. They could generally increase their income by a third by making the change, and in some instances reporters doubled their income. The people who crossed the line into the government service were often reporters who had lost their enthusiasm for journalism and who wanted to establish a new career before sliding into a dim future with their newspapers. Others went into government service just to see how it worked. Having reported on government for a number of years they were curious to see what it looked like from inside. Some who became executive assistants were truly enthusiastic about the qualities of the Minister they went to serve.

But the government's relationship with the Press Gallery was only a part of its dealings with the news media. Beyond the thirty-five news outlets represented in the Gallery there were a myriad of radio and television stations and newspapers out in the province. In many ways these news media were more important to the Conservatives than were those represented in the Press Gallery. These local news outlets were the channels through which the bulk of the province received its information about what was happening at Queen's Park. They did not display the critical attitude towards the information they received shown by the reporters at Queen's Park. Information came in the form of press releases, which often went unedited straight into the newspapers, and Canadian Press copy. Radio and television stations used material from their affiliated stations, CBC or CFTO in the case of television, or clips from freelance or Canadian Press reporters in the case of radio. Generally the emphasis in the material that reached the out-of-town newspapers and stations was on what happened in the House and what programs the government had announced.

The government liked to maintain pleasant relations with these small papers and stations. Government advertising through these media was heavy. Indeed, some of these outlets would have had to tighten their belts without government ads for tenders for road contracts and the like. In Toronto the ethnic press received large amounts of government advertising telling about programs for immigrants. There was obviously value in that. Nevertheless, the government could generally count on editorial support from many of the province's ethnic newspapers. Up north the government dispensed advertising patronage as well; for example, the television coverage of the CTV-affiliated television station in North Bay of the winter carnival there was sponsored by the Ontario Northland Railroad, a government agency.

Davis's office was generally much more concerned about what was said in the editorial columns of the small daily and weekly newspapers out in the Tory ridings than about what appeared in *The Toronto Star* and *The Globe and Mail.*

Even so, Davis kept up an amicable relationship with senior editors of the two Toronto papers. From Davis's point of view it was sensible to give these men some time, so that government moves could be fully explained to them and editorials would not be written on the basis of partial information. But often the dealings went beyond that. It was not uncommon for Clare Westcott, on Davis's behalf, to telephone senior editors on the papers *before* a government decision was finally taken, in order to judge what their editorial response would be. One occasion when this happened was in 1973 when Davis was considering bringing Darcy McKeough back into the Cabinet as Minister of Energy. Before the appointment was made, editors of both newspapers were contacted to see if they would come out against McKeough's reappointment within a year of his having resigned over an apparent conflict of interest. Neither paper objected and the appointment was made.

Newspapers are corporate entities as well as purveyors of information. The larger they become, the more the corporate ethic dominates. Earlier in this book it was mentioned that *The Star*'s fear of the Charitable Gifts Act prompted it to get involved in a by-election in Leeds riding. That was not the only occasion in which *The Star*'s corporate interests seem to have determined what appears in the news columns of the newspaper.

The Star is Canada's wealthiest single newspaper and has the largest circulation. Its money is not only tied up in the machinery needed to produce the newspaper. Some of it is invested in real estate, such as the 400 acres *The Star* owned in the area of Highway 7 and Highway 27 northwest of Toronto. Part of the area was taken up with a plant which did the colour printing for the paper, its magazines, and various supplements, but the bulk of the acreage was vacant and ripe for development.

Then in the summer of 1973 the government produced plans for a parkway belt reaching across northern Toronto that ended development prospects in that area. Much of *The Star*'s 400 acres was included in the Parkway Belt plan. Shortly afterwards *Star* publisher Beland Honderich sent a memo to the Queen's Park bureau of the newspaper asking them to do a story on the problems of the landowners in the area who had had the value of their property cut by the government's action. That was perhaps a legitimate story, as over the whole area millions of dollars in land value had disappeared overnight and the government had refused to pay compensation, but as a corporate entity *The Star*'s position was not one of scrupulous objectivity on this issue.

Slightly more difficult to explain is the number of stories that have appeared in *The Star* since 1972 enthusing over the prospects of development on Toronto's waterfront. In 1972 *The Star* moved from its old offices on King Street West to a spanking new building at the bottom of Yonge Street down by the waterfront. *The Star* owned the land on which the building stood, but the offices were built and owned by Olympia and York Developments Ltd., one of the largest commercial developers in Toronto. In addition to *The Star*'s office space and printing plant there was a large tower of offices, which initially proved difficult to rent. The problem was the isolation of the building. It stood almost alone in vacant land separated from the core of the city by the Gardiner Expressway and the railroad tracks.

After *The Star* moved to its new building, stories began to appear with remarkable regularity about the tremendous prospects that the development of the waterfront offered. Mostly the stories appeared in the real estate section of the Saturday edition of *The Star*, but ultimately one full-page story openly extolling the waterfront development appeared on the front of Saturday's "Insight" section, which was devoted to editorials and commentaries.

Judging the biases of radio and television stations and newspapers is a complex and difficult undertaking. Prejudice is in the eye of the beholder. Professor Stephen Clarkson of the University of Toronto department of political economy attempted to make some judgments of the fairness of coverage of the 1971 election in Toronto, in a report prepared for the Canadian Radio and Television Commission. Clarkson concentrated simply on the quantity of coverage of the campaign by the various news outlets, and on what proportion of that time or space went to each party. He came up with some interesting results.

Clarkson hired monitors to listen to the newscasts from five Toronto stations, and list and time the election items. In Clarkson's view the worst record was that of the private radio station CFRB, which has the largest audience of any radio station in Toronto. His results showed that it devoted the least time to the election of any of the stations monitored, but it also gave the Conservatives four times as much coverage as the Liberals and the NDP. It was normal for the Tories to receive on average twice as much coverage on radio and television as the other parties, which, Clarkson speculated, may have been the result of their being the governing party. CFRB also distinguished itself by concentrating more on the leaders than any other station. Indeed, none of the items monitored dealt with the NDP in terms of anything other than its leader, Stephen Lewis. In the station's coverage of the Conservatives there was also a strong emphasis on Davis. Norman Atkins could not have wished for more. CFTO, the CTV station, devoted most time to election coverage and concentrated least on the leaders. It also aired a series of riding reports, which Clarkson found commendable.

Clarkson's assessment of the three Toronto newspapers showed differences which were not as dramatic as those among the radio and television stations, but which were nonetheless distinct. *The Telegram*, an avowedly Conservative newspaper, printed more than twice as many photographs of the Conservatives as of the Liberals and NDP combined. The amount of general space it devoted to the Conservatives was only marginally less than the total for the other parties. *The Telegram* did, however, devote more space to the election than did *The Star*. *The Telegram* printed 4,079 inches against *The Star*'s 3,348. *The Globe and Mail* came out best–if one believes there is virtue in verbiage –with 4,998 inches of space given to election coverage. In terms of the number of articles covering each party, there was little to choose between *The Star* and *The Globe and Mail*. In both cases the Conservatives received most space, with the Liberals and the NDP not too far behind. In the case of *The Globe and Mail*, the NDP got more extensive coverage than the Liberals. With *The Star* it was the other way around. Of the three newspapers *The Globe and Mail* did best in its photographic coverage of the campaign, since there was only a small difference in the numbers of pictures concerning each party.

Even without any analysis of bias in the writing of articles and news broadcast copy, it was evident from Clarkson's study that there was partiality in the coverage of the election. From the figures, most of the news outlets monitored appear to have made some attempt at fairness; the unbalancing factor seems to have been the Conservatives' ability to generate news coverage by using their position as the government. Nevertheless, CFRB's record remains a model of propagandism.

Biases at election time are perhaps easier to pin down than are general day-to-day leanings of the newspapers. And are those leanings necessarily political biases? Each newspaper has its own character and its own quirks. In the late 1960s *The Star* was smitten by the arguments of the proponents of Canadian economic and cultural nationalism. Such was the newspaper's concern for the subject that every reporter knew that a nationalism story was destined for the front page and should be written with that in mind. Never mind if the nationalism element was only a part of a larger and perhaps more important story; so far as *The Star* was concerned the nationalism angle was the natural lead into the story. *The Globe and Mail* was more modest in its sensitive areas, but perhaps more given to moralizing. Stories on liquor, particularly increases in the price of booze, were guaranteed good play in the newspaper. *The Globe* maintained a catholic capacity for outrage, which had its finicky aspects, but which also drove its reporters towards discovering and revealing a number of unsavoury situations in the government during 1972 and 1973.

Davis's personal relationship with the press operated at two levels. As Premier the Gallery found him difficult to take. Initially he showed no concern for the needs of the press corps in making information available. There was an element of injured pride in the press's surly reaction, and but for the intercessions of Davis's press aide, Don Beeney, the relationship would have deteriorated beyond recall. Davis saw little need to make himself available at regular press conferences, and many members of the Gallery went for months without being able to question him. Usually if a reporter wanted to ask the Premier or a Minister something in particular he could waylay them as they left the House. But Davis took to avoiding even these chance encounters by using a side door from the Conservative lobby to his office. While he slipped out, his entourage would run interference and fend off the reporters, until on occasion the business of trying to talk to Davis reached farcical proportions.

Davis did not suffer fools gladly and the Press Gallery had its share of fools. The Premier felt no necessity to bring them to their senses by explaining his point of view. But while for a period of two years he was seldom generally available to the Gallery, individual reporters whom he trusted, or who could persuade him through Don Beeney that it was important to see him, could always get an audience. Even for the favoured, however, the yield from these interviews was seldom the word from the mountain. The Premier's inborn attachment to circumlocution, his ability to speak forcefully in generalities, his unwillingness to discuss options, made the reading over of notes from an interview a dispiriting job. Pages of nothing. Firm statements qualified to meaninglessness.

At the level of the club, at the social level, Davis and the reporters got on well. He always tried to attend Gallery parties, and always apparently enjoyed himself. In return he had a party for the press each summer, twice at Ontario Place and once at The Grange, an elderly mansion behind the Ontario Art Gallery in Toronto. As long as the conversation kept to football, sailing, or distant political events he relaxed. Indeed, he seemed to find something refreshing about the company of reporters. They were the only people at Queen's Park who did not owe their positions to him and for whom his power was of little direct concern. While even Ministers bowed and scraped and called him "sir" with unctuous smiles, the reporters chatted to him in an easy manner.

Towards the end of 1973 Davis finally realized that his relationship with the press was not doing him any good and he made efforts to make himself more readily available to the

Press Gallery. At the urging of Hugh Macaulay he began holding general press conferences once every two weeks which allowed reporters to shoot any questions at him that they wished. Norman Atkins, unable to resist the opportunity this gave him and the Conservative party, started using edited tapes from these conferences on free-time radio shows—until the Press Gallery discovered what was being done and demanded that it be stopped. But the process that brought Davis face to face with his isolation took two years, and was painful for him and the Conservative party. The series of exposés printed in the newspapers during 1972 and 1973 revealed a side of the Tory character which was not reflected in their public pronouncements about the future being for people, of dialogue with the citizenry, of public participation. Rather the scandals spoke of the assumption that power and authority gave Conservatives rights and privileges beyond those of other people. They spoke of an arrogant disregard for the ethics of public life; they seemed to say that for Conservatives adherence to the letter of the law was sufficient. They showed just how closely the Conservatives were tied to commercial interests and how earnestly the Tories worked to preserve these relationships.

The disclosures of these situations were all made by the press. The changes that were made came largely as a result of insistence by the press. In those senses for nearly two years the Press Gallery at Queens' Park was the Opposition.

17. The Breath of Scandal

From the newspaper's point of view it was a series of lucky breaks that gave the Conservatives problems in 1972 and 1973. The first break, improbably enough, was in Havana, Cuba, on March 19, 1972. A reporter for *The Kitchener-Waterloo Record*, Robert Sutton by name, was on holiday in Havana when he came across a tall, bald man whom he thought he recognized. A second look confirmed his suspicion; it was Bert Lawrence, Ontario's Policy Minister for Resources Development. Sutton engaged the Minister in conversation and discovered that Lawrence was in Cuba as a guest of the government of Fidel Castro. He had arrived in Havana on March 17 with Mrs. Lawrence, his two children, his deputy Dr. Keith Reynolds, Dr. Reynolds' wife and Dr. Reynolds' child. And the entire caravan had travelled from Toronto in an Ontario government aircraft, a Beechcraft.

Sutton thought it worth while sending a story to his newspaper, which he did. The Canadian Press picked up the article which appeared the next day in *The Kitchener-Waterloo Record*. The wires hummed, and before you could say Alexander Graham Bell the Toronto daily papers were hot on the trail. Up at Queen's Park there was a flurry of activity. Inquiries with the Ministry of Natural Resources, which was responsible for the government's aircraft, revealed that the aircraft had flown down to Havana, had come back, and would be returning to pick up the party. The cost of these two trips at $150 an hour was $3,600. The reporters were on a hot scent. Next, telephone a travel agency. The cost of flying eight people from Toronto to Havana on a commercial flight would have been $2,667. What does Premier Davis think of his Ministers carting their families around on government planes? Ring the Premier's office. Sorry, Davis is on a skiing holiday in Stowe, Vermont, with his family. How did he get there? On a government aircraft. The plot thickens.

It is hard to be dispassionate when you see someone destroying himself as Bert Lawrence did when he stood there in the Legislature on March 27, feebly waving his itinerary for the eight-day trip to Cuba. The itinerary showed only one day's holiday at the resort centre of Varadaro Beach, he claimed. He had not announced the visit before leaving because he feared that it might be misinterpreted, but one misinterpretation he hadn't expected "was that the House or anyone else would consider it was a junket just to sit in the sand, or for social fun."

He went on and on to the jeers of the Opposition. He had met with Cuban Ministers, and even though it was not a trade mission he had no doubt that it would bring new trading agreements between Ontario and Cuba. Tory backbenchers began to leave the House, shaking their heads. He had spent the morning of March 22 cutting sugar cane in the fields, as all Cuban Ministers were expected to do. Maybe that was a good idea. Maybe more Ontario politicians should get out there and work with their hands with the people of the province. More jeers. There was hardly a Conservative backbencher with him any more. At the end of forty minutes Lawrence's political career was in tatters. Ultimately there is one thing that destroys a politician, and that is lack of judgment in public.

The situation wasn't entirely Lawrence's fault. The arrangements had been made by Keith Reynolds, who after serving John Robarts for years, just ordered an airplane and thought no more about it. There were spare seats on the plane and a number of social events planned in Cuba, so they took their wives and children. But times had changed. It was a time of responsibility to the public will, a theme which the Conservatives themselves had played on in an election campaign just a few months before.

The Opposition and the press swung at the grapefruit that had been lobbed to them. Why should Ministers be allowed to take their families with them on trips of dubious importance? Who else travelled with Ministers when they flew around in government aircraft? Did senior Conservatives use the aircraft for party business? Did Ministers use the aircraft for holidays? The questions could only be resolved in one way. The government must release the log books of its aircraft for public inspection. It was not a new request; for years Opposition members had been asking for just that, and each year the government had refused.

Davis returned from his skiing holiday a few days later and found uproar. There were tigers lurking in the House as he entered. But he was ready for them; he wasn't going to make Lawrence's mistake of standing exposed for forty minutes attempting to explain the unexplainable. His speech was short. He was Premier of the province 24 hours a day, he told them. It was a necessary part of his job to have a plane on hand. If members imagined that when he was on holiday there was no work, no government business, to be done, then let him assure them that there was. And as for having his family along? Well, the people who advised him on matters of security recommended that he use a private aircraft rather than a commercial carrier. That was the situation, and the House could lump it and like it.

The House wasn't particularly prepared to do either. Over the next few weeks the tigers made swift forays to demand that the log books be produced, but to no avail. The Premier's office got busy on the press. Security was involved, they said. There had been threats on the Premier's life, some of which his Ontario Provincial Police bodyguards took seriously. Revealing the log books might aid an assassin because there was a pattern to the Premier's travel habits. And then the darkest secret of all. A man had been discovered in the basement of Queen's Park, just two flights of stairs away from the Premier's office. The man had a gun in a brown paper bag.

Was this a smoke-screen, a red herring to stop the press and the Opposition from obtaining the log books, which would doubtless show that Ministers and others had been gallivanting around the province, the country, perhaps even the world? Probably. The pressure continued. Finally Davis said that he would allow each Minister to go before the Public Accounts Committee to present and answer for his use of government aircraft. As for himself, no. His use of planes would remain secret.

And so Minister after Minister trooped into the committee room and presented dockets listing their flights. There was only a little in them. Darcy McKeough and James Auld had regularly used the planes to go home at weekends and return on Sunday evening or Monday morning. But, as McKeough said, he gave every waking hour to the service of the province, and perhaps a few hours with his family each week was not too much to ask in return.

The Public Accounts Committee retained nagging doubts about Davis's flights. Unlike the rest of the Cabinet, Davis used a rented jet aircraft which was chartered from Execaire

Aviation Ltd., of Toronto, at a cost of $600 an hour. The Ministry of Natural Resources had been contemplating buying a jet (after all, Premier Bourassa had one), but Davis had vetoed that idea, and they rented one instead. The Public Accounts Committee decided that it really did want to see the Premier's flight records. The Premier's office said no, but James Allan, the senior Conservative on the committee, was invited in, shown the logs and asked to report back. He told the committee that as far as he could see there was nothing in the log books that should concern the committee, but the Premier was prepared to show the list to a delegation of one member from each party. So the delegation was sent. They looked at the logs and reported that everything appeared to be in order.

The strange thing about the affair was the intransigence of Davis when there was nothing there that could hurt his government. The security angle was certainly important. In addition to threats against himself, there had been separate threats against his family. But that had nothing to do with his Ministers. Basically, it seemed to be that he was unwilling to make the information public just because it never had been made public. Revealing the log books was giving ground which could never be recovered again.

In this case what made him decide to send his Ministers before the committee was not the pressure of the press or the Opposition; it was the flow of letters into his office. Somehow the thought that these Ministers had airplanes at their disposal to whoosh them off into the blue yonder touched a nerve in the people of Ontario more sensitive than almost any other. They wrote furious letters to Davis by the score. The scandals of the following months were as nothing compared with the ire Ontarians felt over the planes issue. It stunned Davis and his close advisers until they discovered that only a tiny proportion of the population (one aide said the figure was 12 per cent) had ever been in an aircraft. Having an airplane humming on the runway ready to carry you off to the land of your dreams was the ultimate luxury for most people, and they didn't like the idea of their elected representatives taking tax dollars to indulge in such magic.

The affair that began at the end of July 1972 was more

serious in its implications. A plain envelope arrived at the offices of *The Globe and Mail*, containing a photostat copy of a legal document. It was a deed of covenant between Dalton Bales and a retired postmistress. The document related to the purchase by Bales in September of 1969 of 99 acres of land from the woman. An investigation by the newspaper showed that Bales, then the Attorney-General, and two business associates had bought the land for $252,000. The land in question was in a particularly sensitive planning area. It was north of Highway 7 just east of Markham, in a region designated by the Toronto Centred Region Plan for growth. The obvious question that arose was whether or not Bales had used knowledge gained as a Cabinet Minister when he invested in this particular piece of real estate.

When interviewed by the newspaper Bales insisted that the purchase had not been made as a result of his having the inside track on government plans. He said that as soon as he became aware that the government did have ideas for development in the area, he told Davis about the land, and refrained from taking part in Cabinet discussions on the subject. This was confirmed by Davis.

Coming so soon after the Workmen's Compensation Board inquiry in which, as former Minister of Labour, he had been involved, this revelation did nothing for Bales' reputation. And yet he was an unlikely candidate for the touch of scandal. A tall, thin, sombre man of 52 who had been at law school with Davis, he was one of the Premier's few friends in the Cabinet. Bales was very sensitive of his own honour and of the honour of his post as Attorney-General, and it was with a great deal of discomfort that he explained the land purchase.

In 1969, according to his account of the affair, Bales had been looking out for some land in which to invest money on a long-term basis. In May of that year a man who had been a client of his when Bales was practising law came and asked him if he wanted to become a partner in the purchase of the land. The man was Gerardo Fiorini, a 70-year-old retired building contractor. Bales went out to look at the land and decided it was what he wanted. In September he, Fiorini and the third partner, Armando Boccia, also a building contractor, bought the land.

They each paid $46,666 in cash and assumed a mortgage for $112,000. Fiorini and Boccia sent their quarterly mortgage payments to Bales, who sent them on.

Davis was in Halifax, Nova Scotia, at a Premiers' conference when the story was printed on August 4, 1972. The Premier stated at once that he was convinced that Bales had conducted himself properly over the purchase. But very quickly the issue became not whether Davis was satisfied, but whether the public was. He was asked if he would require all Ministers to make public lists of their land holdings. He would not, he replied, but he would instruct Ministers to make those lists available to him.

The Opposition parties held that Bales had apparently breached the public trust and should resign. When Davis returned from the Maritimes he met with Bales. In a statement after the discussion Bales said he had offered to resign and the Premier had urged him to stay. The Attorney-General said he would make his decision known in a few days.

On August 9 Davis made a statement to the Legislature in which he said that after a thorough review of the situation he was satisfied that Bales had not used any "insider" knowledge in his decision to purchase the land. The Premier said that because of the government's increasing involvement in land acquisition and development, more stringent rules than those then in effect should perhaps be imposed on the Cabinet. Ministers had only been required to declare their interest in any matter under discussion and to refrain from taking part.

Davis said he was considering a number of possible alternative policies to deal with conflicts of interest. It might be necessary to prohibit Ministers from buying and selling land, or to require that all such sales be made public. On the other hand, he said, he might find that the present policy was entirely adequate.

Two days later Bales made a statement to the Legislature saying that he had decided not to resign from the Cabinet. He had satisfied himself that the affair would not impede his ability to perform his duties as Attorney-General. He told the House that his share of the land would be assigned to a trustee who would sell it and the profit would go to charity.

He ended with the statement "A person with public responsibilities such as myself should not today involve himself in land acquisition while holding public office." That was the final word on the matter—but only for a few days.

There is no evidence to suggest that Bales did use his knowledge of government plans when deciding to get involved in the land purchase. At the time he bought the land Bales was Minister of Labour and, according to Davis, was not involved in or privy to any of the studies leading up to preparation of the Toronto Centred Region Plan. When it appeared to Bales that his land might be in a sensitive area, he informed Davis by letter at once. When he didn't get a reply from the Premier beyond a simple acknowledgement, he was justified in thinking that Davis didn't think the situation was important.

Bales abided by the letter of the law. His sin was the same as that of Bert Lawrence when he bundled his family into a government aircraft for a trip to Cuba. It simply never occurred to him to think about what he was doing, and to decide whether it was acceptable behaviour for a Cabinet Minister. There was an obvious disregard for the public in Bales' easy acceptance of land speculation as a fit occupation for a Minister. At a time when housing and land costs were rising, at a time when the government was increasingly involved in planning, it was quite wrong for a Minister to speculate in real estate.

There was another way in which Bales exhibited an insensitivity towards the requirements of his office. He was Minister of Labour when he bought the land. He should have had second thoughts about becoming the partner of two building contractors. It should have been evident to him at that time that labour-management relationships in the construction industry were strained, and he should not have risked undermining his impartiality as Minister by becoming closely associated with employers.

Just what Davis would have produced as a new policy for the Cabinet on conflicts of interest and business activity we shall never know, for he didn't get time to think about it. With the Bales affair quietened down, Davis turned his attention to a trip he was to make to Germany and England with his Treasurer, Darcy McKeough. They were going to the Olympic Games, and also planned to try and borrow some money for Ontario Hydro.

Late one afternoon, just a few days before they were due to leave, a man went into *The Globe and Mail* office on King Street and said he had a story to tell. It was a highly detailed account of McKeough's involvement in land deals in Chatham. As a general rule such information tends to boil down to one-third vindictiveness, one-third imagination, and one-third fact. But when the story was checked out over the following days, it was all found to be true. It was an involved tale, but the essence of it was that while McKeough was Minister of Municipal Affairs, plans for a subdivision in which he had money were approved in his name by his Ministry.

The McKeough family were wealthy, and in looking for some way of investing their capital they bought a third-share of a company called Triple Ten Investments in 1968. Triple Ten acquired a small Chatham subdivision which had already received planning approval and was partly developed. They completed the project, made a profit, and after that "looked around for another good piece of property", in the words of McKeough's brother Stewart.

Together with a couple of other companies involved in housing development Triple Ten formed South Chatham Estates Ltd. In November, 1969, the company gained title to 75 acres of land for $375,000. They subdivided the land into 215 lots and put them up for sale at $6,000 each. With costs taken into account, the company stood to make between $150,000 and $200,000.

South Chatham Estates applied for subdivision approval in May, 1969, some months before it acquired title to the land, and, indeed, before it was incorporated in October that year. Draft approval for the plans was given on December 30, 1969. The approval was given by staff in McKeough's department and the plans were marked with a facsimile of his signature. McKeough was still Municipal Affairs Minister when final approval was given for 19 of the lots in September, 1970. McKeough's successor, Dalton Bales, was in charge of the Ministry when final approval was given for the remaining parcels of land.

Stewart McKeough, in an interview at the time, insisted that his brother's position had nothing to do with the family turning to real estate as a good investment for their money. He also denied that Darcy had in any way aided the approval of the plans, which Ministry officials later remembered as being very bad and requiring complete re-drawing. Nonetheless, the plans did negotiate the rapids of Ministry approval with uncommon speed.

McKeough's position appeared to be untenable. Even though there was no reason to believe that he had interfered with the normal passage of the plans through his department, as Minister he was finally responsible for the work done by his Ministry. Thus when the official stamped a facsimile of McKeough's signature on the South Chatham plans, he did it with McKeough's authority even though the Minister may not have known about it. Though McKeough may not have known the status of the plans at any particular time, he certainly was aware that the company in which he had money was submitting plans to his Ministry. It appeared to be a clear case of conflict of interest.

During the course of *The Globe and Mail*'s investigation, McKeough became aware of what was happening. Partly as a result of that, and partly in response to Davis's request that Ministers supply him with a list of their holdings, McKeough wrote a letter to the Premier outlining the South Chatham Estates situation. The letter arrived at Davis's office shortly before Davis left for Europe and he didn't have time to read it.

Davis left for Europe on Tuesday, August 22, and McKeough followed a couple of days later. According to Clare Westcott, the two men discussed the matter over breakfast on the Saturday morning, August 25. Perhaps it was too much to say that they discussed it. McKeough apparently gave Davis a copy of the letter which the Premier didn't see before leaving Toronto. The Treasurer also verbally outlined its contents, but there was minimal response from Davis. Davis was always a better listener than talker, always unwilling to make off-the-cuff judgments. McKeough left the breakfast table feeling that Davis had no advice to offer him and no wish to be involved in the matter.

The Globe and Mail's story appeared on Monday, August

28. McKeough kept to his schedule and returned to Toronto on the evening of the following day. He avoided the press corps waiting for him at Toronto Airport by slipping out by a VIP entrance, and headed for Chatham. He went to ground for a day in the family compound at Cedar Springs, southeast of the town, while reporters hung around the driveway to his pillared and porticoed home. On the night of August 30 he slipped by the reporters and flew up to Toronto. In his office on the top floor of the Frost Building overlooking Queen's Park, he met with some of his political friends, and they worked late into the night preparing a statement for him. One of the advisers, who had strong federal Conservative links and who numbered George Hees among his friends, commented: "The last statement like this I wrote involved a woman, and she turned out to be a communist."

Although McKeough, feeling that he was going to get no backing from Davis and aware that his situation looked bad, saw little alternative but to resign, he did not make a final decision that night. Gaps were left in the statement that was written. McKeough went home to his Forest Hill apartment, but was up early the next morning. McKeough recalled that it was while sitting in the lavatory that he decided to quit the Cabinet. Down at his office he dictated the final paragraphs for his statement and then telephoned Davis in England to tell him of the decision.

Late in the morning, accompanied by his wife Joyce and a host of aides from his office, McKeough walked over the grass from his Ministry to the Legislative Building. The press conference studio was packed as he read his statement. He said he had not used his position as Minister to aid approval of the subdivision plans, but he was going to resign anyway.

"I am satisfied that I personally have done nothing wrong, but what is at issue here is the confidence and integrity of the system," he said. "I feel that I am guilty of no more than having made an error of judgment. However, it is my conclusion that doubts have been raised and that these doubts may continue to be raised so long as I remain in this Ministry and Cabinet. I cannot tolerate these doubts, knowing in my own mind that I do not justify them."

He refused to answer reporters' questions and left immediately. He and his wife returned to his office. They picked up several cases of McKeough's personal documents and then flew to Chatham in a chartered aircraft.

That night at home McKeough received a number of consoling telephone calls. John Turner, the federal Liberal Finance Minister, called him, as did national Tory leader Robert Stanfield. McKeough's bishop called as well. So did W. Ross Macdonald, the Lieutenant-Governor of Ontario and a veteran federal Liberal politician. McKeough was touched by Macdonald's call, and asked why such an illustrious Liberal should concern himself about a Conservative in trouble. "One of my Ministers has resigned, that is of concern to me," Macdonald replied.

Davis arrived back from Europe a couple of days later to find that events were no longer entirely under his control. McKeough had demonstrated forceful independence in resigning without waiting for Davis to return. McKeough didn't care much what Davis thought, or about public perceptions of the Cabinet as a whole, and it showed. The Premier hadn't even been given the opportunity to officially accept his Treasurer's resignation, and Davis didn't actually do so until September 7.

McKeough had also forced Davis's hand on the question of public disclosure of Ministers' land holdings and other investments. Whatever his statement may have said, by resigning McKeough had tacitly admitted the appearance of a conflict of interest and an unhealthy situation. If within the space of a month *The Globe and Mail* could come up with provable stories of two Ministers speculating in land, the public was justified in wondering how many more such stories might be lurking behind the leather-padded doors of the Cabinet room. The question was no longer a quasi-philosophical one of the public responsibility of Ministers in the 1970s, it was one of confidence in the entire Davis government.

When Davis announced a few weeks later the new policy to govern Cabinet Ministers' business dealings, its cornerstone was disclosure. Ministers were required to make public a list of all their land holdings with the exception of their house and cottage, as well as all their company shares and all mortgages that they held. While the lists showed that land was a popular commodity with Cabinet Ministers, there was no indication that the value of any of the properties could be directly affected by government policies.

Further, Davis banned his Ministers from buying or selling land while in the Cabinet, and he required them to set up blind trusts to administer their other holdings or companies. The idea of the blind trust was that Ministers would hand over control of their affairs to a trustee who would have sole responsibility for administering the concerns. The Ministers would have no right to dictate what should be done, and no right to know what was being done with their interests.

Obviously the blind trust is not a foolproof method of ensuring that Ministers do not use their position for their own gain. A Minister set on lining his own pocket could easily get around its strictures. But Ministers deserve some public faith in their motives. That so little could be left to trust is one of the saddest commentaries on Ontario politics, and on the Conservative regime.

18. The Fidinam and Hydro Affairs

It is a fact of provincial politics in Ontario, and something of a judgment on them as well, that no aficionado can delve much below the surface without having to explore corporate life. Les Frost said, "Government is business, the people's business." But government is also a major client of private enterprise as well. Each year the public accounts list page after page of private concerns from which the province has bought merchandise or services. Everything from thumbtacks to limousines is represented by the hundreds of company names listed in those fat blue-covered books published every spring.

Fidinam and Hydro

But even though some of the individual contracts which are noted in the accounts can run to several million dollars, they are unremarkable compared with some of the major deals in land and office space the government has engaged in. When the Legislature's committee on resources development carried out its investigation of the Workmen's Compensation Board in the spring of 1972 it looked closely at one such deal.

In April, 1970, the WCB was told by its officials that its offices on Harbour Street, down near Toronto's waterfront, were inadequate and would not be able to accommodate its future space requirements. By the fall of that year it became known among office developers and real estate firms that the Board was in the market for new offices, and inquiries were made by a number of firms. They were told that the developer must be prepared to buy the Board's existing land and building at current value, that the Board would like to be able to invest in the mortgaging of the new office development so as to secure its tenancy and because it would be a sound investment. The Board further specified that it would like to own all or part of the land on which the new offices were built, that it wanted a reasonable rental rate, competitive allowances for expenses such as decorating, and room for the Board to take over additional space in the future. Because a lot of the people who visit the WCB come from out of town, the Board wanted the office in a central, easily accessible place. Early in 1971 eight developers made proposals to the Board, and in April the WCB decided it would like to accept the offer of Fidinam (Ontario) Ltd.

The Fidinam site was on the northeast corner of the intersection of Yonge and Bloor streets in Toronto. The office block would be part of a large development that would include a hotel and a shopping area as well. Fidinam offered 220,000 square feet of space at $1,540,000 rental a year with a twenty-year lease. The company offered to sell the WCB 56,000 square feet of the land on which the building would stand for $5,600,000. It said it would also accept a $15 million mortgage from the Board at 10 per cent for 35 years. In turn, Fidinam offered to buy the old Harbour Street offices and land for $3.5 million.

The Legislative Committee examined the deal from every possible angle. The members found the amount of money involved breathtaking and the complex details of the deal daunting; but they eventually came to the conclusion that Fidinam's offer was the best of the eight. If they had reached a different conclusion, it is hard to see what could have been done—because the agreements had been approved by Cabinet in the summer of 1971, a year before the committee's inquiry, and the contracts had been signed in the fall of the same year. Work was already well under way at the site only a few blocks from the room where the committee (whose approval was required) was straining to understand the niceties of the deal.

The matter appeared to have been concluded when, late one morning towards the end of October, 1972, copies of two Telex messages were delivered to *The Globe and Mail.* The first, dated November 23, 1971, was addressed to Fidinam, for the attention of Elizabeth McDonald, the secretary-treasurer of the company. The first message said:

"Re IP account c/o TDB. Please inform me per Telex about cheque issued to M. Kelly—July 23 EEEE 13 for dlr 50,000 Thanksbibi. Ina."

The second was the reply from Miss McDonald sent later the same day. It was addressed to Miss Piattini at Fidinam's parent company in Lugano, Switzerland. It said:

"Dlr 50,000 payment out of IP A/C July 23 was political donation related to UCP/WCB. Will be repaid before end of year."

For *The Globe and Mail* reporters this was treasure indeed. They had no doubt that UCP/WCB meant Upper Canada Place (the name of the Fidinam Development) and WCB meant Workmen's Compensation Board. Miss McDonald was clearly saying that Fidinam had made a political donation of $50,000 to M. Kelly related to Fidinam's agreement to build offices for the Workmen's Compensation Board. A look at the newspaper's files showed that the money had been given four weeks after the Cabinet had approved the deal.

There were a few problems, however. The reporters knew one Kelly involved with fund raising for the Conservatives. That was William Kelly, the party's chief bagman. The reference to M. Kelly might just be a mistake, or it might be another Kelly altogether. If the parent Fidinam company had been in the French-speaking rather than the Italian-speaking part of Switzerland, the M. could have been the abbreviation for Monsieur. So "M. Kelly" was a problem.

But the biggest problem was to decide whether or not the Telex messages were true. They had arrived during the last week of the federal election campaign. There was no doubt that when the story of the messages was printed, it would be of considerable embarrassment to the Ontario Conservatives, who for the first time in many years were actively helping a federal Tory leader, in this case Robert Stanfield. Might there be some political motivation behind the sending of the messages to *The Globe and Mail*? It would be very easy for anyone who knew how to operate a Telex machine to sit down and type out the messages without transmitting them. There was no guarantee that the two pieces of paper in the reporters' hands were genuine—and without that confirmation the story could not in conscience be printed.

The reporters contacted Pat Saunderson, president of Fidinam (Ontario) Ltd., and asked about the connection between the donation and the contract with the WCB referred to in the second Telex message. "That's pure nonsense," he replied. "I'd love to see it [the message] myself if someone has it . . . and I'll tell you this, it would be the first time I've seen a copy of it."

The reporters also contacted Premier Davis and William Kelly. Kelly refused to discuss individual contributions made to the Tories. "In my experience there has not been at any time, any connection—direct connection—between a specific decision of Government and a contribution of any sort or a level of contribution. It's just ridiculous."

Davis said, "All I can say is, I know nothing about Mr. Kelly's activities. There is a very clear understanding, and that is that those people who do assist the party do it on the basis of wanting to help the party from the standpoint of agreeing with its general objectives and not related to any future or past activity of government."

The reporters were still unable to write a story. They could not confirm that the Telex messages had been sent or that the donation had been made, and everyone who might be concerned refused to discuss the matter in anything other than generalities.

Then, at the beginning of November, Miss McDonald wrote to *The Globe and Mail.* Her letter was followed by a telephone interview between one of the reporters and Saunderson, who defended Miss McDonald. Saunderson said there was no connection between the donation and the development. Miss McDonald had answered the question from Switzerland incorrectly. "She was sent a question to ask what the money was for. It was a political donation but she made an assumption that was not right."

Miss McDonald said in her letter, "At no time during the past three years has any political donation been made by the Fidinam Group in return for or even the expectation of any political favour. Any impressions to this effect contained in correspondence from me would be completely erroneous."

In stating that the wording of the Telex message was a mistake Miss McDonald and Saunderson had confirmed that the message was genuine—and that the donation was made. On November 2 *The Globe and Mail* printed a story which began:

> A Toronto-based investment company, Fidinam (Ontario) Ltd., donated $50,000 to the Ontario Progressive Conservative Party last year nearly a month after the Ontario Cabinet approved a property deal between Fidinam and the Workmen's Compensation Board.
>
> Fidinam president P. A. Saunderson confirmed yesterday that the donation was made but said that a Telex message relating the donation to the deal was an error made by a company official.

Despite the denials of all concerned, this was an extremely serious situation for Davis. The $50,000 donation had been made to the Tories and it had been made shortly after the donor had received a large government contract. This meant that people involved were open to investigation for a possible breach of the Criminal Code. Section 110/2 of the Code says:

> Every one commits an offence who, in order to obtain or retain a contract with the government, or as a term of any such contract, whether express or implied, directly or indirectly sub-

scribes, gives or agrees to subscribe or give, to any person any valuable consideration for the purpose of promoting the election of a candidate or a class or party of candidates to the Parliament of Canada or a legislature.

The maximum penalty for such an offence is five years' imprisonment.

The Opposition parties were incensed. Robert Nixon said the situation was "bloody shocking . . . It's the crassest kind of political corruption." Stephen Lewis was a bit more moderate. He said a Royal Commission inquiry would be useless, because the Tories would do what they had always done with such inquiries and whitewash the whole affair. The only answer, he said, was to change the law regarding political donations. There must be limits on the amounts that parties and candidates could spend on elections, and all contributions must be disclosed, he said.

The battle in the House went on for days. The Opposition pressed Davis and the Attorney-General, Dalton Bales, for an investigation and information about what quickly became known as the Fidinam Affair. The government remained as tight-lipped as it could. Davis did make a statement a few days after *The Globe and Mail* published its story. He said he had discussed the matter with William Kelly and that he was assured by his fund-raiser that Fidinam had neither been offered nor received any favours in return for the donation. The Premier said he also remained firmly against the idea of making public the sources of political contributions. That statement was made on November 21.

A few days later Albert Roy, a Liberal backbencher, charged in the House that Bales was neglecting his duty by not investigating the affair for breaches of the Criminal Code. On November 30 Bales made a statement saying that he could not allow the thought to be left in the public's mind that the government was doing nothing, since that thought could undermine confidence in the administration of justice. He said he had therefore instructed his law officers to conduct an investigation.

By ordering the investigation Bales headed off a plan by the Liberals to bring their own criminal charges and fight the affair out in the courts. Stephen Lewis didn't like the Liberals' plan; he intended to bring a motion of no confidence in the government. This would necessitate a debate in the House, when the wider implications of the matter could be discussed.

The debate on the NDP's motion was slated for late afternoon on December 12. A number of Conservative backbenchers had been listed to speak, and they had all taken as their text Davis's statement of November 21 when the Premier came out against any changes in election legislation that were not foolproof, and particularly against disclosure of the sources of contributions.

But at 1:30 p.m., half an hour before the House was due to meet, Davis called his Ministers to the Cabinet room and told them he had changed his mind. The Election Act would have to be studied by the Ontario Commission on the Legislature to see if it could be changed, since he had decided that there must be disclosure of the sources of funds. There was little the Ministers could do, except troop into the House with the Premier and listen to him read a statement setting out what he had told them a few minutes before.

Davis's statement took the wind out of the sails of the NDP, who had been preparing themselves for an afternoon of hitting the government. The Premier had capitulated and there was nothing much left to say. Of course the people worst hit by the statement were the Tory backbenchers; there they were with their speeches all prepared on the basis of Davis's statement of a few days before, and now Davis had changed his position entirely. As the hour of question period before the debate proceeded the Conservatives could be seen scratching away at the texts for their speeches, changing all the "should nots", "cannots", and "will nots" to "should", "can", and "will".

One Conservative, Bernt Gilbertson from Algoma riding, found the editing job too taxing, and gave it up. He delivered his original speech against disclosure, to the great enjoyment of the Liberals and the NDP. John MacBeth, from York West, found that his speech didn't read quite right with just the "nots" cut out, but he struggled through with a smile that masked his anger at Davis for having made them all look so stupid.

Meanwhile Dalton Bales' investigation was getting under way. The man put in charge was a Crown Counsel named Clay Powell. To assist him he obtained the services of Inspector J. E. Grubb, of the Criminal Investigation Branch of the OPP, and Brian McLoughlin, a chartered accountant with the firm of Touche, Ross and Co. The trio spent a month looking into the circumstances surrounding the donation and the granting of the WCB office contract to Fidinam. They looked into Fidinam's corporate situation, and exactly how the donation was made by Saunderson, and they attempted to find out how *The Globe and Mail* came by the Telex messages.

Fidinam and Hydro

Patrick Saunderson had been involved with two companies that assembled the site at the corner of Yonge and Bloor Streets with a view to developing it. In 1968 a Swiss group of companies, headed by the elusive Lugano banker Dr. Tito Tettamanti, bought the property for just under $4 million. Fidinam (Ontario) Ltd. was set up to manage the two corporations through which Tettamanti owned the project. They were Berhold Investments Ltd. and Upper Canada Place Ltd. Fidinam (Ontario) was controlled by Fidinam S.A. of Lugano. Saunderson's own company, P.A. Saunderson and Co., was hired on a consulting basis by Fidinam (Ontario), and Saunderson himself became president of Fidinam.

Dr. Tettamanti was president of Berhold Investments, but Upper Canada Place Ltd. was controlled by a Panamanian company called Upper Canada Corporation. Both Berhold Investments and Upper Canada Corp. were in turn controlled by another Panamanian company, the Yonge-Bloor Development Corp.

Yonge-Bloor Development Corp. was a vehicle for investment for a number of banks and financial institutions in Europe and Canada. The major shareholder with 20 per cent was Banca della Svizzera Italiana, a Swiss subsidiary of the Commercial Bank of Italy. Another large shareholder with 15 per cent was Cantrade A.G. of Zurich, a subsidiary of the Union Bank of Switzerland, and then there was Tifina Handels Anstalt, of Liechtenstein, with 13 per cent, a holding company administered by Dr. Tettamanti. There were a number of other Swiss banks involved, as well as a French subsidiary of Continental Grain of the United States, and the Royal Bank of Canada.

Yonge-Bloor Development Corp. was putting up $7 million towards the estimated $50 million cost of the project. The rest of the money was coming from the Workmen's Compensation Board, $15 million, and the Canadian National Railways pension fund, $33 million.

What was of concern to members of the Opposition parties at the time was that there was no way of knowing whose money it was that Dr. Tettamanti was investing in the development. Lugano is just inside the Swiss frontier from Italy, and it is a town that specializes in banking and investing abroad money that takes the short journey over the border. Much of it arrives in Lugano in the form of cash; it arrives in suitcases, trunks of cars, even in people's pockets. The money is very anonymous, and the Lugano banks and investment houses make sure it stays that way.

Fidinam S.A. was the largest of three companies in the town specializing in investment in Canada, and it controlled altogether more than $70 million in property in Toronto. There was no doubt that much of Fidinam S.A.'s money came from Italy. Dr. Tettamanti had a subsidiary, Fidinam Italia SpA, in Milan, Italy's wealthiest city, only an hour's drive from Lugano. According to the Lugano financial houses the bulk of the money that came to them was from foreign companies and governments. The question that remained unanswered was why governments and companies should wish for the staunch anonymity that the Lugano houses provided.

While Clay Powell's investigation did set out in its report the companies involved in developing Upper Canada Place, it was strangely silent on the subject of the ultimate sources of the money. One might not have expected the inquiry team, with its limited resources, to open up the Lugano situation. But one could expect that they would think that the Attorney-General would like to know something about the money running into the Swiss town. For example, with anonymous money it is always legitimate to ask whether it was come by honestly.

The inquiry into how Saunderson came to give $50,000 to William Kelly also leaves a lot of questions of detail unanswered, questions which are not answered in the resulting report. The report said that in the spring of 1971 Saunderson attended a number of meetings at the Albany Club at which the philosophy of the Conservative party was presented, and active and financial help for the party solicited. There were usually about thirty people at these meetings and Kelly, among others, spoke about the need for funds. Among the speakers who regularly addressed these gatherings (although the report doesn't mention it) was newly-elected Premier Davis.

Fidinam and Hydro

The report continues: "Mr. Saunderson and three other guests were invited by Mr. Murray Webber to attend a dinner meeting at the Albany Club on June 7. At this meeting, Mr. Kelly and Mr. Norman Morris made the presentation on behalf of the Conservative Party. . . . After the meeting concluded, Mr. Saunderson as president of Fidinam (Ontario) Ltd. made a verbal commitment of $50,000 to Mr. Kelly and Mr. Morris."

Those few sentences leave out a wealth of detail. Norman Morris was identified in the report simply as comptroller for the Tories, and there is probably no reason why the report should have said that Murray Webber had been Darcy McKeough's bagman during the leadership campaign and had been drawn into Kelly's fold at the time of the re-unification of the party. The Attorney-General might have liked to know how the figure $50,000 was hit on. Whose suggestion was it? Was it to be a single donation, or was Kelly already using the system of annual payments that became most talked about after the election? Was the $50,000 commitment the first of four or five equal payments? The Tory fund-raiser's methods of operation were known at the time. They had been written about and were on file. They were questions that could logically be asked.

The report goes on to say that there was no further discussion between Saunderson, Kelly, or Morris about the matter. Then, on July 12, over a month after the dinner when Saunderson had made the commitment, he asked Miss McDonald to make out the cheque for $50,000 to Mr. Kelly in trust. After it was prepared Saunderson gave it to Kelly.

A little more detail here might have been helpful to Mr. Bales as well. Why, for example, was there a gap between the commitment and the making out of the cheque of over a month? It is hard to imagine that the fact that he had promised the Tories $50,000 slipped Saunderson's mind. What was he waiting for? And what was the situation under which the cheque was given to Kelly? The wording of the report indicates, but does not flatly state, that Kelly was in the Fidinam office at the time. It might have been worth mentioning in the report that both Kelly and Saunderson had offices in the same building, the Royal Trust Tower on King Street West. Kelly's office was suite 1019 and Fidinam's suite 4208. Under those circumstances one can see Kelly slipping up in the elevator in a free moment to collect; $50,000 was surely worth the trip. But by the same token, why had he waited over a month to do so?

The cheque given to Kelly was drawn from a Fidinam trust account for clients. At the same time $50,000 was transferred from another client's trust account maintained in the name of Ina Piattini, the woman in Lugano whose query to Miss McDonald sparked off the whole affair. Saunderson apparently intended that Fidinam (Ontario) would not ultimately pay the $50,000. He intended that one of the client companies, either Berhold Investments or Upper Canada Place Ltd., would reimburse him. Saunderson told the investigators that as a result of the Telex inquiry he talked on the telephone with Dr. Tettamanti, but the matter was not finalized until he visited Switzerland in December, 1971, and talked with the Doctor. As a result, Berhold Investments assumed the charge and reimbursed the Ina Piattini account.

In view of this trans-Atlantic telephone call and this visit to Switzerland it is hard not to marvel at the confidence with which Saunderson told *The Globe and Mail* in the first interview in October, 1972, that he had never seen a copy of the Telex message from Miss McDonald to Lugano. It was the kind of document he might well wish to acquaint himself with, before dashing off to Switzerland to explain to Dr. Tettamanti why he had spent $50,000 of the Doctor's money.

Another criticism that can be levelled at the report is that it does not deal with events in order. Attorney-General Dalton Bales might have found it useful in his zealous search for the truth to have a list of the dates when the important happenings occurred, to assist him in coming to his judgment. If he had been given such a list it would have gone like this:

February 18, 1971:— Fidinam made its proposal to the Workmen's Compensation Board.

April 6, 1971:— The WCB accepted the Fidinam proposal.

June 7, 1971:— Pat Saunderson made a verbal commitment to donate $50,000 to the Conservatives.

June 28, 1971:— Cabinet approved the deal between Fidinam and the WCB.

July 5, 1971:— The WCB informed Saunderson that his offer had received final approval.

July 12, 1971:— Saunderson gave Kelly the $50,000 cheque.

August 17, 1971:— Lawyers were appointed to draw up the legal descriptions of the land involved.

October 17, 1971:— The order-in-council confirming the Cabinet's decision was issued.

October 22, 1971:— The agreement was completed, with the exception of Fidinam's purchase of the old WCB building. The government had decided in the meantime that it wanted to turn the old building into a new headquarters for the Ontario Provincial Police.

The Powell inquiry ended its report by saying, "There is no evidence to indicate this donation constituted a breach of any section of the Criminal Code."

Dalton Bales released the report on January 5, 1973, and said there was no basis for him to authorize a prosecution.

Within the space of four months the Conservatives had been hit with three major scandals, and it did their public image no good at all. Even a few senior Tories were beginning to wonder what was so wonderful about Davis's vaunted new wave. It seemed much worse than the old wave, and what was more the people who made up the new wave were getting caught. The party that just over a year before had proclaimed that the future was for people had shown by its actions that it believed in something rather different; the future was for the Tories and the corporate élite. Nothing demonstrated that the Conservative party czars and the emperors of business were in fact the same people like the events of the months following the Fidinam affair.

On April 28 and 30, 1973, *The Globe and Mail* printed stories which said that developer Gerhard Moog, a friend of Premier Davis, had gained a contract to build a new $44.4-million head office for Ontario Hydro under circumstances which were anything but straightforward. The newspaper said that Moog had been given the advantage over other competitors from the start. His company, Canada Square Corp. Ltd., had been working on its proposal for months before other developers were invited to make submissions. The three other developers were only allowed to make outline proposals, and these did not receive serious consideration by Hydro. One of the unsuccessful bidders was told by a senior Conservative to keep quiet about the situation or he would never get another government job.

Davis was furious, and his close associates were treated to the unusual experience of hearing him swear. The object of his curses was not the developer, or Ontario Hydro, but *The Globe and Mail*. *The Globe*'s story raised questions of his own personal integrity, since Moog had been a friend of his for many years. He had stayed at Moog's Florida apartment before he had bought one of his own. While Davis was Education Minister, Moog had built the lavish new offices for the Ontario Institute for Studies in Education on Bloor Street at a cost of $60 million.

Obviously, Davis was under some pressure to clear his own name in the matter; but there was also the question of the "threat" to one of the unsuccessful bidders to keep quiet —or he would get no further government work. If that were true, it was the most damning indictment yet of the Tories.

It is one thing to use your power to help your friends. It is quite another to use the power to silence your critics.

Fidinam and Hydro

The day after the second of *The Globe*'s stories appeared Davis ordered that a select committee of the Legislature investigate the entire matter of Hydro's new head office. The committee of eleven MPPS (seven Conservatives, two Liberals, and two New Democrats) sat for fifty days, between May 22 and September 17. It heard forty-four witnesses, amassed 7,500 pages of transcribed evidence and collected 239 exhibits. The committee hired one of the country's leading lawyers, Richard Shibley, to prepare the evidence and question witnesses, and it engaged a firm of chartered accountants to assess the contract between Moog and Ontario Hydro.

The hearings were held in a low-ceilinged basement room at Queen's Park. From the start it was packed day after day with reporters and with some of the most expensive legal talent in the country, representing people who most certainly would be called to testify and people who were afraid that they might be called to give evidence.

The chairman was Conservative John MacBeth. It was his first big job since he was first elected in 1971, but the guide for the Tories on the committee was James Allan. Allan had been on the committees that investigated the Workmen's Compensation Board and the Ministers' use of aircraft. He, as much as anyone in the Conservative caucus, was concerned about what was happening to the Tory party, and his inclination was to put no barriers in the way of a full and open investigation. The other Conservatives followed his lead, although one or two of them showed no great enthusiasm for doing so. Lorne Henderson, the Tory MPP from Lambton, attended the hearings only sporadically, but when he was present his role was generally to run interference for government or Conservative witnesses who were having difficulty answering questions.

Much of the committee's time was taken up with hearing detailed and complicated evidence about the procedure Hydro had adopted for choosing the developer of its new building, why it needed a new building, how it would be financed, and what the contract with Moog really meant.

But mingled among the drab recital of facts and figures were moments of high drama and sometimes even of farce.

Early in the inquiry the committee began to deal with the main reason for its existence: the line in the second of *The Globe* stories which said that one of the bidders for the project had been told to keep his mouth shut or he would never get another government job. The two reporters who had been involved in the story (this writer was one and Gerald McAuliffe was the other) were called before the committee and asked for the source of this statement, and for all other notes and files they had which might bear on the investigation. The committee was not at all happy when their requests were refused. It was the first refusal to answer questions that the committee experienced. It was not to be the last.

There was drama also when Moog tied up the hearings for several days when he refused to give information about where the money to finance the building was coming from. His lawyer, Donald Finlayson, was one of the star turns of the hearings; for days on end he interrupted committee counsel Richard Shibley's questioning of the developer with objections about the unfairness of the questions.

Moog also provided farce. For one striking example, there was Moog's story of being on holiday in Europe with Davis in the summer of 1971. One day they had a leisurely and very liquid lunch in a restaurant overlooking Lake Constance. Davis wanted to meet some Swiss bankers and they had an appointment that afternoon in Zurich. They started out rather late after their long lunch, with Moog testing the capabilities of the powerful sports car he was driving. Unfortunately, they had a puncture along the way and arrived in Zurich at the bank's closing time. The two men were, in Moog's words, "well fortified" from their lunch (which could have meant anything from tipsy to drunk) and dishevelled from changing the tire. Consequently, the security guard at the bank was not impressed with their account of the importance of their visitation, and was reluctant to let them in. Eventually, however, he was persuaded to do so, and they met with senior officials of the bank.

While Davis discussed international finance at one end of the room, Moog took another official aside at the other end.

Speaking in German (which Davis did not understand), Moog asked about the likelihood of getting financing for the Hydro building. Even though Moog's dealings with Hydro were then in the very earliest stages, these "gnomes of Zurich" might be forgiven for feeling that there was little doubt that Moog would get the job. Wasn't he sitting in their offices with his friend the Premier, and wasn't it obvious that they had been having a very good time together?

This episode outraged a lot of backbench Conservatives. While they believed that Davis did not know what Moog was doing, they found it extraordinary that Davis had allowed himself to be used in this manner. In the course of their investigation the committee came to the conclusion that while Moog was a good developer with fine products to sell, he was also a very smooth operator who used every tool that came to hand. It turned out that one of the tools that came to Moog's hand was Vernon Singer, the deputy leader of the Liberal party.

Late in the hearings it came out that Singer had done legal work for Moog for some years. But in November, 1972, when rumours about the Hydro deal were already circulating, Singer agreed to accept a retainer from Moog of $25,000 a year. The retainer for Singer's services as a lawyer were primarily concerned with one of Moog's developments at Yonge and Eglinton, but Singer also acted as an observer for Moog at the Legislature. Whenever anything about the Hydro deal came up, Singer would quickly pass on the information to Moog. On December 1, Bob Nixon, Singer's leader, put a series of questions about the Hydro deal on the order paper of the Legislature. He did not know about Singer's retainer from Moog, and the deputy Liberal leader did not volunteer the information. In fact, Singer did not give up the retainer, even when it became obvious that the deal would become a political issue.

The revelation of Singer's involvement came as a complete surprise to the Liberals on the Hydro inquiry committee, and the news poleaxed them. James Bullbrook, especially, was just flattened by the stunning information. He had played a leading role in the inquiry, but when the news that Singer was in the pay of Moog came out, Bullbrook felt politically emasculated. He felt that he, as a Liberal, no longer had the right to take the strong stands he had done previously, since the deputy leader of his party was involved in the affair they were investigating.

The man who revealed the ties between the Conservatives and the business world was Don Smith, president of Ellis-Don Ltd., a London construction company. Smith had built his company on government work during the Robarts years, and he became outraged when he found it impossible to get even reasonable consideration of his proposal for the Hydro building. He pulled every political string he knew of, and as a member of the London Conservative establishment, he knew a lot. When that didn't work, he put *The Globe and Mail* on the track of the story, first by anonymous telephone calls, and finally in an interview.

Smith first approached Hydro late in 1971 and was told that just a general outline would suffice and that he should submit his proposal in that form within a month. This he did. But a few days later he was told by a friend that Moog's company was being handed the contract on a plate, and that no rival proposals were receiving serious consideration.

On April 14, 1972, Smith wrote to John Cronyn who, as well as being chairman of the Committee on Government Productivity, was also a director of Smith's company, Ellis-Don—and, it might be mentioned, a director of almost every other London company of significance. In the letter Smith said he had talked with Colin Brown, an extremely active Tory and the main agent for London Life Insurance Company (which handled most of the government's insurance plans for its 52,000 civil servants), of which both Smith and Cronyn were directors. Brown, Smith wrote, had talked to his friend and golfing partner George Gathercole, the chairman of Ontario Hydro. Smith asked Cronyn to put in a good word for him with Darcy McKeough, a pal of Cronyn's. All this string-pulling didn't get Smith very far, however, and on July 14, 1972, he wrote again to Cronyn. He said he had talked to Ernie Jackson, Robarts' old right-hand man, and also to Joe Barnicke, who had been in the Robarts coterie of close friends. It was finally through Jackson that Smith did get to talk to Gathercole, but it didn't do him any good. Moog had the contract sewn up by that time.

What the bulk of Smith's evidence showed was not that he was upset at not having an equal opportunity to bid for the project; rather, he could not understand why the political string-pulling, which he had used to great effect for so many years, no longer worked. Smith's company was founded and thrived on government business, both provincial and federal, and Smith kept feet in both the Conservative and the Liberal camps. Smith was astounded to find that all those provincial strings that he had so carefully laid close to hand in the Robarts era were no longer attached to anything at the Queen's Park end. The seat of power had moved from London to Brampton. But this only slowly dawned on Smith as he frantically searched for someone who could get him a hearing.

The central figure in this piece was John Cronyn. Cronyn, 52 years old at the time of the inquiry, was the epitome of the London Conservative-business establishment. His grandmother had been a Labatt, and so in addition to his many other directorships he was vice-president of that famous old brewing company. When he was called before the committee halfway through the hearings he presented a testy impatience with its members and its counsel, mixed with a complete lack of appreciation of the committee's powers and rights. He was found in contempt for withholding from the committee letters from Smith which he (Cronyn) felt to be of no significance. Being found in contempt did not lead to any punishment for such a distinguished Conservative.

One of the questions the committee asked him was about his political activities. He admitted to being a Conservative, but said the extent of his activity was limited to driving people to the polls at election time. His involvement in the 1967 federal Conservative leadership campaign apparently slipped his mind. He and Richard Dillon (then the dean of engineering at the University of Western Ontario and, ironically, the chairman of a committee looking into Ontario Hydro's organization) planned the convention-day organization for Duff Roblin, the former Manitoba Premier. Another Roblin supporter at that convention was Darcy McKeough.

Cronyn was appointed chairman of the Committee on Government Productivity by Robarts. When Cronyn was looking for someone to chair the sub-committee, Task Force Hydro, it was natural for him to think of Dillon. It was equally natural for McKeough, when he was made Energy Minister in 1973, to also think of Dillon and appoint him deputy Minister of Energy. McKeough and Cronyn were old friends and lunched together regularly, generally once a week. In the fall of 1973 Cronyn was appointed to the board of directors of Union Gas, which operates in western Ontario. When the company wanted rate increases it had to apply to the Energy Board, which came under McKeough's department.

When the aggrieved Don Smith gave the committee a list of his recent political donations it showed that he had made a couple of sizeable gifts to the federal Tories through a London lawyer named Albert E. Shepherd. At one time Shepherd had been a dummy director of a company owned by James Fleck, who was brought into government circles by his friend John Cronyn, and who eventually became Davis's chief executive.

Smith's political connections had served him well over the years. His entire company had been created on federal and provincial government work. He built almost the entire University of Western Ontario during the Robarts era. He was not ungrateful for the opportunities he had been afforded. When the social sciences building that his company constructed was opened in 1973 he contributed about $20,000 to the festivities and associated events.

Although Smith was a large financial supporter of the provincial Tories and had many friends within their ranks, he was most closely associated with the federal Liberals. He was president of a federal riding association, the larger proportion of his political donations went to them, and he was a fund-raiser for them. Obviously in the Ontario business world the prudent and ambitious man saw to it that his bread was buttered on both sides.

One of the main reasons why Davis ordered the committee inquiry was the quote in one of the original *Globe and Mail* stories: " 'I was told to keep my mouth shut or I would never get another Government job' the company official said." After several days of fencing between committee counsel Richard Shibley and Smith, Smith conceded that he had probably said something like that to the *Globe* reporter. But, he said, he hadn't really been threatened. John Cronyn had told him to deal only with facts and not hearsay when dealing with the press. That was all. The committee accepted that Cronyn had not threatened Smith in the words the contractor relayed to *The Globe and Mail.* However, the committee said, "Smith may have interpreted what was said in these terms." Whether they thought Cronyn intended his advice to Smith to be interpreted in those terms the committee did not say.

The committee found no evidence that Premier Davis had used his influence to get Moog the contract, but it did gently chide him for not keeping a closer eye on what Hydro was up to. It was apparent to the committee that Moog had used his friendship with Davis to impress Hydro officials, but the report adds that this was only a partial factor in Hydro's decision to go with Moog.

While the committee cleared Davis—and there can be no doubt that they were thorough in their investigation—there had been just too many scandals that came too close to the Premier's office for Davis's image to survive without taint. From this point onward the increasing loss of popularity of Davis and his government was pronounced.

19. The Opposition Whet Their Knives

As scandal followed scandal in 1972 and 1973, it seemed to the Liberals and the New Democrats that the collected poisons of thirty years were finally weakening the Tory party to the point of death. The skin of youth and agility with which the Conservatives had wrapped themselves in 1971 had been pierced by the sores that festered underneath. At last, their opponents felt, the public could see the real nature of the Conservatives, the arrogant misuse of power, the shady deals, the corruption. Surely the election had been the last hurrah.

Their optimistic feelings were a long way from the bleak numbness that had seized the Opposition leaders in the weeks following the election. At that time Nixon was to be found moodily ploughing his corn fields, and thinking how pleasant it would be to roll up the driveway to the farmhouse behind him and forget about it all. For his part, Lewis remembered what a fine thing it was to teach in Africa, how much he'd enjoyed it, and how there were many more interesting things to life than wanting to be Premier of Ontario. Both men came close to quitting over the winter of 1971-72. Indeed, Nixon did say he would quit. At the annual meeting of the Liberals in Ottawa in the early spring he told the delegates that he was stepping down, that a leadership convention should be organized as soon as possible, that he had had enough.

He seemed relieved and relaxed after he had taken that decision. His performance in the Legislature perked up, everyone remarked on it. It was as though some burden of duty had been taken away and he was his own man. When he was reminded later of the comments about his improved performance he said: "I just don't know what that means. I find it vaguely offensive, quite honestly. I have more confidence in the Legislature, but I think it's because of experience. I can't imagine it's because I said I was getting out, because I always intended to stay on as the member for Brant."

Nixon wanted the convention in the fall of 1972, but a number of things conspired against him. The main one was the federal election, which would have clashed with a leadership convention, preventing Liberals from giving their full attention to selecting a successor to Nixon. And the Mitch Hepburn messiah complex rose again. There was no great enthusiasm among Liberals for anyone in the caucus except Nixon, and there wasn't much enthusiasm for him either. Perhaps the long-hoped-for event would occur, and some charismatic Minister would descend from Ottawa and save them all. The Liberals were the Cargo Cult of Ontario politics, always waiting for some great leader to descend from a magic machine bearing gifts and power. And so they waited out the federal election to see if it would free a deliverer.

Unfortunately, the result of the federal election was so tight (Liberals 109 seats, Conservatives 107) that no Ottawa Liberals could leave for Queen's Park without upsetting the balance of power. John Munro, the chain-smoking Health Minister from Hamilton, did flirt with the idea of running for the provincial leadership. He had a couple of agents scurrying around for several months testing the provincial waters, but they didn't find that they were hospitable to their man.

Early in 1973 the provincial Liberals again met in Ottawa. A year had passed since Nixon had said that he was going to leave, and he was still there. He was embarrassed about having yet again to go before the delegates as leader of the party, and was astounded by the warm reception he got from them. There was a strong demand that he reconsider his decision, and he made a spur-of-the-moment decision to think again.

One result of the 1972 federal election was that there were two vacant seats at Queen's Park. Allan Lawrence's moment of glory had been swept up with the litter at Maple Leaf Gardens after the Conservative leadership convention. Voluble, impetuous and ambitious, he couldn't stand the obscurity and inactivity of being Policy Secretary for Justice. So when the federal election was called he was the Conservative candidate in Northumberland-Durham, a riding with which he could claim an affinity because he had a cottage there. As it turned out, his was one of the Tory gains in Ontario. Lawrence went to the Opposition backbenches in Ottawa, leaving St. George riding vacant behind him.

Charles MacNaughton also wanted to get out of politics. Nobody could argue that he had not served his term. When the reorganization of government had been under way at the end of 1971, he had been the rock in which the anchor was set. When McKeough had resigned, he had stepped in for a few months as Treasurer, to tide Davis over until a successor could be found. But in the spring of 1973 MacNaughton, at 61, wanted to get out and get home to his family in Exeter. So he too resigned from the Legislature.

Premiers have a fair amount of leeway in deciding when they should call by-elections to fill vacant seats. The wording of the act is vague enough to let them put it off indefinitely if they wish. Hepburn, for example, was a great man for putting off by-elections. But Davis called the by-elections in St. George and Huron quite promptly, calling them both for March 15. Both seats were traditionally Tory in their own ways.

St. George was an extraordinary riding which encompassed much of the snob area of tree-lined Rosedale, as well as some of the rattiest, most drunk-littered areas of downtown Toronto. In the past such notable Conservatives as Roland Michener had represented it, and it had been in Conservative hands for a long time. But the Party could no longer count on its loyalty. The lawyers and stockbrokers of Rosedale were still there–as were the apolitical drunks–but every year it gained more and more highrise apartments, whose population changed and fluctuated politically as well as physically.

Huron seemed a safe seat for the Tories. It was the western buckle of the 34 seats in the Tory belt, and it had been represented for years by MacNaughton, kingpin of the government. Huron was good solid rural Ontario, and the Conservative candidate was to be Don Southcott, MacNaughton's executive assistant and therefore a man very much in touch with the riding. When MacNaughton couldn't personally do those small favours for his constituents that are half the trick of getting re-elected, then Southcott did them. So it seemed safe to assume that he had almost as many friends in the riding as MacNaughton himself.

In St. George the Conservatives nominated Roy McMurtry amidst much ballyhoo. The nomination meeting in the St. Lawrence Market at the south end of the riding looked like a replay of a rally from the 1971 election, with noise, colour, hundreds of delegates primed with booze before they were urged onto the buses to take them to the meeting, the lot. Meanwhile, up the road at the quiet and grimy Legion Hall on Church Street, a rather grumpy chain-smoker with an aggravating drawl by the name of Margaret Campbell was getting nominated by a handful of Liberals.

Anyone with the stamina to attend both meetings would have been justified in thinking McMurtry was a shoo-in. Young, handsome, clever, sensitive, a Kennedy-Irishman, he seemed tailor-made. And look at the hundreds of people that turned out for the Tory nomination, all enthusiastic! Never mind the parties and free drinks that got them there, they were obviously having a whale of a time and enjoying their politics. That's what counted.

But McMurtry had some liabilities. One, he was a Tory, and two, he was a close friend and confidant of Davis. In the spring of 1973 neither could be considered attributes. While the scandals of 1972 might not mean much out in Huron, they loomed large in Toronto. In Huron the Fidinam affair was an abstract idea; in St. George many of the constituents went past the site of Fidinam's new commercial complex every day. In Huron land prices hadn't rocketed the way they had in St. George, where speculation was a dirty word. The name of the Big Blue Machine, once encouraged by the Tories because it gave them the feeling of invincibility, had become a pejorative phrase in Toronto, and McMurtry was part of that machine. Everyone knew it. And everyone knew Maggie Campbell too; they knew her frizzy grey hair and the cigarette ash spilling down her shapeless front. She had represented the area for years on City Council, and when she was defeated in a bid for the mayoralty she had become a family court judge. But she had never lost touch with her constituency. All the people who kept the chains on their apartment doors when the Tories came to call, with their sheepskin coats, ski-slope tans, and flashy smiles, flung the doors wide when they saw Maggie's ample form. She was an old friend.

Nothing much happened in St. George. The candidates rang doorbells till their fingers ached. How else could you fight a by-election in such a secret place of solitary apartments? But in Huron things got a bit more raucous. Southcott made a few stupid blunders. He didn't live in the riding, so his tenancy was vicarious, through MacNaughton. On one notable occasion he was asked if his commitment to Huron was so strong that he would move there if he lost. He said he wouldn't, thus gaining one point for honesty, and losing a dozen for not lying. Such are the demands of politics.

He was also up against a mortal fear among the voters. They feared the advent of regional government like they feared hoof and mouth disease. Try as he might to tell them that the government had no plans to introduce regional government in Huron, they wouldn't believe it; they were certain that regional government was coming. Somewhere in the caverns at Queen's Park was a plan labelled Huron, they were sure of it, and nothing Southcott could say would change their minds. They had seen it happen. They had seen Darcy McKeough and John White lump these plans on the table and that was it. All your treasured traditions went down the drain. Even the names of the places that were part of your childhood, part of your being, were taken away. Look what had happened in Northumberland and Durham counties. Only a few weeks ago White had fanned out his maps, and there it was, one great mammoth thing from Scarborough to Port Hope. No Northumberland, no Durham any more, just this artificial blob on the map. Tory loyalty or no loyalty, they weren't going to do that here.

The Liberal candidate, Jack Riddell, and his campaign manager, Murray Gaunt, fed this discontent with great success. So on March 15, when the results came in, they had won Huron and Margaret Campbell had won St. George as well. The Liberal win in Huron especially frightened the Conservatives. It was because of ridings like Huron that they were still in power. If they started losing those ridings to the Liberals, they were heading towards defeat. Despite the ineptitude of the Liberals, they were the only party that could replace the Tories in those southwestern rural ridings and create a power base. The New Democrats didn't have the basic level of support to be able to hold those ridings firmly election after election.

The new Minister of Intergovernmental Affairs, John White, immediately changed the government's approach to the introduction of regional government schemes. There were two plans already on the table, Northumberland-Durham and Hamilton-Wentworth. White gave these areas a much greater role in deciding the outline of those plans than had been the practice before, with the result that both schemes were radically altered before they were approved. There was one other scheme pending, Haldimand-Norfolk. White made sure that the area had its full say in what it wanted before the plan was implemented, with the result that there was hardly a whisper of criticism. Previously the introduction of the schemes had been marked by shouts of pain and anguish from the areas affected and cold intransigence by Queen's Park. After the Haldimand-Norfolk scheme had been dealt with, White announced that Queen's Park had no immediate plans for more regional governments.

The overnight change in Queen's Park's attitude towards the introduction of regional governments, from the authoritarian to the consultative, contained a large element of fear on the part of the Tories. It also had something to do with John White. White, a ruddy-faced bull terrier of a man, was the leading red-Tory in the government and his socialism, paternal though it was, gave the New Democrats the uncomfortable feeling that they would have to look over their left shoulders to see his spot in the political spectrum. Within a few months White completely changed the relationship between the government and the municipalities. In law the municipalities are the creatures of the province, and successive Ministers of Municipal Affairs had treated them as just that, creatures to be bullied and occasionally thrown a sop. White loosened the apron strings and gave the municipal politicians more authority over their own futures than they had ever imagined in their wildest dreams.

The by-election results and the scandals heartened Nixon. He began to believe that the Conservatives could be beaten, the first time he had really felt that in over ten years in the Legislature. The Liberal Leadership convention was booked for October, 1973, and by late summer there was no doubt that Nixon would be a candidate to succeed himself. It looked as though his main opposition would come from one of his caucus members, Donald Deacon, a 53-year-old lanky, bespectacled investment dealer, who had represented York Centre since 1967. Deacon had never made any secret of his ambition to become leader, and he had been working away for some years to build himself a basis of support among provincial Liberals. He was in charge of hunting out candidates for the 1971 election and had won many friends across the province in the process. But his experience as an MPP had done nothing to give him facility as a speaker or debater. In both departments he was painful to listen to, but he had gained a reputation in the party as a diligent and tireless organizer. He gathered support from those Liberals who felt that it would be hard work and not Hepburn pyrotechnics that would defeat the Conservatives.

Shortly before the convention a Hepburnesque character did appear on the scene—Norman Cafik, the federal member for Ontario riding. Possessed of a gravelly voice and a glib tongue, Cafik swiftly usurped second place in the betting from Deacon. Nixon was still considered ahead, but with Cafik in the race his chances of winning diminished. Cafik's descent from the heights of Ottawa was enough to impress the Cargo Cult Liberals, and they could start a stampede towards Cafik.

In fact, Cafik might well have won. What stopped him was the revelation the day the convention started that his bankruptcy debts had been paid off by some wealthy friends. In private life it is a measure of your fine character if friends bail you out. In public life it only means that you owe people, and are not your own man. The story of Cafik's indebtedness was put around by the Tories, especially by William Newman, the provincial member for Ontario South riding, which corresponded with much of Cafik's federal constituency, and which would have been Cafik's most obvious target in a provincial election.

Even though Cafik had been discredited, Nixon's eventual victory in the leadership vote on October 28 was not overwhelming. On the first ballot Nixon won 730 votes, Cafik got 574, Deacon got 402 and Michael Houlton, who entered the contest for laughs, got 11 votes and was eliminated.

On the second ballot votes began to drift away from Deacon, but Nixon and Cafik gained almost equally. Nixon got 768, Cafik got 613 and Deacon got 316. Tearfully and reluctantly Deacon threw his support to Nixon.

In the final ballot Nixon won 922 votes and Cafik got 675. It was no great mandate for Nixon. If an opportunist like Cafik could come in at the last moment and come that close to winning, obviously the party was less than delighted with Nixon. It was a hard way for Nixon to learn the lessons of his mistakes, but in the aftermath of the convention Nixon promised the Liberals a new regime. He appointed Deacon deputy leader of the party, with responsibility for organization. He promised that he would travel the province much more than he had done, and he made a Maclean-Hunter executive named Bob Reid his executive assistant.

Reid was one of the few provincial Liberals around with any record of successful political organization. He had planned one of the most successful events in the 1972 federal election, the Trudeau rally at the Maple Leaf Gardens, which was probably the most lavish political event in Canada's history. Reid had also been Margaret Campbell's campaign manager in the St. George by-election, and quite a bit of the credit for her win had rubbed off on him. Nixon picked up Reid after the by-elections and made him his campaign manager for the leadership. As well as being a tough political professional, Reid enjoyed a position that none of Nixon's former executive assistants had had—Nixon listened to him.

One of Nixon's problems had always been that he would not take advice from the people he employed to aid him. Sometimes they felt he hardly even listened to what they said. Nixon always gave the impression that if he ever did become Premier he would run the province with only a secretary to help him. He had always been aware that there was strong opposition within the party to his leadership, but he had never had it so plainly demonstrated before as on the night of the convention, and it shook him. Now he became open to Reid's suggestions about organizing the leader's office and the leader's time, and he listened to Deacon's plans for boosting the party and the caucus.

But old habits die hard. For a while after the October convention Nixon slumped back into his old ways of inactivity, until the press began to question in print what had happened to Nixon's great resolutions to stomp the province whipping up grass-roots support. He got the message, and early in 1974 began travelling a great deal, generating considerable local news coverage.

Reid and Deacon arranged for many more people to be employed as organizers and research assistants for Nixon and the caucus. Slowly the feeling grew among Liberals that they were beginning to do the right things. Now when Liberals asked questions in the House, they knew at least something of what they were talking about. So often in the past it had been easy for the government to slough them off with half answers, but in the spring of 1974 that wasn't happening as often. More work was given to the Liberal backbenchers, and they liked it. They began to feel that they were going somewhere.

After the leadership convention, Nixon moved to split up the Liberal party in Ontario. In the past it had covered both federal and provincial politics, but Nixon felt that the only way he could build an organization with any hope of defeating the Tories was to split with the federal group. In the province the emphasis in the combined party had always been on Ottawa, so that provincial politics was largely ignored by Ontario Liberals. Nixon held that he had to have his own group of supporters and organizers who could be welded together, and whose loyalties to provincial politics could be counted on.

Even though the Liberals had struggled out of thirty years of torpor, the most that could be said was that they were awake. Thirty years of blundering is not a way of life easily discarded, and at the beginning of 1974 the most time they could hope for before an election was twenty-two months. They still had a leader who had been twice defeated in elections. They were still faced with a Conservative party of great strength that was defiantly shrugging off the impact of the successive scandals. To the Liberals' left there was still the NDP. All that could be said of the Liberals was that they had finally made the break with Hepburn. Whether their new tack would make them any more acceptable to the voters was quite another matter.

Opposition ... Knives

Meanwhile the New Democrats had been going through a metamorphosis of their own. What emerged from the chrysalis was a less exotic creature than the one that had cocooned itself after the 1971 election. Instead of making the old dramatic lunges for the Tory artery the New Democrats now attempted to cultivate respectability and public acceptance. In place of dogma, they tried to substitute policies based on the real world of Ontario. They also lowered their sights. Instead of the grand leap for power they recognized that they must extend their power base from industrialized areas, and that they must have solid strength in wide areas of the community before they could hope to form the government. Their aim now was to become the official Opposition party after the next election. Their mood was restrained, quiet, but still resolute. The years stretched ahead of them. They would wait.

The air of tranquillity that hung over the NDP came from its leader, Stephen Lewis. The years 1972 and 1973 were as much years when Lewis came to terms with himself as years when the NDP re-plotted its future. Lewis toyed with the idea of leaving the leadership for over a year after the election. He was hurt by the interpretation that he personally was largely responsible for his party's bad showing in the 1971 election. A devoted and joyous family man, he disliked what the demands of politics did to his home life. He found the divisions within the New Democratic party intolerable, especially the back-stabbing of the Waffle group.

The Waffle had started out as a ginger group of ultra-socialist, ultra-nationalists, but it had become a party within the NDP. It maintained its own membership lists, issued its own policy statements (which were often at variance with the NDP line), and collected its own funds. It seemed as much to be against the NDP as against anyone else. After the election, the Waffle's chairman, Stephen Penner, commented that the electorate "couldn't tell who was the Conservative and who was the socialist". So when Lewis attempted to resuscitate the party, his first decision was that the Waffle must go. In March of 1972 he told an Oshawa meeting of the party's provincial council that there must be an end of the internal division and that he was prepared to meet the issue head on. "Groups within the party are meeting separately and secretly. Nominations are being fought on whether you are a member of the Waffle wing or not," he said. And he made it clear that he would not tolerate this situation.

After some weeks of turmoil, the Waffle question came for resolution before the provincial council of the party when it met in Orillia at the end of June. Lewis told the delegates, "I can't cope with the present situation any longer," and they voted decisively to oust the Waffle. At the meeting Lewis told reporters that if the Waffle had not been dealt with, he would not have continued as leader. A few weeks later the Waffle met near London and decided to leave the NDP, and to set itself up as a movement for an independent socialist Canada rather than a party. But in December, 1973, the Waffle decided to become a political party and field candidates. After the group was forced out of the NDP it dropped from public sight. It had been highly visible, and had used the internal conflict within the party which its presence generated to gain publicity. Once it was on its own little more was heard of it.

In the fall of 1972 there was an automatic (by constitution) vote on the NDP leadership. For a while Ian Deans, the MPP from Wentworth, mused with the idea of running against Lewis, but decided against it. Lewis was re-elected unopposed. In the spring of 1973 there was speculation inside and outside the party that Lewis would quit, but in June that year he told a provincial council meeting that it was his intention to lead the party into the next provincial election.

The style of his leadership changed markedly. Lewis spent much less time in the Legislature verbally eviscerating the Tory Ministers. Even when he was at his seat in the House, he was much more composed and controlled. "I don't feel like jumping across the floor and assaulting John White more than once a week. That used to happen three or four times a week," Lewis said with a grin on one occasion. Instead of flaying the Conservatives in the confined and confining arena of the Legislature, Lewis spent two days a week out in the province talking to people, meeting groups like the business men from Hawkesbury in the Ottawa Valley. The same Hawkesbury, mark you, where Lewis's facetious election pledge in 1971 was to drop hay bales for the animals. But in 1973 the businessmen of Hawkesbury felt able to have lunch with him without fear that their trade would disappear overnight.

Lewis devoted much more time to his family than he had before. He decided that his top priority was his family, and not politics. So he didn't leave for work until his children had gone to school, and he often nipped back home to have supper with his family before returning to the Legislature for evening functions. He gave much more time to looking after the people in his Scarborough West riding as well. They had nearly turned him out in 1971, partly because he had devoted so much time to being leader, and not enough to being an MPP. Once he got into the swing again of being the local member and dealing with all the problems, great and small, that his constituents brought to him, he got a great deal of pleasure from the work. More pleasure, indeed, than he got from any other part of his political work.

Lewis, in 1973, became convinced that the new low-key New Democratic Party was gaining acceptance among the voters. The province was ready to accept the NDP, and prepared to listen to them. He thought that NDP successes in Manitoba, British Columbia, and Saskatchewan, and the federal party's role as holder of the balance of power in Ottawa, had a lot to do with giving the party credibility. For years the Tories had warned Ontario that if the socialists got in, there would be economic chaos and worse. But three provinces had NDP governments and seemed to be doing rather well on it. They hadn't collapsed in poverty or condemned their people to egalitarian servitude, or invented salt mines for bourgeois offenders to toil in without remission. On the contrary, there was a steady stream of people leaving southern Ontario for the good life in British Columbia.

So by the end of 1973 both the Liberals and the NDP felt pretty good about themselves and their prospects. But what were those prospects in terms of votes? On the face of it, the ground available to the NDP was more abundant than the ground open to the Liberals. As a young party they were untainted by the stigma of history and could go proselytizing anywhere. Their rocky ground was rural Ontario, which had never shown any real inclination to go socialist. But if the New Democrats could break the loyalty to the Tories in rural southeastern Ontario especially, they might well make significant gains.

The Liberals could not expect to gain anything much east of Toronto, since the historical feelings of the area were too strongly against Liberalism. The cities, and rural western Ontario, were the areas open to the Liberals. And the Liberals had always been the Conservatives' primary enemy. The Tories always tried to convince the electorate that it was otherwise, by raising the straw spectre of socialism, but that was just a hoax. Even at their worst period in the thirty years, 1951, when they won only eight seats, the Liberals had got 32 per cent of the popular vote. The 1971 election, when they got 27.75 per cent of the popular vote, was their worst showing since 1926, when they got 25 per cent. There was a constant and large portion of the electorate that would faithfully follow the Liberals. But in 1971, facing a flagrantly anti-socialist campaign, the NDP got 27.15 per cent of the vote, only marginally behind the Liberals.

If both parties are going to live up to their promises and make gains at the next election at the expense of the Conservatives, then the voters of Ontario may be faced with the question of whether or not they want a minority government. There is no precedent to suggest that Ontarians are enamoured of such a situation. They seem to like their governments to be in control and stable. Should the voters decide it is time for a change, then either the Liberals or the NDP must become ascendant—unless the Conservatives are to be decimated, which seems hardly likely. Their record for keeping a hefty chunk of the people with them, even when out of power, is considerably better than that of the Liberals.

There is, as well, the question of the changing nature of politics. Political philosophy has largely gone out of the window, so that the Waffle spokesman was right when he said that it's hard to tell the Conservatives from the socialists any more. A Conservative platform, a Liberal platform, and a New Democrat platform differ in method rather than intent. In an abundant society the only political philosophy is pragmatism, and the only choice for the voters is who do they want to administer the cornucopia. It is a question of leadership. But the world of politics and economics is changing so rapidly that the questions may be entirely different come the next election.

20. *Future Prospects*

There is a temptation to see the period from 1970 to the summer of 1974 as a progression towards defeat for William Davis and the Tories. The slim leadership victory, the undeservedly large election win, the retribution of the scandals —there is a dramatic wholeness to the picture, whose logical outcome in Act Five is defeat at the polls in the next election. It would give a roundness to the thirty years, too. The passage from Drew's bright promises to a stultified, inbred, and isolated Davis regime has a certain dramatic appeal. It is a classic picture of the fate of proud dynasties, of politics as theatre.

Without a doubt there were strong elements of decline in the Conservative government in 1974, and without a doubt one day the collected abuses of their years in power will defeat them. It is hard to forget the passage from Dalton Camp's book *Gentlemen, Players and Politicians,* which has been so often quoted as to become trite:

> When men in power lose their touch, their facility in determining the political climate, the tragedy is that they are the last to know it is gone. For a while, their power and reputation will sustain them, or the gift of their opponent's folly may rescue them, but when decay of judgment sets in, it permeates the bones of the public man and he has not long to last. It is a terminal condition and no amount of luck may save him.

Are the Conservatives in this twilight period? Has their feeling for Ontario gone? Have they been supported by the two staffs of their power and the folly of their challengers? Again, this paints too theatrical and too simple a picture. While the scandals of 1972 and 1973 say a lot about warped thinking (and lack of thinking) in the Conservative cloisters, there is no reason to suppose that such affairs will be the Tories' downfall.

In September, 1973, at the time of the Hydro inquiry, Peter Regenstreif conducted a poll for *The Toronto Star*. The poll said that, despite everything, William Davis was still far and away the most popular political leader in the province. Thirty-one per cent of the people questioned expressed their preference for him, while twenty per cent preferred Lewis, and only fifteen per cent were for Nixon. Even so, Davis's personal popularity had declined considerably since the 1971 election, when forty-six per cent of the sample liked him best. The public's estimation of Davis had gone down quite markedly, but he was still well in the lead and could count on almost the same following as both Nixon and Lewis together. In general, the poll showed Davis and the Conservatives in about the same position they had been in in 1971, before the election campaign began–in a strong jumping-off point for an election victory.

It's also true that such a mid-term decline was to be expected. In 1971 Davis was untried. Through the summer of that year the new Premier and his party were orchestrated superbly by the Camp-Atkins machine, but it is impossible to maintain that kind of charade of efficiency and unity between elections. Inevitably the voters came to know something about Davis and his new government and, equally inevitably, it didn't live up to the technicolour promises of Norman Atkins. There is nothing unusual in that.

Yet hardly anyone knew much about Davis personally, even after he had occupied the Premier's office for three years. Senior Cabinet Ministers, when asked what he was like, would somewhat sorrowfully reply, "I can't say. I don't really know anything about him." There was in Davis a degree of self-containment that was at once a protection and a weakness. It sustained him, because he created no illusions in his relationships with people that could later be torn apart; he disappointed no one because he offered nothing. At the same time, there is a limit to the length of time people will support a leader who offers nothing of himself.

Sometimes Davis's personal isolation has been explained by saying that he lacks any philosophy; that he never says what he thinks about things because he has no ideas. It is a judgment that has infected even his closest aides. They would place on his desk abridged versions of reports, they would go to him with various ideas, he would listen and say nothing. Then the decision would be announced. He is a great listener and a lousy talker.

There were many examples of his one-way communication and his reluctance to be discursive with the people around him who had some right to know what he was up to. There was the Spadina decision, the decision to opt for disclosure of the sources of political contributions, and in 1973 the plan to introduce a seven-per-cent sales tax on energy. This latter scheme had to be withdrawn when Davis found himself faced with a full-blown revolt in his caucus and Cabinet. It was an ignominious retreat, and an unnecessary one, since the whole situation could have been avoided.

There is an oppressively austere side to Davis's character, and it shows in public. His statements and speeches have a measured, plodding progression to them. Nothing much is ever said lightly. He has no facility for the sparkling aside, and even though he has claimed that he enjoys the cut and thrust of debate in the House, he has never been much good at it, and has tended to avoid it when he could.

But in private he is far from a dull man. He can turn his own circumlocutory verbiage into sly, dry wit aimed both at himself and at other political figures, but none of it is ever spiteful. There is an excessive small-town gentility about him. Only on the rarest of occasions, once in point of fact, did he ever really lash out at his opponents. The occasion was a meeting of the provincial Conservatives at Elgin House in Muskoka in September of 1973. It was a private, closed meeting of the Tory family and he felt safe. The meeting was at a time when morale within the party was low because of the scandals, and Davis rose to the occasion and gave the best speech of his career. During the speech he hit out at Nixon and called him a hypocrite on the issue of the sources of political donations. "Where does he think his funds come from—the United Appeal?" he chortled, to thunderous applause.

It was an unusual attack for Davis to make, as slight as it may seem in the records of political vilification.

Davis is at his most relaxed in small groups when he can control the situation. He has a phenomenal memory, and can recall word for word conversations that have taken place months before, and he stores up thousands of obscure facts about politics and about football, his other passion. Crowds, which traditionally set a politician's adrenalin flowing, do nothing for him at all. They dry him up, make him unsure, and uncomfortable. Orators excite audiences by first being enlivened by the people before them; Davis is no orator.

He is a rather unsophisticated man who is awed by successful cosmopolitan men. In the past he has enjoyed the company of men like Gerhard Moog and James Fleck, and this was something of a failing. Their dazzling appearance tinted his judgment of them. Yet there is no evidence that Davis himself covets wealth. He is well off, with his pleasant but ordinary house on Brampton's main street, his island cottage in Georgian Bay with its boats, and his condominium apartment in Florida. But he could be bought and sold several times over by most of the people around him.

Even Davis's bitterest critics, Stephen Lewis for example, have always maintained that the Premier is absolutely honest. The events that swilled around him smelling of corruption never touched him personally. His mistake has been to imagine that everyone had the same principles that he had—so he didn't bother to worry about what they were doing.

There is a complacent strain there as well. He drifted easily and comfortably into the unthinking use of the trappings of power. It took a long time for Clare Westcott and Hugh Macaulay to persuade him that he had cut himself off from his Ministers, his caucus and the voters. At first he found it hard to believe, and because he felt sure in his own mind that he knew what was going on in the Legislature and the province, he couldn't understand why people should think he was remote. Davis probably did know exactly what was going on, but it was a vicarious understanding. Again he was listening and sharing nothing.

When he did, at the end of 1973, restructure his office at the pleading of Westcott and Macaulay, he didn't come to grips with the basis of the problem. True, he brought in genial, down-to-earth people who gave the office a more open-collar-and-shirt-sleeves image. Retired MPP Arthur Wishart, one of the old charmers of the party, came in to serve as liaison man with the caucus; Jim McPhee, a public relations man beloved of the news media from the news room to the executive offices, came in as chief press officer; and the Tory organization's political realist Paul Weed was made Davis's appointments secretary—the man who controlled Davis's time. But really nothing had changed. Davis was still blocked from doing the thing that he does so well, meeting people.

It was a source of great frustration to Davis's greatest fans. Westcott, for example, once said: "Hell, if he's driving along in the car and he wants a packet of Rolaids, he sends Bob (one of the bodyguards) into the shop to get them. Why can't he go in himself? Davis once went into a shop a year or so ago to buy some cigars and the guy who owns the shop has been telling everyone who goes in ever since."

The assumption of the right to rule that permeates the Tories is there in Davis, but it is tempered by a streak of humanity. He may be cavalier in his dealings with the Legislature and his fellow Conservatives, but he finds it emotionally upsetting to get rid of incompetents or those who have served their time and should leave. For example, he found it a gut-wrenching experience to dump John Yaremko and Dalton Bales from the Cabinet early in 1974. Yaremko, despite a brilliant record as a law student, had never achieved the promise of those early years while he was a Cabinet Minister—and he was a Cabinet Minister for a very long time. He was first appointed by Frost in the early sixties, and it was said that he owed his longevity not to his efficiency (many of the departments he ran became disaster areas), but to the fact that he could pull in a considerable ethnic vote.

The dumping of Bales was even more painful for Davis, and it shocked Bales too.

Davis was also astoundingly tolerant of his enemies within his fold. He was well aware, for instance, that McKeough never missed an opportunity to express his dislike for Davis. It never took much prodding to launch McKeough into a tirade against Davis and the way the Premier's office was run. But Davis ignored this, and concentrated instead on McKeough's undoubted abilities as a Minister.

It has been believed by many inside and outside the party for a long time that Davis's personal ambitions lie in the direction of Ottawa and federal politics. There is evidence to support this view. His first interest in politics was at the federal level, he seriously considered being a candidate for the federal leadership in 1967, and the main interest of many of the political figures around him–Dalton Camp, Norman Atkins, Roy McMurtry–is federal politics.

He made a lot of the motions of a man eager to succeed Robert Stanfield as national Tory leader. He maintained friendly relations with Quebec Premier Robert Bourassa, which could be useful at a federal convention. In 1972, for the first time since Frost campaigned for John Diefenbaker, Davis, Premier of Ontario, went on the road to help Stanfield in the federal election. As it happened, Stanfield was very successful in Ontario, and Davis got a lot of the credit. Such efforts are not forgotten by party loyalists, and help them make up their minds at leadership conventions. Down east Davis and Richard Hatfield, Conservative Premier of New Brunswick, have been known to sit around of an evening in Norman Atkins' cottage, chewing things over. The West, of course, was the preserve of Davis's main opponent in the minds of the soothsayers, Peter Lougheed, Premier of Alberta.

But against this weight of evidence must be set Davis's own firm denials of any federal ambitions. On a number of occasions before, during and after the federal election campaign in the summer of 1974, Davis made clear statements that he was not looking to succeed Robert Stanfield. At the same time the people close to Davis, who a few months before would hedge when asked about the Premier's intentions, had no hesitation in saying that Davis was not interested in going to Ottawa.

Future Prospects

The defeat of Stanfield by the Liberals on July 8, 1974, made the Conservative leadership available; but even if Davis were to seek it, there is a strong possibility that he could not win it. The low ebb of his popularity in Ontario is one reason. Another is that he might even have difficulty in getting the support of his own organization. His people will continue to support him as Premier of Ontario, but a number of them feel that he could not be an effective leader of the Opposition, and that's what being federal Tory leader means. Davis could not wage a no-holds-barred battle with the Ottawa government from the Opposition benches. He has no stomach for delivering the final blow in any debate. If an argument cannot be won by reason he is not interested. He is not the kind of man the Conservative party is looking for to defeat Pierre Trudeau.

Yet there is a strong competitive streak in Davis. If it looked as though, say, Peter Lougheed, was going to walk away with the Tory leadership unchallenged, Davis might well throw his hat in the ring and damn the consequences.

In the summer of 1974, however, Davis's main problem was getting re-elected in Ontario, and the result of the federal election in July did nothing to help his chances. It was Davis's machine that failed to make Robert Stanfield Prime Minister of Canada. The last ballot was hardly counted before it became apparent that there would be great turmoil in the provincial party. There had always been a significant number of Ontario Tories who had resented the way Davis had brought in the Camp-Atkins machine, and who disliked its methods. But now that the machine had failed, the detractors' confidence was bolstered. It seemed as though Davis would have difficulty preparing his party, leave alone the province, for his re-election.

All other considerations aside, he can expect to lose some of the seventy-six seats the Conservatives held in mid-1974. In 1971 the voters were asked to support the promises of a new age under Davis, which they did. The reality has proved to be something less than the promise, and a fair amount of disenchantment can be expected. Davis, however, has a number of hedges against the disenchantment being enough to throw him out.

Perhaps Davis's most important asset is that despite inflation, oil shortages, and the rest, Ontario still offers the good life to the bulk of its inhabitants. And there is little wrong with the prospects for the future. Ontarians can look around them at the United States and at Western Europe and see nothing but political and economic turmoil, in which Ontario is one of the few islands of stability and promise. Significantly, Davis's own theory about general elections is that the voters are concerned less about issues than about who is running the government, and whether he can be trusted to keep dishing out the goodies. With that analysis Davis can feel some confidence that so long as things keep ticking along, the electorate is unlikely to get angry enough with him, or enchanted enough with one of the Opposition leaders, to want to change storekeepers.

Davis could certainly be forgiven a smile of confidence as he looks across the floor of the Legislature at Robert Nixon and Stephen Lewis. "The gift of their opponent's folly" Camp called it. Neither of the Opposition leaders nor their parties seem capable of arousing the excitement of the voters to defeat the Tories. Neither of them has expressed a vision of Ontario that is much different from that of the Tories. A pragmatic government is difficult to fight, particularly when it uses pragmatism well, and the Tories use it well. Looking at the three parties, the voters have little reason to suppose that the Liberals or the NDP would materially improve life in Ontario.

There are no strong signs that the twenty-two seats between Toronto and Ottawa have lost any of their traditional Tory allegiance, and that is a fearsome advantage to have at the start of any election campaign. In other rural areas there is not much reason to suppose that the voters would desert the Conservatives in numbers sufficient to bring defeat.

The Conservatives' liabilities are less concrete than their assets, but they are none the less real. Though the rural ridings may not be in revolt, there is discontent. The heavy-handed introduction of regional government plans has left a persistent anger. Centralization of schools and social services is often aggravating to rural people who have to drive many miles to facilities which previously may not have been palatial but which were at least close. The Conservatives have to a large extent lost touch with their rural constituency. They have attempted to impose the values of the cities, which they have learned from thirty years at Queen's Park, without questioning whether the bounty that they offered was what the towns and villages wanted.

The Tories have become too managerial, too technocratic. They have their eyes on some spot in the future and have neglected the problems that are around them. When they do move, it is late and slowly.

The housing crisis was an example. For years the Tories watched house and land prices climbing while they did nothing but thump their chests over their inadequate, shoddy, and socially reprehensible public housing projects. For years they were told that the reason for the scarcity and high price of housing was that there was not enough land serviced with hydro, water, and sewers. They did nothing until at the end of 1973 the situation reached crisis proportions—it was estimated that in Toronto a family earning less than $10,000 could never hope to own a home—and then they embarked on a crash program. The success of this program, which is all geared to 1975, could have a considerable impact on the outcome of the election. The chances are that even then there will not be many completed houses to show the voters, only lists of "housing starts"—which can mean holes in the ground.

There was no excuse for the province having got into the housing business so late. They were well aware of the situation—so much so that one or two Cabinet Ministers were making quite a bit of money out of it. When planning and local government reform became the government's pet project, they should have recognized their responsibilities to make sure that housing was also provided. They did nothing to help private housing plans through the mill of planning approval, either. The Municipal Affairs department was notoriously slow to process plans, adding to costs and keeping houses from getting built, while the province's efforts to provide serviced lots were meagre in the extreme. At the same time large amounts of money were spent on questionable enterprises; the $33 million spent on Ontario Place could have provided a healthy number of serviced housing lots.

Davis can also expect trouble from his decision to stop Spadina. Come election time the experimental test track for the intermediate capacity rapid transit system may not even be in operation around the grounds of the Canadian National Exhibition in Toronto. Four years after Camp penned his delicate phrases in defence of better ways of moving people around cities than in motor cars, all there will be to show of these better ways will be, at best, an exotic and expensive side-show. And however much Davis and his transportation mandarins insist that their futuristic system of magnetic levitation and computerized operation will work, the chances are that it will go through severe growing pains. The Montreal-Toronto Turbo train with its constant hilarious breakdowns has entered the Canadian lexicon of standard jokes, while the BART system in San Francisco, with all its bizarre computer-age foibles (such as the doors flying open while the train is speeding along, and computer black-outs halting the entire system), is an ominous example that should tell Davis and his men that they are in for trouble. Eventually, no doubt, Toronto's Go Urban system will work, and be a great boon to a society slowly strangling in a noose of automobiles. But in 1975 Davis is going to have to face up to what Dalton Camp told him in 1971. He has no readily available alternative to the Spadina Expressway. He decided then that he would rather live with that than with the Expressway creeping south, and in 1975 he is going to have to.

Peter Regenstreif's poll of September, 1973, showed Davis's popularity to be considerably less in Toronto than it was in the rest of the province. In Toronto he had a following of twenty-five per cent of the residents, the same as Stephen Lewis. Robert Nixon, with twenty per cent, was, like Lewis, stronger in Toronto than in the rest of the province. The housing crisis and the rapid transit situation could radically change the political scene in Toronto, where the Conservatives made most of their gains in 1971.

Planning, housing, transportation, these are the unsolved issues of George Drew's design for Ontario in 1943. Frost built it, Robarts added to it, and surrounded it with an air of grandeur. Davis has been given the job of putting the finishing touches to it. Davis's are the final problems of the boom years of population growth and industrialization. There is no sign that the Tories know where to go after that. They will undoubtedly clean up the legislation in some areas to provide more equality. Perhaps in time they will implement the only promise that Drew made that is still outstanding, to provide dental care. They may well spin out the seventies on these issues, grooming and polishing their work. And then, like Mitch Hepburn in 1943, they will be able to stand back and say that Ontario has reached a plateau in its development where it will stay for a generation. And then, like all political parties that believe that nothing remains to be done, they will be defeated.

21. Epilogue

Monday, May 7, 1973, was a clear bright spring morning. It was the kind of day when people leave their coats at home because the spring sun is so inviting, and they want to show their faith that winter has finally gone. But once outside they find there is still a chilling bite to the wind, and quietly wish they had shown a little less faith. On this particular day, out of Toronto, there was a new brilliance to the grass and a shimmer of green haze as the trees swayed. One couldn't be quite sure whether it was evidence of spring or an illusion—an impatience for summer that tinted the vision.

Out on Highway 401, the Macdonald-Cartier Freeway, Leslie Frost's road, the work crews had come out of hibernation. Eight lanes in each direction north of Toronto were marching steadily towards Oshawa, and that meant diversions, lines of trucks churning loads of concrete, and bulldozers snorting back and forth across the road and holding up traffic. But finally the traffic cleared and the way was clear to head north on Highway 35, past the white clapboarded farm house at the junction where they have relics of the Fenian raids, on through the rolling Durham County farm lands. Every few minutes a chauffeur-driven limousine would go swooshing past the other cars, its passengers sitting back in the shadows, vague unrecognizable outlines of impressive faces. Further on, one of the limousines had pulled off the road and the chauffeur was handing out sandwiches and whisky from a hamper in the trunk. The passengers, silver-haired men in neatly tailored black suits, stood around sipping and eating. They didn't have time for lunch later, and people experienced in attending decorous events plan against rumbling tummies.

Near Lindsay the volume of limousines increased. They headed purposefully into the town, turned left onto Kent Street and passed the one-cent parking meters and the shops. A policeman directed them up Cambridge Street, a quiet avenue roofed with trees. Along the sidewalks people were walking up the hill towards a small red brick church. The limousines crawled through the crowd that was gathering in the patches of sunlight. At the church steps the limousines stopped, and the reporters and photographers hanging around gave the dismounting passengers searching looks and then argued among themselves about who the dignitary was.

Some of the dignitaries provoked no arguments. John Diefenbaker emerged from one sleek black motor, the light of thought in his eye. It seemed for a moment that he would speak, as some vision twitched the muscles of his mouth. But the words did not come, and he carefully bent his steps to climb to the church door. Others arrived—Governor-General Roland Michener, Premier Davis, Lieutenant-Governor W. Ross Macdonald, former Lieutenant-Governor Earl Rowe, former Ontario Treasurer James Allan, Ontario Cabinet Ministers innumerable, worthies past and present.

Inside, the church was packed. The seats were full and the crowd spilled out into the lobby. Sprinkled among the dignitaries were men in more roughly-cut dark suits. Their faces were ruddy and creased, marked by Ontario's summer suns, and when they took off their hats their foreheads were white; farmers from the concession roads.

Standing on tip-toe and looking over the crowd one could see down the aisle of the church. On a plinth just in front of the altar rail was a coffin. It was made of dark wood, highly polished. The design was massive, with sweeping round terminals at each corner. It was Victorian, gothic, like the furniture in the farm houses just out of town. Draped over the coffin was a flag, the red ensign of Ontario. On top was a deep purple cushion on which lay a row of medals.

Somehow that coffin had little to do with Leslie Frost. It didn't say anything about the easy comforting voice or the strong hands.

The service was brief. There was no eulogy. "He emphasized that he wanted a service of joyous thanksgiving," said Rev. Lorne Dorsch, the minister of the church. There was a hymn, a reading, and a prayer. Then the nineteen honorary pallbearers left the church and flanked the steps down to the sidewalk and the hearse. The coffin was carried out by eight members of the Queen's York Rangers. They winced as the heavy load bit into their chain-mail epaulettes. Frost was the regiment's Colonel-in-Chief.

The crowd outside the church had grown and was full of children who had been given the afternoon off school. They stood silent as the cortege moved slowly off down Cambridge Street, the light flashing through the trees on the gleaming paintwork of the cars. At Kent Street, the main street, they turned left and drove past the shops and stores. Mid-afternoon shoppers stopped and watched. Storekeepers came out and stood on the curb. The fire brigade had pulled their shiny trucks out onto the station forecourt, and the firemen were lined up in front. Somewhere amongst the awnings and weathered red brick on that street there was a barber shop.

The cortege moved on past the gas station to the edge of town, and the Riverside Cemetery. The limousines stopped and the people gathered by a grassy slope overlooking the Scugog River. There was one grave there already; the slab of granite said Gertrude Frost, and that she had died in 1970. The breeze chilled the spring sunlight as the honorary pallbearers and mourners gathered under the elms.

"I used to call him Old Man Ontario, and I'm two days older than he is," murmured John Diefenbaker to an acquaintance.

The coffin was carried to the grave. Rev. Dorsch said a few parting words which were whipped away by the wind. The soldiers saluted. The honorary pallbearers filed past the small group of members of Frost's family, shaking hands, exchanging a few words. Then everyone moved slowly away, breaking up into groups.

Then for a split second the frame was frozen. Up under the elms Ernie Jackson was standing by himself. Ross DeGeer was down by the river. Allan Lawrence and William Davis were caught in mid-stride walking away from the grave. Hugh Latimer, A. D. McKenzie's aide, was shepherding someone towards a car. Two generations of Conservatives. And in that brief moment came the recognition that the continuity of the thirty years had gone. There was no longer any relationship between the present and the past.

Index

Index